SPEAKING IN PUBLIC

Books by Reid Buckley

Eye of the Hurricane
Servants and Their Masters

SPEAKING
IN PUBLIC

*Buckley's Techniques for Winning Arguments
and Getting Your Point Across*

REID BUCKLEY

HARPER & ROW, PUBLISHERS, New York

Cambridge, Philadelphia, San Francisco, Washington

1817 *London, Mexico City, São Paulo, Singapore, Sydney*

FIRST EDITION

Designer: Sidney Feinberg

Copyeditor: Holly Elliott

Index by Alberta Morrison

Library of Congress Cataloging-in-Publication Data

Buckley, Reid
  Speaking in public.

  Includes index.
  1. Public speaking. I. Title.
PN4121.B778   1988   808.5'1   87-46123
ISBN 0-06-015930-8

---

88 89 90 91 92 HC 10 9 8 7 6 5 4 3 2 1

L. Brent Bozell

the most impassioned orator of his generation

who with painstaking affection coached me through the Buck
and Ten Eyck oratorical competitions at Yale

Wm. F. Buckley, Jr.

the consummate debater of his time

who has been a loving staff of support since our boyhood

with gratitude

Contents

Acknowledgments

The late historian Rollin G. Osterweis patiently and shrewdly coached the successful Yale debate teams of the late 1940s and early 1950s, teaching me much of what I still find valuable. He is lodged in the affectionate memory of us all.

Christopher Taylor Buckley, my nephew, gave the original manuscript of this book a thorough critical reading, which was just what it needed. Bless him!

My secretary, Mary Jo Place, proofread half a dozen or more versions of each chapter; when there were long silences between giggles, or puzzled frowns, I was advised that work yet had to be done. Beth Chapman despatched some difficult research with wonderful efficiency. To both, my gratitude.

Frank E. Forsthoefel, M.D., who introduced me to Frank Chesno, Ph.D., who in turn introduced me to the Myers-Briggs Type Indicator test.

Professors Raymond G. Smith and Paul L. Soper; professor of philosophy and logician Michael A. Gilbert; publicist Jack Valenti; corporate executive Herb Schmertz; and William O. Rusher, the formidable polemicist; have all written excellent books on aspects of public speaking, which I have read with profit, and which I recommend to the reader in Appendix I.

I fought ferociously with my editor, Daniel Bial, over the concept of this book. He was right. I have sobbed and groaned over, and kicked and screamed at, his relentless textual criticisms and suggestions . . . but I have accepted almost all of them, and this book likely would have been better had I balked at none of them. I am grateful.

Justin McDonough is the rare agent who makes one feel that he actually likes one's writing! (And moreover, has read it.) Thanks: for his tact and good cheer in dealing with a prickly client.

My wife, Tasa, is that rare mate who truly does not resent long fits of total absence of mind in her spouse, who murmurs no protest when he clambers out of bed at pitch-black hours of the last watch, stumbling over furniture and banging into bedposts as he williwaws his way to the word processor. XXX.

SPEAKING IN PUBLIC

Prefatory Notes

Demosthenes

A trouble with books by nonacademic authorities on public speaking is that they tend to devolve into a litanous account of the cleverness of the author, which is boring.

If anything bores more than other people's dreams, it is other people's witty sallies, dextrous ripostes, biting repartee, smashing rebuttals.

I solemnly undertake to indulge in as little of this as possible (for one so noted for his obliterating rebuttals, withering repartee, lightning ripostes, and blistering sallies).

Another and generically repellent trouble with these books is that they are written by folk who have been elevated to that awful pop status called "celebritydom," incurring, as it seems, the all but inevitable consequence that the pages are littered with name and place dropping. "Late one evening in Marrakech . . ." "At an intimate supper in Lutece a week before the Oscar ceremonies, Chuck Heston said to me . . ." Not to worry.

What can't be helped is some personal biography.

I am what the British would style Buckley Minor, the fourth son and eighth child of our parents, who inflicted ten Buckleys on unsuspecting mid-twentieth-century America without once apologizing. I have two very distinguished brothers and a slew of distinguished and accomplished sisters, almost all of whom talk and write almost all the time.

Bill is the third son and sixth child. He and I strongly resemble each other. The timbre of our voices is eerily similar. Once, in his New York town house, we tinkered with a new tape recorder that I was to use on an assignment, and when we played the tape back over supper, neither he, nor I, nor his wife Pat was able in every instance to certify who the speaker was, Bill or I. When I am plagued, as so often, with the observation, "My, how you look and sound like your brother!" or, as at times, accusingly, "Do you realize how much you and your brother sound and look alike?" I smile a tight smile and quip, "Same mother, same father."[1]

Don't recall when this asinine retort occurred to me, but for some reason it bemuses people and gets me off a tedious hook. (Tedious hooks are more annoying than sticky wickets.) But there are those who persist, demanding—as though some nefarious genetic scheme was perpetrated by our parents—to be told how it is that Bill and I so evoke each other, in expressions and even in certain mannerisms. I then say to them what I now relate here, namely: that we are neither twins nor clones; that Bill is five years older and two inches taller than I, and brown-haired where I was a redhead; and that, crucially, the specific gravity of his brain is sevenfold mine. The little gravity with which I was endowed spilled before I was six years old, when I first saw fat Hardy massaging skinny Laurel's feet, thinking them his own. I have never got over it.

Buckleys were not born with silver pebbles in their mouths, courtesy of Demosthenes. *Toute au contraire.* We were born with orthodontic jawbreakers cramming the space between palate and tongue, which probably had the effect of improving our diction. If you could so much as enunciate Demosthenes so as to be understood whilst the roof of the mouth was plated with a hard rubber retainer, and whilst molars were clamped and cemented in silver jackets to which tough round little elastic bands were hooked, these stretched to attach to similar metalwork on canines, achingly vising the jaw together with the effect that lower and upper sections slowly accommodated into a correct bite, you were a blinking wonder of diction.

It really was tremendously difficult to use the tongue properly in enunciating some consonants and the *s*'s in combination with the *th*'s—as for example *Demotheneeths*. My argumentative kid sister Maureen until well into her freshman year at Smith College (where she excelled as a debater) was incapable of pronouncing the second

---

1. Bill tells me he is made weary unto death by the remark "My, how your brother Reid looks and sounds like you." In fact, one of the revelations of this book is that Bill hasn't been seen on the lecture trail in twenty-nine years. It has been I. This finally explains his prodigious productivity.

d in *didn't* (*dint,* she would say) or the *d* at all in *shouldn't* (*shount* came explosively from her). These natural and prosthetically imposed impedimenta to clear speech were aggravated by our father's adventurous business career. Following his unreasonable expulsion from Mexico in 1921, with the confiscation of everything he owned,[2] he roved the financial capitals of the world in search of financing. These included London and Paris, where he sojourned long periods: which is why *color* or *labor* still look funny to us, because there ought to be a *u* in them someplace, why we all had to be taught that two negatives don't make a right, and why when a princess kisses me I turn into a frog.

I was born in Paris—on 14 July, Bastille Day, a courtesy so Gallic that it prompted the mayor to present my mother with twenty-five francs (five dollars) and a pencil chased in gold. (Mother spent the francs; when I went away to boarding school she gave me the pencil, which I have lost.) I was three before we moved back to Sharon, Connecticut, and were once again installed in the huge pre-Revolutionary farmhouse called "Great Elm." Ever seeking to civilize his wild brood, and sparing no cost in this reckless endeavor, our father set up a schoolroom under the supervision of a Miss Penelope Oyen and the British-strict Miss Constance Cann, whom we detested. We were taught literature and history, and just adequate mathematics, which instinctively none of us (except brother James) much took to because there is no arguing with 2 + 2 =ing 4, quite taking the zest out of life. We were a disputatious lot, with hot tempers that we lost in several languages several times a day. Listening perplexedly to little Maureen boil over one suppertime with my latest aggravated assault of infamous intent (I had desired to brain her with a croquet mallet, in which ambition I had been frustrated by my beastly older sisters, who took turns sitting on me out on the lawn while I raged and bawled and bit and kicked), Father remarked to his long-suffering consort, "Does it occur to you, Aloise, that we have not been able to understand a thing our children say for several years now?"

To tell the truth, he was hard of hearing. Nevertheless, we did jabber in a most awful and at times incomprehensible mash. The younger ones of us were brought up by Mexican nurses, though we were all under the general supervision of Mademoiselle Bouchex, who patiently drilled us in the subtle tonal difference between *accent*

2. He was charged with the peccadillo of starting a revolution, which, had it been successful, would have spared Mexicans ninety years of misery.

grave and *accent aigu,* while responding to our leaden Anglo-Saxon *oo*s with exasperated *eu*s. We were afflicted with the curse of polyglot upbringing, unable to keep to one language when the choice expletive occurred to us in another. "Mi Papa," cried Janie in a tantrum one evening, "que es el grande idea? Tu eres un grand bully, y este no es pas tu business!" We not only mixed up our languages, there was a foreign intonation when we spoke English, and our tongues could become quite tied in knots when we were excited, which you will have gathered was more often than not. Before one of us could chant How Now Brown Cow, brought to "Great Elm" were a succession of what I suppose today would be called "voice therapists," but in those days tended to be operatic divas *manqué* with tremendous lungs and exalted temperaments, who had us bawling, "Oh To-by, Don't Ro-ll in the Ro-ad," across the hall from, and against, Mdme. Bouchex's no less determined "Ne parlez pas avec la bouche pleine!" (as we blew bubblegum bubbles through our *ou*s), developing into a kind of linguistic reenactment of the Battle of Crécy.

Father was home rarely during the week from the New York offices, but he could not stand this. It happened that business again demanded his presence in Europe that winter of 1938; so those of us still young enough to be pulled from formal institutions of learning in the cavalier fashion to which our sire was wont were packed off to England, there to be instructed in the King's English.

Bill was sent to Beaumont, Jane and Patricia to St. Mary's in South Ascot. Sister Maureen and I were enrolled in a London convent day school, where we were summarily subjected to tough British pedagogy that would put all U.S. institutions of learning, public and private, in a state of permanent shock. I was eight years old, Maureenie just five. So what? We were expected to memorize whole scenes from Shakespeare's lighter plays, and much other difficult poetry, because the English were, and I gather are still, no-nonsense about the heritage of their language, inculcating its glories into their children almost from the day they are able to pronounce Neither Leisured Foreigner Seized Either Weird Height. To our mutual disgust, Maureen and I were required to play-act the balcony scene of *Romeo and Juliet* ("Romeo, Romeo, wherefore art thou—ugh!—Romeo," she spat down at me, while I grew sick and pale with *vergüenza*). Our teachers cared less whether we understood what we were mouthing; the important thing was to flex our tongues, challenge and exercise our mnemonic capacities, and implant in our skulls the sounds and rhythms of English at its most sublime.

This is why Brother Bill and I share the same quasi-British accent, with many of the same intonations and speech patterns. We were brought up paying attention to words—discovering new ones with the excitement of finding a silver dollar on a beach, treasuring them, promiscuously employing them in letters and school papers to test out their possibilities. We learned the music of language first, then its sense. We all read omnivorously (there was an absolute rule that no one was ever to be interrupted for any reason short of the out-break of war when that person was buried behind the pages of a book), and we were passionately opinionated. No opinion was by our reckoning worth the name that wasn't worth holding with all our hearts and souls, so that at every meal we argued ferociously about novels and poetry and the latest "flick" we had seen. They mattered desperately to us, and we could be reduced to tears if our siblings mocked a favorite character or put down a favorite author. Oh, yes: the younger ones of us sometimes fled from the table shedding tears of humiliation and rage when our pet ideas were lanced by the dreaded barbed wit of sister Allie or the no less wounding sarcasm of our brilliant eldest brother, John. It was a lesson for us all in cool, but I, for one, rarely kept mine, having yet to develop that sense of one's personal ridiculousness in the scheme of things that is the foundation of humor and the salvation of the ego.

Within the bosom of the family, we were a quarrelsome bunch; outside, we closed ranks. We were mavericks—and proud of it. In the largely Episcopalean and mainline Protestant, Anglo-Saxon Connect-icut of the time, we were Catholics, Irish, and Southern. And new-rich Texan. In England, we were Irish Catholic yanks, a cross of inferior breeds. In France, we were Yankees Go Home. In Mexico (where we spent 1941, and where I went to school), we were *Texan* gringos, the worst species. Wherever our parents took us we were an embattled brood, defending religion, country, origins, and, in poli-tics, our father's frontier republicanism. We were not exactly out-casts, but wherever we found ourselves we were different for certain, and we grew up ever watchful of the slight or insult, ready on the instant to fly to the defense of family and beliefs. By the time we went away to college we were practiced, and for our age pretty fair, polemicists. It helped, of course, that our Catholic faith was the True Faith, our country the greatest and most virtuous country in the history of the world, our father a hero, and our mother a saint. We never wasted time doubting our convictions, because how could we be so stupid as that when they were in every jot and tittle absolutely and sempiternally correct.

Given this background, it shouldn't be surprising that I have been engaged almost all my adult lifetime as a writer and lecturer promoting the unpopular political view, which was the conservative political view. There were some dark decades during the forties, fifties, sixties, and seventies for people of our persuasion, as the saying used to go. This is, of course, not a political book, but it would be as unreal for me to forgo adducing my experiences in that arena as it would be for D'Artagnan to write a treatise on swordplay without mentioning Porthos, Aramis, and Athos. Deep modesty causes me to resist making the claim that in 1980, with the election of Ronald Reagan to the presidency, conservatives "prevailed"—true though that may be; suffice that the once scorned and intellectually discreditable conservative political position has now become well-nigh establishmentarian—to the queasy discomfort of many of us. Prominent Democratic legislators who just yesterday were among the blithest spenders in the Congress are today harrumphing solemnly about balanced budgets. Liberal scholars who for half a century promoted an ever larger and more pervasive central government have rediscovered the principle of subsidiarity. How much of this can be dismissed as lip service is beside the point. The parameters of debate have absolutely undergone a transformation, a political reality that the troubles of the Reagan Administration these past two years do not in the least alter; from which I don't think it is incorrect to infer that we (conservatives) "won" the decision as to what political course this nation should follow. And this suggests either (a) that our case was self-evidently correct, a proposition that will be unpalatable to some readers, absurd and indigestible to others, including conservatives, or (b) that we prevailed because we argued our case better than the opposition theirs. The fact of the matter is that we, aided by events, convinced the People. The political ethos of our country has been revolutionized. Conservatives did something right—which cannot be explained away by Richard Viguerie's mailing lists.

Among my deepest concerns is that a triumphant Right will degenerate into a complacent political orthodoxy, boring and unimaginative. Good heavens, what if it becomes no-contest! The long and once virile tradition of American liberalism must be rescued from its dialectical doldrums. That—if the reader will grittily suspend his disbelief, the writer promises not to snip it off—is a not entirely disingenuous purpose of this book. I hope to impart equally to *mes amis à gauche* as well as to *mes confrères à droite* some of the practical rules I observed when I was actively engaged in the ideological wars, because what were Achilles without Hector, Caesar without Pompei, the Prince of Orange without Alba, Wellington without Bonaparte, Grant without Lee, or Laurel without Hardy? A written tract will never take the place of one-on-one instruction and live interaction, but I trust some usable information can be gleaned from these pages.

If one comes looking for heavy pedagogical essays on speech theory, however, one will be disappointed. One can go to the library for that. Oh, I will touch most bases, and indicate (see Appendix I) where to repair for further study, but: I have made a living on my feet, writing and speaking; and I know from my thirty years' experience facing hostile audiences what works and what does not work, what is useful and what is of little value. I bring you the tips of a career spent tilting at windmills, and even, astonishingly, bowling down one or two, trusting that you will have as much fun as, in the lists, have I! *En garde.*

1

Making a Fool of Yourself

The notion came to me four years back while watching NBC's evening news.

The Union Carbide toxic gas leak in Bhopal, India, which killed two thousand people, had just taken place. The grisly footage of dead and dying victims was appalling enough to sit through; well nigh as appalling, from my point of view as a professional speaker and debater, and, of course, in a vastly different way, was the sheer incompetence of the high Union Carbide functionaries who were paraded before the cameras that night and during the following weeks. I was dumbfounded by how, by turns, they squirmed or blustered; by how they seemed never able to get their story straight; and even, in their anxiety to shunt corporate blame, by how insensible they at times gave the impression of being to the horror of what happened.

Now, they did not mean to bluster. Not for the world would they have wished to appear to be squirming. I am sure they were as shocked as anyone by the accident's toll in human death and misery. And one could understand how difficult it must have been in the immediate aftermath to ascertain from a distance of several thousand miles what the facts were, where and how the leak had occurred. Nevertheless, the spokesmen for this mammoth international corporation, despite their undoubtable competence as technicians and executives, were bumbling sciapods when subjected to the nationwide scrutiny of the television camera, from whose glare they seemed helpless to shade themselves.

How often have you writhed to witness such pitiful and pitiable performances by eminent people whose accomplishments otherwise command, or merit commanding, utmost respect? (How often have you been infuriated by the superior smirks on the faces of glib TV anchor folk when they have finished wiping the floor with a sweating official whom they have trapped in contradictions that should have been easily avoidable yet somehow were not foreseen?) The sophistication of James Burke, chairman of Johnson and Johnson, who handled the Tylenol cyanide deaths so expertly, is rare. The masterful humble pie of Donald Keough, Coca-Cola's president, when in July of 1985 he professed over public television his gratitude to Coke's loyal customers for demonstrating to the company what a mistake it had made in abandoning the original syrup formula, retrieved a monumental corporate blunder (and earned Keough about $3 million in "performance units" from the Coca-Cola board, which otherwise might reasonably have been moved to fire him, along with Brian Dyson, Coke's U.S.A. president, and Roberto Goizueta, Coke's chairman). A born huckster with demagogic rapport like Lee Iacocca, who positively revels in controversy, and whose ego visibly inflates in the spotlight, is a phenomenon. So is Ed Koch, mayor of New York, who seems to relish even the scandals in his administration, so long as they keep him stage center. But then there are the Geraldine Ferraro's, whose reputation an *apologia pro vita sua* one hundred thousand words long is insufficient to repristinate. Public officials of every description need only to have crisis hit them to come apart: to squeal loud protests or denials as the news of, say, a kickback on some municipal construction contract first breaks, then to equivocate, and then to blunder—to the cumulative disgust of the public. Yet they may be as blameless as Snow White. Which the public may ultimately accept, but only after it has concluded that they are as stupid as Snow White. Large corporations especially can be—or give the impression of being—utterly insensitive to the effect of language and the importance of the words they use, in their delivery and in all their connotations. This failing sometimes spills over into commerce itself. Can anyone imagine a major pharmaceutical company, with its long experience in marketing new products and its resources in selecting sexy brand names, dubbing a salve for the relief of hemorrhoids *a-n-u-s-o-l?* Sure, Parke-Davis insistently pronounces it in TV ads as *an-you-sol,* but the spelling of the word—the look of it—ineluctably has one pronouncing it differently. You know, as in, "Tennis, all?"

My frustration watching worthy folk make blithering idiots of themselves in public moved me to found the Buckley School for Public Speaking. We hold concentrated seminars usually beginning Wednesday afternoons and terminating late Friday afternoons, at which blessed release faculty and "conferees" (for lack of a better title) virtually collapse from exhaustion, having completed twenty-six hours of the most intensive exercises.

Few come through without bruises. On the other hand, the survivors have learned how to think and talk on their feet. By generating intellectual friction right from the start we at the school break through rhetorical blocks and mitigate what are often psycho-emotional impediments that prevent many people from being as effective on the platform as they are capable. The happy surprise for us over these past three years is not how few people possess talent for public speaking, but how many—latent within them—have what it takes.

Now, great public speakers, like great actors, are born. Talent can be discovered; it cannot be "taught."[1] There is no such thing as a "creative" writing class, for example. "Creative" writing courses may be life's blood for the impecunious novelists hired to conduct them, but they exploit vain hopes and conceits, and for the student are a waste of time.

Nobody can impart creativity to anyone who hasn't got it already. There can be useful instruction in how to put together decent English sentences; but just as nobody can be given a syllabus on breaking rules brilliantly after the genius of William Faulkner, no one can be taught to orate like Douglas MacArthur, polemically fence like John Kenneth Galbraith, synthesize the essence of an opponent's case and demolish it under a barrage of fact and logic delivered in accents of withering scorn like my brother Bill, or, contrarily, like the uncanny Ronald Reagan (prior to Iran), smooth feathers and bring aboard one's ship even the most obdurate ideological foes. But: everyone, with almost no exception, can be taught how not to make a fool of himself in public discourse.

We accept a maximum of twelve students per seminar. They may be professional groups or phalanxes of promising executives from major corporations. Our youngest participant so far was in his early

---

1. Normally the school bestows a certificate of completion to conferees. In the past four years of operation only twice have we awarded a diploma in which the Buckley School certifies that the person therein named is a speaker (or debater) of "high forensic skill."

twenties, a law school student, the oldest—the chief executive officer of a Southwest manufacturing concern—in his mid-sixties. Priests, psychiatrists, educators, professional politicians (two of our graduates won their races in 1986!), dentists, doctors, scientists, physicists from the JFK space center, engineers, lawyers, editors, publicists, successful entrepreneurs, and even teachers of speech on the sly—these sundry folk, and men and women from many other career fields, and from all over the country, and as far away as Sierra Leone in West Africa, have written in and applied, which is ample evidence that A Lot of People Out There Need Help.

We don't waste time. Participants have hardly pinned their name tags to their lapels before they begin performing. Faculty and assistants number six—one to every two conferees—and there are guest experts who teach such matters as how to organize materials into a strong case, how to handle oneself at a press conference, and how to stand up to the invariably disingenuous and often openly hostile grilling of a program like "60 Minutes."

The principles we teach are equally applicable to the board room or to the faculty conference; to the editorial, or sales, or policy review meeting: in short, to any professional situation where a person is called upon to state his or her case, or promote his or her idea, or sell his or her product, or defend his or her record, and may be put on the spot.

(May we make a deal? May we simply assume that anyone who was the youngest brother of six talented and opinionated sisters cannot have remained a male chauvinist and survived, and in the future omit clumsy equalitarian fussings with personal pronouns?)

Our method is confrontational. For example, students are given scenarios in which they assume parts. One may be the point man for a corporation proposing to establish a highly unpopular paper plant on the banks of a river that is heavily used for recreational purposes— a pet estuary of Sierra Club types. Another may be the state senator or federal representative who urges bringing the plant to the region, or the chairman of the local chamber of commerce. A third may take the part of the chief detractor of the plant, a biologist who claims that all ecological hell will bust loose if the atrocity is permitted.

Each role is complicated with a background in which there are muddy areas conducive to ugly as well as favorable interpretation. The world would be simpler if facts were always hard and people so selflessly disinterested that their motives were purer than a spring well. Alas. The corporation may have been charged with repeated violations of the 1963 Clean Air and 1967 Clean Water acts in the past, though it resolutely protested its innocence and counter-charged the Environmental Protection Agency with conducting a vendetta against it, and, anyway, a broom has since swept the old (wicked) management out; the state senator may have received a heavy donation to his most recent campaign from a pulpwood industry PAC, though his vote is on record against protectionist legislation for the textile industry; the biologist may have a long history of association with the radical fever swamps of no-growth ideology, which prejudices acceptance of his evidence (though these associations shouldn't be permitted to: conferees learn how not to let dastards get away with this kind of smear by innuendo, otherwise known as the illicit *argumentum ad hominem*).

The rôles are elaborated; the journalists are privy to some of these crepuscular areas, not to others. But from the moment the fiercely hot klieg lights are turned up, and the TV camera focuses its pitiless opaque lens on the rostrum, the conferees are on their tenterhooks, never knowing when a barbed dart may be tossed at them by folk who are expert at pinning their victims to the board and who enjoy watching them wriggle. A videotape camera is, of course, running almost all the time throughout the two and a half days of exercises, recording for speedy remedial attention where conferees have faltered.

I repeat: the entire faculty, including guest instructors, make their living doing what they preach. They are pros, not academics.

It is amazing how people come to identify with their assigned roles: how the perspiration breaks on their foreheads when their integrity is challenged or when their position is damaged by verbal abuse. The reward is that when once our students have been subjected to this ordeal, for which they have been fortified by concentrated coaching in what to expect and how to deal with it, they need never fear being roasted by the press or bullied by officious do-gooders again. In a true-life showdown, they will be competent—alert, cool, feisty, and unflappable.

What I have been describing in operation is the first principle of successful public speaking: the speaker's emotional and intellectual faculties must be exercised. They must be aroused. They must be (1) heated, (2) harnessed, and (3) coolly but forcefully deployed. A person cannot hope to give a good speech or to perform ably in any public circumstance unless he or she digs into his or her nervous temperament, excites it, disciplines it, and deliberately uses it to charge the spoken word with energy and interest. And when this is accomplished, guess what? Self-consciousness evaporates.

We send out detailed questionnaires to our conferees weeks in advance of the seminars, which we insist on having completed and returned to us ten days before their session takes place.

They are means of cutting through to problems most bothering people—in cases, paralyzing them. Repeatedly we see described as major impediments:

1. nerves,
2. the panic of stage fright,
3. lack of self-confidence,

(these three are all intimately related stumbling blocks)

4. trouble convincing people of one's sincerity and credibility,
5. a perceived inability to get one's point across,
6. difficulty in organizing one's materials.

(These three problems are also related to each other.)

The final three areas of concern:

7. difficulty in fixing the interest of one's target audience,

(which difficulty derives from a combination of [a] lack of self-confidence, [b] the failure to tap the temperament and exercise the imagination, [c] trouble communicating well-organized materials),

8. a tendency to antagonize people,

and, last,

9. giving an impression of arrogance.

You who have picked up this book may have special devils to exorcise, but these are the ones most often listed by our students, who, I remind you, are almost all people of consequence. I want to comment here on the first three, which bear on temperament.

It takes us about ten minutes—truly—to eliminate stage fright from the list of almost anyone's worries. (Not, please note, abolish it altogether, which we would decline to do for reasons to be elaborated on.) We accomplish this by engaging the speaker's mind and heart. Once we have done that, fears wash out, nerves become catalysts instead of obstructions, and the words flow.

In Shakespeare's plays, when emotional stress in a character builds to its most rendering intensity, that character—Macbeth, Hamlet, King Lear—tends to soliloquize in powerful, image-rich iambic pentameter that generally terminates in an aphoristic couplet, much as a bullfighter completes an inspired faena with a *paso de pecho*. *Emotion—or what we may describe as the nervous temperament, which is the key in the lock of artistic temperament—releases in us all a rhetorical eloquence that we never dreamed we were capable of.* [2] When Sonny Liston, the thuggish heavyweight champion, was taunted beyond endurance by the brash and obnoxious Cassius Clay (who promised to dance like a butterfly but sting like a bee), the "big, ugly bear" was finally moved to a burst of marvelous exasperation, which I paraphrase from memory. "He say he fast? He so fast he can kiss a bullet? He so fast he can go through Hell in a asbestos suit and not get burnt?" Never mind that Liston lost the fight. He won that round of verbal sparring, for which he will be more honorably remembered than for his two dismal performances against Muhammed Ali in the ring.

Hold on, say you. This is all very well. But what if one happens to be dispassionate by nature, of a "cool" or even "dry" temperament. And what if one's quotidian fare is dull, dry stuff, like maybe actuarial tables, or virus cell counts, or military regulations regarding the approved correct digging of field latrines—how does one sweep people off their feet with that kind of raw material!

Let's deal with the second objection: that a body is saddled with boring material.

One is in life insurance. One's daily fare is actuarial tables. Or one is a CPA, whose principal job is auditing company reports.

Stop feeling sorry for yourself. There is no topic under the sun that cannot be made interesting. Some topics just demand more effort on the speaker's part. *The interest quotient of any speech is in direct ratio to the interest and energy put into the topic by the speaker.*

---

2. I am using "temperament" in its two senses, which can be confusing, because they overlap: as denoting that spark, or verve, or fire (the "nervous temperament") that we associate with the personality type ("temperament") of artists, actors, and other passionate folk, and which is derived from it, though not exclusively a property of that type, in that all human beings possess nervous temperament in degree (the absolutely phlegmatic person having ceased to breathe); and I am using it to denote the natural, or traumatically acquired, inclinations of a speaker.

Even corporate balance sheets can be made of gripping moment. If one is reporting on the sickly rate of a company's return on investment, one need not just set it forth. One can compare it with the historical rate for the company, with the rate of return in the industry, and with—for example—a much more favorable rate posted by a competitor. This may require some research, but the sweat one puts into any report or paper tends to be reflected in the energy level with which one delivers that report or paper, and it is the energy in the speaker's voice—the note of keen interest on his part—that ignites interest in the audience.

When a speaker is imaginative in his presentation, the audience will sit up and pay attention. One does not simply reel off the figures: one assigns a priority of significance to them, shaping the presentation in an intelligent manner. "Sales are at record levels, production is up, the backlog of orders is satisfactory, but the area in this past quarter's performance that bears watching is this: the return on investment. It isn't good. It hasn't been good for the past five quarters."

What one is trying to accomplish is to bring down to whomever one is addressing what the dry figures, when interpreted, signify personally to them. This is always the speaker's object: bringing his thesis home to the audience, making the abstract concrete and therefore real. It is in fact easy enough to capture and hold the attention of soldiers when one instructs them in how and where to dig field latrines, because it is evident to the dumbest recruit that the consequences are far from dry. Nor are they abstract. Other matters aren't so easy. When one discourses on budget-breaking government programs, for example, the subject is dull dull dull. The same horrendous figures have been deplored over and over again, going back, it sometimes seems, to one's earliest childhood. And what's the use? The billions of bucks bandied back and forth are so absurdly beyond mortal ken that their meaning is quite lost. Eyes glaze over . . .

In such cases the speaker has to reduce the vast abstract to something within the average person's powers of comprehension. One such reduction that I have used for twenty-five years is this. I ask the audience, "Do you know how high a pile one million bucks would make in thousand dollar bills?" I pause to allow for uh-ing and uh-huh-ing as some people whisper guesses to each other. Then I announce, "Seven inches." I let that sink in. "Now: do you know how high a pile one *billion* bucks would make in thousand dollar bills?"

They don't. They can't begin to guess, because this is the incomprehensibleness of the astronomical sums of money that we talk about these days. "Well, twenty-eight feet higher than the Washington Monument."

"Wow!" is the never-failing reaction. People even look up at the rafters of the auditorium, as though they are envisioning that tottering pile of greenbacks windblown above the shining marble obelisk.

This illustration isn't original with me, and I have no idea whether it is strictly true, never having had the pleasure of a million bucks at one time in thousand dollar bills to pile up, not to speak of a billion. But it serves the purpose, because we lose sight that one billion is one thousand times one million. Everybody has his favorite analogy to reinvest with concreteness what has become so worn from use that it is virtually skinned of meaning, the object being to give the audience something that will flare, if only for a moment, vividly in the imagination. "Gee, whaddayou know!"

Each case has its proper mode, but keep in mind also when you ponder how to make fascinating stuff out of cell counts or balance sheets that every audience is different and requires treatment tailored to it. How to trim one's talk to the audience will be discussed in Chapter 10. Suffice here that the intrinsic or implicit interest of any topic can be dug out by the hard-working speaker and made dramatically explicit; and there are as many ways to do this as there are to skin a cat.

Returning now to the question of temperament, what about the first objection: that one is diffident by nature, *un*dramatic, *un*passionate, and *un*exciting. How does this self-effacing, understating, shy and introverted personality summon up that emotional and intellectual commitment to what one is saying that we assert is the indispensable operating principle of an effective speaker?

The first thing to remark is that there is a difference between the nervous temperament and temperament denoting one's personality type, which will be discussed in the following chapter. Within—or, if you like, despite—whatever one's personality type may be, the nervous temperament must be excited.

By exercising one's imagination. Anyone can learn to do this. It is work. It requires practice, though at last it becomes a matter of habit. If you are an eco-freak, don't drone on about damage to the ozone from atomizers, which the audience will doze through, they have heard it so often. Make it vivid to them, for Pete's sake! Search for that sharp image and fresh analogy. You cannot be lazy. That is the inadmissible sin for a speaker. One must give of oneself. One must force oneself to feel first in the gut, then speak. See in your mind's eye the ravages being wrought throughout the ozone; picture the unshielded infrared rays pouring through those rents to wither vegetation, to strike tender human skin and radiate into it, producing the sores and lesions of cancer. As you tell of these damages—you do not "recite" them; you make them graphic—in the course of relating the terrible consequences, picture them to yourself, envision your own crops baked to dry straw, feel your own flesh blister. You must yourself in the imagination experience the horror in order that your audience feel it. Dry and diffident that your personality type may be—sometimes the dryer and more diffident that it normally is—the more palpable to the audience your imaginative evocation of the environmental damage. (When a strong man weeps . . .) One need not wax overdramatic. One need not fear waxing overdramatic in the strenuous exertion of vividly expounding a case with the intention of engaging the audience's imaginative faculties, so that the audience sees the matter and participates in it as clearly as the speaker. When the speaker incarnates in his private imagination what he is talking about, he will not be forcing his emotions. He may to the contrary have to restrain them, about which more later.

This takes work also. The price of activating the imagination is mental sweat. Let's be honest, you and I. Most people are not "diffident" by writ of nature; they are by nature plumb lazy, having permitted themselves over long years to become deficient in the habit of imaginative projection and in its derivative, compassion, for want of exercising the faculty. I grant they may have been driven into this by circumstances, such as a broken home or physical disfigurement, causing them to fly from human company into the cave of their own suffering. Nevertheless, if a person has seen one slum, he hasn't seen them all, unless what he is revealing about himself is that human suffering has become to him an abstraction. Nothing must ever be abstract to a speaker. One has to reactivate the imagination in the same manner that Christians every Lententide freshly conjure up the tortures of death on a cross, and Jews during the observance of Yom Hashoah every April oblige themselves to recall the Nazi persecutions, so that successive generations may not become inured to their monstrousness. Just so for speakers. They must by shaking up their imaginative faculties engage the temperament. The nervous temperament. They must also, if they are advocates, dig down to their humanity—and in the process of accomplishing the first, the more likely will they access the second.

The imagination proceeding from the intellect trips also the moral imagination. This is not an inevitable happy result—there are plenty of cases of brilliant creative minds lacking in compassion, George Bernard Shaw to, well, wit—but the heat of the one, I think it is fair to propose, will tend to engage the other. (The opposite is more commonly not so: the sensitive moral imagination often almost typically is never accompanied by intellectual discrimination, Eleanor Roosevelt being a famous example.) Speakers who are advocates must not only cultivate the habit of vividly experiencing and thus compellingly expounding the cause they favor, they must cultivate this same sympathy for the opposition; even, for the enemy. (We will expand on this point later.) Lee, watching the slaughter of Union troops from his hilltop position at Fredericksburg, murmured, "It is well that war is so terrible, else men would learn to love it too much." For soldiers, this has ever after been the model.

Cultivating the habit of exercising the intellectual imagination on any subject, the driest, will endow that subject with unexpected interest. This much does follow inevitably and ineluctably. Temperament, even the most desiccated, or most refractory, will be tapped, and it will flow into the content. The rewards are more, as I have been suggesting. The practice of exercising the intellectual imagination even on subjects of no intrinsic interest to the speaker prepares him for the occasion when he is fighting for something he deeply believes in. Moral passion will then naturally enter the talk. Moreover: the awakened intellectual imagination helps the rational intellect become supple, more cogent in its own behalf while at the same time engendering tolerance for contrary opinions; and the hoped-for awakened moral imagination helps engender compassion for others in their humanity. The speaker's presence undergoes a transformation. He will be himself, but as a speaker he will have acquired intellectual and moral faculties, and attitudes of mind, that provoke a sympathetic response. It is to an essential decency that most audiences favorably respond, no matter how it is packaged according to the individual speaker's personality. One will have discovered not only how to deliver an interesting speech on what are ordinarily forbiddingly dull topics; one will have acquired the traits of mind and character that help win an audience round to one's point of view.

Do not misunderstand me, please. I am not making forensic skill contingent on virtue. It would be downright ridiculous to hold that mesmerizing speakers are necessarily fine and decent human beings. Nonsense. Think of Hitler—or Satan. Marcus Cato and Marcus Quintilian were acutely aware of the dangers of eloquence in the service of evil, preaching cultivation of virtue as a first requirement. Plato before them prohibited the teaching of dialectics to young men, "lest they should taste the [dear] delight too early," in their foolishness leading them to abuse the discipline for their "eristic" pleasure. "To the incontinent," huffed Aristotle, "knowledge [read: forensic skills] brings no profit."

So, OK. Granted good speakers don't necessarily make good men, those same exercises of compassion and imaginative projection that enhance one's humanity nevertheless do enhance one's forensic powers. Every time an advocate prepares to get up on a platform, he must compel himself yet once again to reimagine his material, on which maybe he has discoursed oft and oft. As, in the privacy of his motel bedroom, he mulls over what he is going to say that night— even as he is mounting the steps of the podium, or, seated there, enduring the fulsome and overlong introduction—he must intimately reidentify himself with that material, and by cudgeling the slow, recalcitrant processes of the imagination, compel himself one time more to think his text through and accord it that degree of passion or commitment that it warrants.

Once again, this is hard work. It is necessary. The imagination seems sometimes to be subjected to the temperament of personality type, and if that is sluggish—that is, if the nervous threshold of that personality type is recalcitrant, hard to access—oh god, there is heavy weather ahead.

At the school, we have ways of helping people arouse their dormant nervous temperaments that cannot be translated into print.

We can be rough. We bait some speakers. We attack their premises, their prejudices, their most sacred beliefs. On occasion, we grasp them by the shoulders; and shake them; and push our mugs right into their kissers. We risk having them take a punch at us, which assuredly some of our conferees have itched to do. (We do not deploy these desperate tactics with everyone, please understand: only in hard cases.) I can't through the written word shake and taunt and bully the reader out of his complacency, obliging him to really think about what he is saying, and hence feel what he says. I cannot compel him in these pages to tear himself from the web of his own prejudices or moral and intellectual obtuseness the better to project himself into an awareness of the other's condition, and the kindred human claim, if not the validity, of that condition, thus intimately relating to his audience. But this is what one must go through on one's own when preparing a speech. One must shake oneself up. One must sensitize oneself to the feelings, beliefs, and conditions of the audience. Even the introverted personality—bluntly speaking, the self-engrossed and egotistical personality—will benefit from the hard exercise of activating his imagination, though it should cross his grain.

Digging into oneself to touch the nerve of temperament, exerting oneself to make as interesting as possible even "dry" or "dull" material, and customizing one's approach to one's particular audience while keeping clearly in mind what one's objective is—what it is that one desires the reaction of the audience to be—is the recipe for successful public speaking. It's the same in writing. I know. I was bored silly by the prospect of this chapter, in which I have been obliged formally to set out the process I put myself through every time I give a speech. (Which is why, being incurably lazy, and no masochist, I hate giving speeches.) But once I did a little sweating myself, I discovered that I had learned more than at the beginning I knew.

2

Making the Most of Your Fool Self

We are not through with temperament.

There is the matter of individual personality type to discuss, as well as more to be said on the role of emotion.

Well-disciplined emotion—organized emotion—is what all people who use their voices professionally aim to achieve, whether they be actors on the stage, or coaches of athletic teams, or politicians and statesmen, or spokesmen for businesses: if you want to exercise to the fullest your inherent capacities for counting, for amounting to something in a public way, or plain leading, you must be able to communicate with a conviction that carries your audience. This means that you must contrive to unlock the wellsprings of passion. You cannot allow yourself to be phlegmatic, even though this be your "nature."

We boast at the school that we try to help everyone realize to his maximum potential what by genetical determination comes naturally to him—the cool man his cool, the hot man his heat, the intellectual his ratiocination, the folksy fellow his wit—but in this crucial matter of the nervous temperament, there is no alternative. It must be excited. If you would speak so that people listen, and so that they act on your recommendations, or adopt your conception, or even buy your wares, you have to learn to rouse yourself—to excite yourself intellectually, and thus emotionally, about what you are doing, what you are selling, the case you are making—in order to spark the interest of your audience.

Furthermore, you must accomplish this within character: that is, according to your born (or acquired) temperament. Hams and demagogues incur our fastidious disdain, but no speaker carried any crowd without being a bit of both. Read Mark Anthony's oration to the Romans at Julius Caesar's funeral; read Henry's summons to glory before the Battle of Agincourt. Read the great orations of Winston Churchill in the bleakest days of the Battle of Britain. Do not read President Jimmy Carter on the moral equivalences of war.

That, by the way, it has been pointed out to me, was not so bad a speech as memory deceives us into believing. Where President Carter failed was critically in his vain efforts to defy his natural temperament, that deeply—puritanically—moral. This created a dissonance between his character and his delivery, which was too bad. I am not here speaking of one being "true to oneself" in the moral sense. I am speaking of the theatrical effect. Men as different as Churchill and Franklin D. Roosevelt were able each in his way to give a stirring oration, and to half the world each in his way was a mountebank. There are as many good styles as there are good speakers; and it is the unfortunate commonplace that intellectual content and logical rigor may weigh pittance in the pull on an audience of a powerful platform personality. *What one must never do is step out of character.* The hortatory earnestness of his Bible Belt upbringing warred against Jimmy Carter's attempts to humanize himself. Recall that awful, inappropriate grin. Recall in contrast the weak, nervous rictus of Richard Nixon, expecially during the Watergate collapse. Carter, in whose stony blue eyes there lurked Cotton Mather, tried to relieve his essential earnestness by putting on just folks. Nixon, who desperately desired to convey sincerity and integrity, but who was aware that people distrusted him, endeavored to identify himself with common folk in a way different from Jimmy Carter, assuming a one-of-the-boys public persona that suited him not at all, complete with that godawful "game plan" jockstrap lingo that in the privacy of his office quickly degenerated into gross vulgarity. Attempting to put on a character that was not his own—the folksy bit—fatally damaged Jimmy Carter's delivery; but, though some of Nixon's speeches were textually well wrought, it was his suspect character itself that betrayed Nixon's platform personality: one in fact did not trust the man, even when he spoke the god's truth—there was something disingenuous about him, his own seeming awareness of his falseness surfacing in that fugitive grin. We will return to these important considerations in a moment.

It may be that we should draw a distinction between *commitment* and *passion.* We hear from Nietzsche that commitment is *the* moral virtue, because it presupposes the seriousness of he who holds it; and this *serieux* ness is communicated to the audience, which responds in kind. Commitment need not be rabid, nor undiscriminating, as passion can err in being. Passion is a dangerous weapon. If overdone, it can embarrass and alienate an audience. It can invite mockery and become for the speaker a disaster. In debate, an incautiously passionate opponent is my meat. Never lapse into sentimentality. You will be chewed up and spat out, and you will deserve your inglorious fate. But without the passion deriving from commitment there was nothing ever done, nor any adventure even embarked upon, because unless the speaker's own heart is moved, never can he expect to move the hearts of his fellow men.

Wait a minute!—you object. In the last chapter didn't I say not to worry about becoming overemotional? I did: speaking of the person with a dry or diffident nature. That person must excite himself; the person with a Latin or Irish temperament has to practice control.

How to walk this tightrope? The way to avoid the dangers of slopbucketing emotion is to activate the heart second by engaging passionately the intellect first. Which is the process by which commitment should be arrived at. This compels intellectual rigor. Summon people to your crusade against the Sandinistas of Nicaragua not because you detest Daniel Ortega or Miguel d'Escoto, those scruffy tyrants, but because you abominate the philosophical underpinnings of the totalitarian government they practice, which you have subjected to the most severe examination—severe on your own prejudices—and found despicable for being intellectually false, or morally evil, and therefore repugnant. (You also, it's true, don't like the self-righteous sons of bitches, but that is in the way of a delicious prerogative, which you have earned.) Loathe and abominate Fidel Castro not because of the hideous accounts you may have lately read about his treatment of political dissidents, which, have they surprised you, you should be chewing yourself out for not having long suspected, but because of the merciless dialectic that promotes such horrors.

(Those readers of liberal-leftist persuasion may substitute General Pinochet for Castro in the second example, General Alfredo Stroessner of Paraguay for the Nicaraguan dictators in the first. Just a blink ago we might have cited also Imelda and Ferdinand Marcos of the Philippines, or Baby Doc Duvalier of Haiti, but the villains of the right, generally, endure only the life span of their rule, and sometimes, like General Chun Doo-Hwan of South Korea, get, as it were,

religion, whereas such happy resolution is unknown among their
counterparts on the left, whose evils, in their ideology, live after
them . . .)

A speaker must have roused his forensic passions in a clinically
intellectual manner, and he must then marshal those passions in the
most succinct and well-organized way. If the audience catches in him
for a single instant what it perceives as drift in the direction of his
logic; if for one split second the audience suspects that he is unsure
of himself, or concerned for the spectacle he may unhappily imagine
he is making of himself; or if he is diffuse, and repetitious, and like
so many preachers unable to wind down to an end, that poor soul is
lost.

At the school, we teach disciplined use of temperament through
the vehicle of debate. Debates accomplish two objectives. Not only
do they compel people to organize their materials, to speak to the
point, to say in the fewest and most striking words possible just what
they intend to say, debates ignite intellectual and emotional heat: a
person becomes less self-conscious as he forgets himself in the case
he is trying to present.

There is the school of thought that holds, quite the contrary, what
folk need most is to learn to relax. People function optimally within
a range of tension, neither too little nor too much. The nerves that
are overstrung by stress can cause people to hyperventilate, to lose
their composure, their aplomb, and their very voices, reducing them
to pale-faced, trembling hunks of vertiginous terror. This school of
thought—notably espoused by Speakeasy in Atlanta, which was
founded and is still run by the redoubtable Sandy Linver—recommends several means of relieving anxiety short of bladder and bow-
els, such as exercises in breathing and muscular distension. These are
useful. Composing oneself in an elevator as one is whooshing up for
an important interview by filling the lungs deeply and expelling the
air evenly can indeed beguile nerves and keep one's pipes uncon-
stricted. It does no harm to take several deep breaths before entering
one's boss's office, reminding oneself the while that Thomas More
kept his cool all the way to the chopping block.

Ms. Linver addresses herself to very specific stress "situations"[1]
that are commonly experienced in the corporate world and that

---

1. In her two books, an occasion to speak is so invariably a "speaking situation" one
is curious how a visit to the Mustang ranch outside Las Vegas might be described by
her.

usually occur in interaction between a subordinate and a superior. There is a difference between looking forward to a contest of wills essentially between equals—going to battle with a light in one's eye, so to speak; looking forward to the fracas—and being scared, well, witless because the other fellow has power over one. There is a difference between pleading or defending an abstract cause, such as a political position, and defending or pleading for oneself.

In the corporate and professional worlds, the relationship is generally between petitioners and masters of destiny who are in a position to deny or grant the petition. One may be selling some financier an idea. Everything depends on the outcome of one's meeting with the mogul. Years of work, maybe a heavy personal investment in the business, all hang in the balance. Or, worse, one is an employee, a junior executive, and one has flubbed. One has messed up. Nobody enjoys a chewing out. It's scarier yet if one's mistake triggered serious financial repercussions for the company. One's career may come crashing down. One may be demoted, even fired. There are some tough hombres out there in the corporate world.

Physical exercises that help relax the body, and thereby the nerve centers, are dandy, and I use them, such as rolling one's head on the socket of the neck, or massaging the nape of one's neck, or even lying down on one's back, legs out before one, resting the arms beside the torso, palms flat down by the hips, and s-l-o-w-l-y arching up the small of the back, as high as one is able, until one's whole body is strung in an arc from heels to base of neck, holding that position for a few tense moments, and then s-l-o-w-l-y letting the small of the back down in such manner as to touch the floor at the base of the spine first, just above the coccyx, and then—vertebra by vertebra (hear them individually crack!)—pressing the spine hard on the floor, and with a clenching of the pelvic muscles, and a scrunching up of the gluteal muscles, keeping the spinal column flat and straight. At which time one releases breath that has been pent with effort, totally relaxing.

Having completed this excruciating exercise three or four times, each time winching the pelvis higher, one swings hands and arms back over the head, reaching with them (butts of palms foremost) for the back wall while simultaneously reaching with the legs (heels first, toes curled up) for the front wall, as though one were strung on a rack by thongs attached to wrists and ankles—maintaining this tension a few tremulous moments before utterly letting oneself go.

Oh, it's delicious. The danger is that one can drift right off to sleep! Which is not a bad idea. No no no, I do not mean flopping down on the sumptuously carpeted floor of an executive suite and under the astonished eyes of the receptionist launching into what can be misinterpreted as an erotic ritual borrowed from some steamy Middle Eastern rite. When I am waiting in somebody's antechamber for an important interview, and have been told that Mr. Bigshot will be able to receive me in just a few moments, would I like a coffee? or a bagel? or last summer's *New Yorker?* I just as politely decline, sitting there and popping inconspicuously off to sleep. A mere catnap, sometimes not quite slipping over the rim of consciousness, from which I am instantly roused by the announcement that I may now be admitted. I have taught myself how to do this. I relax neck, shoulders, arms, and legs, each in turn—breathing quietly but deeply. Shut my eyes. Pray to—or informally commune with—my God (yours, too). Compose my mind, permitting it to dwell on pleasant matters, such as cool water, or a jubilee year during which the Congress of the United States goes on twelve months' vacation. Hesto presto, I have slipped into slumberland—which is not only wonderfully refreshing, taking the edge off the business at hand, it flabbergasts rivals and adversaries. The competition may be nervously shuffling papers, or jotting down last-minute notes, or glancing at one out of the corner of his eye. He may attempt light banter, because he is himself in need of reducing stress; or he may decide to attempt intimidating one with a scowl or a sneer. Pay him not the slightest attention, save for an insufferable smile. If one relaxes back in the plush executive couch, shuts one's eyes, and actually dozes off, he is no end disconcerted.

But this is all outside the compass of this book, which is about putting together and delivering public speeches. We will stick to our last. People with acute phobia about getting up in public—people who suffer from what is called dysfunctional anxiety—may need the help of a psychologist. They will undergo treatment that comprises systematic desensitization, promoting deep interior relaxation. The patient is then bit by bit introduced to what is again styled a "speaking situation," learning how to handle it.

I don't quarrel with this treatment, which will work for many people. I prefer, however, attacking the same problems with a competing response. It is significant, I think, that a typical sufferer from speech phobia is the introvert—the ultra- or morbidly sensitive person who is absorbed by himself, and his problems, and his acute, anguished perception of the poor fool he is or before a public (he is convinced) is certain to appear to be. That person needs to be brought up out from the crippling syndrome of these fears. The importance or urgency of what it is that one has to say must compete with those morbid fears, ousting them. Which is why I believe that most people need keying up, not calming down, when they are called upon to deliver a talk.

I am lucky. I find it comparatively easy to light a match to my temperament. More often than not, because of my politics, I have had hostile crowds to contend with. On radical campuses, during the height of student unrest, I've run the gauntlet of rotten epithets, packaged in obscenities; I've been greeted by a stage on which had been sprayed in crude giant letters: FACIST PIG (sic). Almost any businessman or professional person is destined to face an inimical audience also. At the top, one must expect that, and one is not destined to stay long at the top unless one can take it. I always try to psyche myself before a performance. I don't mind waking up cranky on the morning of a debate. I want to feel like snapping at someone. I want a fight. It suits me just fine for somebody to make a crack at me as I walk down the aisle to the platform, or for people in the audience to jeer when I am being introduced. The adrenalin flows. Irish pugnacity—or whatever—takes over. I hunch my head down between the shoulders. I feel like weaving and bobbing, sticking and jabbing. But one does not have to be Irish, or Latin, or Jewish, or Hungarian, or by any combination of genes and upbringing combative, for the same flow of adrenalin to be activated. One must believe strongly enough in what one has to say for it to make a very big difference to one. If one does not conceive that commitment, one never will move a crowd in an auditorium—or, for that matter, carry an unpopular decision in a conference room.

Temperament (in the first, the nervous sense) is the *sine qua non* of public speaking. It is the absolute necessity. The trick is to learn to tap temperament without losing one's temper.

But—returning to the plaint in the last chapter—what if one is built differently, *un*pugnacious, pacific and sanguine by nature? Well, one is now talking in terms of temperament as personality or character.

The trick here is to work with one's natural bent withal learning how to tap that other species of temperament: the furnace in the belly consisting of ambition, despair, fright, desire, and genius, or at the least some embers thereof, that produces great divas, great comedians, great industrialists, great statesmen, and too many demagogues. (Read Pericles' famous "Funeral Oration.") This is not impossible even for one who is, say, placid by nature. That's not necessarily a disadvantage, depending on the kind of talk one most suitably (to one's character) delivers: a sanguine disposition, which is highly praised by the inventor of the Socratic dialogue, may permit a person to reason more tightly and ultimately advance his point with greater authority, tapping that excitement in the beauty or classical purity of the ratiocinative process itself.

But how does one know what kind of a personality one truly possesses?

In those questionnaires I spoke of last chapter, we also drop a number of impertinencies aimed at digging out a personality profile on our students. Necessarily, what applicants answer is how they perceive themselves. I'm not sure what we are entitled to be amazed by more: how often people have a realistic view of who they are, or how often they are wildly wrong. One dares say most people are (blissfully?) unaware of their true looks, for example. They are surprised by the photographs others choose as best depicting them, or as most flattering to them; and they are sometimes deeply offended, because in our "self-image" we are generally much more attractive than is the case.

This is probably natural protection. A girlfriend of my elder sister Jane labored under the pathetically mistaken illusion that she was good-looking. In reality, she was as plain as dishwater: a tall and willowy blonde, but tallow-skinned, insipid of feature, spare of frame, stooped, and devoid of those subtle pheromones that spin the male animal around in his tracks. Nevertheless, her self-confidence was such that she secured dates for dances and proms with ease, married young—which in those days was a maiden's goal; in those days maidens not yet qualifying for the endangered species list—and has since, if I am not mistaken, divorced and got rehitched twice over, maintaining through every conjugal vicissitude a cheerful though quite mistaken estimation of her attractiveness. Maybe the moral is this: only neurotic people truly have a realistic view of themselves.

But to whom does one go to get a handle on the kind of person one in fact is?

In the old days one might have suggested one's preacher or priest, or one's family doctor. Sadly, these relationships do not any longer exist for most of us. The steely eyed specialist with eyeballs like the digital displays of cash registers has taken over from the doctor who knew one's father and grandfather before one; in many parishes, the Catholic church, to speak for my denomination, yanks its pastors every several years, so that no personal relationship with a father confessor is possible; substantial numbers of people no longer attend any church regularly enough to develop such a close relationship; young adults flock from hometowns to impersonal cities where from Adam they are by none known, suffering the first shocks of Rousseauian alienation; and modern peripatetic corporate and professional careers tend to shift people so fast they scarcely strike roots before reserving their lot in Sun City.

Where, then, if one is between the ages of twenty-five and forty-five, does one turn for help in determining what one's true personality is?

Lover or mistress is not recommended, unless the affair is of common-law duration. One's spouse of five, ten, or fifteen years may have a realistic view of one, but it may also be a warped and cynical view, and therefore little as reliable. Depending on one's faith in witchcraft, one can repair to a clinical psychologist. There are eleven personality types represented in psychiatry: paranoid, schizoid, schizotypal, histrionic, narcissistic, antisocial, borderline, avoidant, dependent, compulsive, and passive/aggressive. (I fit the parameters of them all.) One's psychologist may put one through the MMPI test, as it's known (the Minnesota Multiphasic Personality Inventory, known also as the Minnesota Waltz)—and this may be helpful. If one is diagnosed as having an "adequate" personality, one may be encouraged to reenforce certain traits that will help in public speaking.

Excepting the hardest cases, I don't advise that route. For our purposes, it isn't necessary. Go on and check with that old shoe, your spouse, unless it is embarrassing for you to do so. Inquire of your best friend, if your humility is such that you can do so and retain him as a friend. Take a fresh and unbiased gander at your corporate or military effectiveness reports, or ask your business partner what he would describe as your principal strengths and weaknesses, and beyond that, his or her impression of what type of personality you most—or best, or potentially best—represent. This research may be an eye-opener, but it should be sufficient.

A terrific additional aid can be the Myers-Briggs Type Indicator test, which one can take on one's own.

m reduces the human personality to four basic variables,
ırrived at by establishing opposite ways of *perception*
ıgs out) and *judgment* (making decisions).

e second first, some people prefer to arrive at their judg-
.... *inking* ("T"), others by *feeling* ("F"). Some people prefer
to find things out by *sensing* ("S"), others by *intuition* ("N").

Right off, types of personality are suggested:

If in matters of perception one prefers *sensing,* one tends to be
(according to Myers-Briggs) "practical, observant, fun-loving, and
good at remembering a great number of facts." A speaker of this
character type should be especially good at debate and at conference
or board meeting free-for-alls. That speaker, because of the fun-
loving trait, will manage to avoid antagonizing colleagues or audiences, even when taking exception to the prevailing view, and can
risk being a mite outrageous. If in matters of perception one prefers
intuition, however, one tends to "value imagination and inspiration,
and to become good at new ideas, projects and problem-solving."
Such a speaker is likely to be talented at puzzling out and presenting
original solutions to dilemmas of long standing. He should emphasize
this natural bent by pushing the frontiers of his imagination until the
synaptic connections click with fresh formulations for tired concepts,
in turn suggesting new angles of approach that may be fecund with
possibilities.

If in matters of judgment one trusts to *thinking* over feeling, one
tends to become "logical, objective and consistent," and to make
one's decisions "by analyzing and weighing the facts," including
those that do not please. This character type should be excellent in
any polemical situation involving dispute over concrete matters,
such as debate respecting the results of a program or policy (but not
necessarily of the validity of the concept of that program or policy).
A person of this mold should emphasize in his talks closely reasoned
passages of deductive thinking, deriving his excitement from the
rigor of his analyses. He should avoid topics in the numinal, pneu-
matic, or metaphysical fields, with which he will be less comfortable.
This speaker should above all resist conjecture and hypothesis. If in
matters of judgment, on the other hand, one is more comfortable
with *feeling,* one tends to become "sympathetic, appreciative and
tactful," and to attach high importance to the personal values that
may be involved. A person of this character type should be effective
as an advocate, and as a speaker will perform best pleading a cause,

especially that of some person or worthy interest. He or she should be especially good as fund raisers—giving any pitch that relates to a humanitarian appeal—and as political candidates. Such people do well to emphasize human values in their talks, because these they will genuinely feel, and will therefore be able to convey to the audience the urgency of the values put forward and their sincerity in promoting them.

The plot thickens. From these four variables multiple combinations ensue, among them: "ST," "SF," "NF," and "NT."

People who prefer the combination of *sensing* (the manner of perception) plus *thinking* (the manner of judgment)—according to the Myers-Briggs taxonomy—focus their attention on facts, and handle these with impersonal analysis. They tend to the practical and matter-of-fact. They are at home with technical matters, and they are best suited for such career fields as applied science, business, and construction. Significant for these "ST" character types, as far as public speaking is concerned, is their need to cultivate the left-hand side of the brain—the side in which the imagination and conceptual powers are located. (Democrats, of course, in their interpretations of reality, are very good at using the left sides of their brains.) They will tend to be too dry, too reliant upon the power of sweet reason, out of its self-evident correctness, to convince, and to assume that an orderly setting forth of the premises in scrupulous syllogistic sequence does the job. On paper—as a text—and for other like-minded people it may, but the job this will do for the average audience is somnifacient. Whereas this character type must apply imagination to his public performances, he should be wary of getting entangled in emotional disputes. By natural bent he will not be good at them.

People who prefer the combination of *sensing* (perception) plus *feeling* (judgment) focus their attention on facts also, but they handle these with personal warmth. They tend to be sympathetic and friendly, and are happiest finding scope for these generous traits in giving practical help and services for people. These "SF" personalities should be in patient care, community service, sales, and teaching. They are the Marthas of this world, the good-hearted, but the practical and down-to-earth. As speakers, people of this type should indulge in few flights of fancy, talking always from concrete cases, permitting the facts to speak for themselves but drawing also to the audience's attention the human considerations contained in those facts.

People who operate by the combination of *intuition* (perception) plus *feeling* (judgment) focus their attention on possibilities, which, like the sensing and feeling type, they handle with personal warmth. They tend to be enthusiastic and rife with insight. They are good at understanding and communicating with people, and they find their niches in the behavioral sciences, research (according to Myers-Briggs: I find this curious), teaching, literature, and the arts. This "NF" category, to which I belong, is composed of exceedingly pleasant folk, who are also in the main half starved. They speak well, however, having so little else with which to occupy them. Their forte is inductive reasoning, which they are advised to use generously in their talks, and in establishing instant, personal contact with audiences. Their logic is as little to be relied upon as their income, though they make for uxorious husbands and forgiving wives.

People who prefer *intuition* (perception) plus *thinking* (judgment) also focus their attention on possibilities, but like "ST" character types above, handle these with impersonal analysis. They tend to both logical and ingenious, finding scope in theoretical and technical developments, and their place is in the physical sciences, research, management, and forecasts and analysis. These "NT" folk have the makings of superb speakers—that combination of ratiocinative daring coupled to close scrutiny of all evidence, pro and con. They must cultivate humility, because their failures are (1) intellectual impatience, nothing which, if transpiring, can be more damaging from the platform, and (2) difficulty in establishing empathy with the audience.

Now, some people are unsure which category fits them best, and others either deny the most appropriate category because they hold it in lower esteem than others, or indulge in wishful thinking—liking to believe that they answer to a character type for which (since they know subconsciously they are deficient in those particular qualities) they have exaggerated respect. (We all tend to prefer the intellectual over the moral virtues, having succumbed to the prevailing inversion of values, which happens also to be—I'm happy you asked—the great ontological heresy of our time.) These are the tragic folk who all their lives make the same mistakes, who expend their energies vainly pushing the square corners of their true selves into round holes. They are unhappy and unsuccessful, or if they are successful doing what they do best, unhappy because they are not allowed to do also what they are rotten at, which, were they permitted to indulge in the fantasy, would quickly render them unsuccessful (though possibly happy). (I trust this is clear.) Typically, the genius-founder of a Silicon Valley high-tech company comes to mind—the man of visionary imagination—who likes to conceive of himself as a corporate executive too. Thus went the Osborne Computer company. Thus almost went Apple, had it not been for the shakeup that removed the genius-founder (Steven Jobs) from management functions, ultimately— because we are stubborn in our delusions—bringing about his resignation.

Wishful thinking about oneself in a different way can wreak havoc with one's delivery. Recall the examples of Richard Nixon and Jimmy Carter: if one persists in the folly of one's illusions or delusions about oneself, one will attempt to convey a platform impression, or to speak in language and in manner, that are not true to character. There will be a dissonance. The audience will at once sense the anomaly. And either (a) the sincerity of the speaker becomes suspect, as in the case of Richard Nixon, or (b) the delivery will suit the character of the speaker so ill, as in the case of Jimmy Carter, that he comes off ridiculous.

Using Myers-Briggs with scrupulous honesty about oneself can pile up benefits for the speaker. Perception, we are reminded, precedes judgment. The system advises: *"Use your sensing* for facing the facts, being realistic, finding exactly what the situation is. . . . Try to put aside all wishful thinking or sentiment." The system advises: *"Use your thinking-judgment* in an impersonal analysis of cause and effect. Include all the consequences of the alternative solutions, pleasant and unpleasant, those that weigh against the solution you prefer as well as those in its favor." This is the recipe for *building* a case.

The system further advises: *"Use your intuition* to discover all the possibilities—all the ways in which you might change the situation of your handling of it or other people's attitudes toward it." And: *"Use your feeling-judgment* to weigh just how deeply you care about the things that will be gained or lost by each of the alternative solutions. . . . Consider also how the other people concerned will feel [and] include their feelings [along with] your own feelings . . . in deciding which solution will work out best." (Emphasis in the original.) This is a recipe for *delivering* the case. A useful rule of thumb to keep present: "The clearest vision of the future comes only from an intuitive, the most practical realism only from a sensing type, the most incisive analysis only from a thinker, and the most skillful handling of people only from a feeling type."

The Myers-Briggs character analyses are elaborated into sixteen taxonomical designations by tossing in the wild cards of the *introverted* ("I") and *extroverted* ("E") personalities, and by adding to the definitions previously established folk who are more partial to judgment ("J") than to perception ("P"), or vice versa. Thus, among "sensing types" there are those "with thinking" as an auxiliary process, such as an "ISTJ," as well as those "with feeling" as the auxiliary process, such as an "ISFJ." Among "intuitives" there are folk "with feeling" as an auxiliary process, such as an "INFJ," and those "with thinking" as the auxiliary process, such as an "INTJ." These subtypes each head a column, in each of which are included three other subtypes. All are valuable to know, and the reader is directed to the Consulting Psychologists Press, Inc., 577 College Avenue, Palo Alto, California 94306, which publishes Isabel Briggs Myers' *Introduction to Type,* for further study. Sufficient for this book, however, are the categories we have examined. They give one a handle on one's temperamental make-up. They suggest one's strengths and weaknesses on the platform.

What's left to consider is how the audience perceives of one, and if the shoe of any of these broad personality types fits better than it pinches, what one should do about it to capitalize on one's perceived character.

This requires personal coaching by a professional. In Appendix 4, however, the reader will find distillations of three personality types, which I label "Hail Fellow, Well Met," "The Sensitive Neurotic," and "Eeyore." Their self-perception and the perception that audiences will form about them are discussed, along with their strengths and weaknesses as public speakers, and what they can do to improve. From pursuing these, the reader can educe others to fit the sixteen personality types recognized by Myers-Briggs—and sundry more from his own experience with the human comedy. The exercise should help him discover himself.

There are simply too many permutations of the human personality—they are infinite, as any novelist will attest—to encumber this book describing and analyzing. Each of us must exploit our given temperament, polishing the virtues, mitigating the faults. We can never hope to step out of character, nor should we try; rather, the aim, once having determined what our true character is and how we are perceived by others, is adroitly to make use of the potential. Our model might well be Ernest Wuliger.

Ernest who? Wuliger. W-u-l-i-g-e-r. His face and form fit the somewhat ludicrous Elmer Fudd–sound of the surname he bears—has borne up bravely under, maybe, lifelong.

I do not know the gentleman personally, but my delight is in the thirty-second TV spots featuring his late-middle-aged unmemorable self, with the bland, upper Ohio Valley voice and the self-deprecatory air. His hair is gray and thinning, his complexion pale and gray. "You won't remember my name," he says in one of these ads (I think the first)—which he proceeds to mumble in such manner that, indeed, we do not remember it (I had to ask our kind librarian to look it up for me), we scarcely hear it. But he goes on to say, "I do hope you remember the name of my mattress company, Stearns and Foster," telling us betimes with a disarming sincerity what a fine mattress his company makes. He quite wins one over. In another ad, he is presented lounging comfortably (though, it somehow transpires, a trifle embarrassedly) on a mattress, saying, "Hello, I am Ernest Wawuff-mumble [we never do get the name], and my business is putting people to sleep." Which the viewer is hilariously quite sure that this eminently nice gentleman would!

This is what's called "brilliant packaging." The firm that designed these spots for Mr. Wuliger exploits his character type, which he courageously (and, viewers are confident, humorously) plays before the cameras. The result is a sincerity that commands our affections. But whereas I will look into a Stearns and Foster mattress if ever I have need of another, I hope never to be asked to endure a formal half hour after-dinner address by Mr. Wuliwhat's-his-name, unless he is able to tap the temperament (first sense) within, or serves a 1977 Graham's port!

3

Where to Go Looking for What You Need and Discovering and Using Fresh Material

Finding a fresh idea is about as easy as spotting a red-cockaded woodpecker in Central Park.

Fresh ideas are scarce, yet no one wants to listen to stale content if it can be helped.

Writers and speakers have an obligation to discover as original a perspective on whatever they are talking about as they are capable. They are equally obliged to get their facts straight.

Nothing But the Facts, Ma'am

The straight scoop about anything can be the damnedest, most elusive bird of all, but finding it, if one is lucky enough, requires sifting through newspapers, periodicals, monographs, and books.

Everybody is well advised to sift these sources critically, however. Books, monographs, magazines, and newspapers can be pest-places of error that the magic of print perpetuates. (I used to believe anything I read in a library was true, or it wouldn't be there.) "My good friend Dr. Palache wrote a doctoral thesis about paralysis in paraplegics," won't do, because if it wasn't published, it was never subjected to broad critical examination. "It was in the newspapers" likely may not do either, because newspapers are mine fields of misinformation that harried editors have no time to verify and correct. "I read it in *Time*" or *Newsweek* or *U.S. News and World Report* is safer, but a glance at the letters columns shows how often even these reputable journals, despite their elaborate infrastructure of researchers and copy editors, can make a hash of fact, and sometimes print fabulations as fact (twice I've had personal experience of this in the case of *Time*). To their shame, they are guilty also of shaping stories for the politically sensational effect, a vice to which *Time* and *Newsweek* are notoriously prone. And even books from reputable publishing houses aren't totally safe. Whereas the factual content has probably been rigorously checked over a period of months, there is still no guarantee against error, and books about historical events, current issues, and political figures are almost always written not only by someone who has cultivated a strong perspective, which can have the effect of distorting evidence by selection, but sometimes also by a writer whose perspective has long deteriorated into bias, his bias into ideology, tingeing and distorting almost all evidentiary material.

Down the road a piece, I will be coming back to this. Suffice now that a person has to cross-check. One has to use one's judgment.

Dangers in the Attractive Anomaly

This is especially so in the search for original material. The piquant datum may be piquant because it is wrong, or deceiving. Everyone should have suspected right off that onetime Soviet Premier the late Yuri V. Andropov's touted closet enjoyment of scotch whisky and American jazz was as much in mitigation of his totalitarian nature as Adolph Hitler's love of good music his, and in no way entered into the balance of, by way of redressing, Andropov's background as the merciless hangman-in-chief of the KGB. Yet this goes on all the time, peripheral irrelevancies obscuring substance. (Read *Time*'s grovelingly fulsome interview of Mikhail Gorbachev two years back.)

Still, the person who is likely to be called upon to give a speech, or a pitch, does well to collect oddities of fact and fancy. Jack Valenti (see Appendix 1) keeps a journal filled with the culled pithy sayings of famous folk, tidbits from which he trots out to embellish his talks or drive home points.

It's a good idea. It can intimidate opponents in debate or in board rooms. One must be careful about erudite references from the platform, however. In this illiterate age, they have a habit of sailing over people's heads, so that one's satisfaction becomes quite private. And speaking of board rooms, never underestimate the cultural ignorance of anyone who did not major his four college years in the humanities. Irritated one afternoon by a business partner's negativism, I snapped that we had enough problems without him playing the Mercutio in our own garden. He was a redheaded Irish-American lawyer, a graduate of Georgetown, no less, where he had lost his religion apparently to no comparative effect. He turned beet-red with ire. I thought he would slug me. I still can't figure out what he imagined I was accusing him of, maybe masturbating, but the thrust of my jibe was utterly lost on him.

Be prudent. Don't pretend to an erudition you do not possess. Unless one has truly read the author or work referred to, one is liable to misunderstanding and misuse of the fancy allusion (as in Lenin's famous prediction that the contradictions of capitalism would of themselves bring those economies down, which he never made—I am told, I have not read Lenin through—and as in Lord Acton's oft-quoted "Power corrupts, and absolute power corrupts absolutely," which he never said in that categorical manner).

The Perilous Quotation

There is no embarrassment quite like having one's half-educated conceits pricked by authentic scholars who listen through and then calmly rise to demolish one, as in: "Mr. Buckley's speech was imaginative, but there is scarcely a word of truth in it. He has grounded everything he has told you on a derivative and quite wrong reading of Lord Acton, from which he has drawn his characteristically perverse conclusions. What Acton actually said was that power corrupts, and absolute power *tends* to corrupt absolutely, which is a far cry from the dire inevitability of this occurring, as Mr. Buckley would have you infer . . ." Oh, no rebuttal is so humiliating, and can throw a speaker into such confusion, as having his facts blown to smithereens and the accuracy of his citations of authority discredited by an opponent who is thus able to flaunt superior knowledge. The advantage is surrendered to him, never to be recovered. The audience will not fully trust Mr. Buckley thereafter if he timidly suggests that the sun rises in the East.

Regarding Lord Acton's treacherous aphorism, one's only recourse is to pull out a facsimile of the gentleman's 1887 letter to Bishop Mandell Creighton, wherein he wrote, "power tends to corrupt, and absolute power corrupts absolutely."

Those Treacherous Generalizations!

Be careful. Hasty generalizations from oft-heard adages that are misquoted, or when quoted correctly, that convey only part of the truth, and, because wrested from context, inaccurately reflect the author's real views, have not only embarrassed a lot of folk, they have damaged promising careers by exposing the unwary mouth to ridicule. We take for granted that J. S. Mill is the apostle of popular government, for example, but we would be mistaken to assume his benediction for many of the egalitarian political practices that have crept into our system, and that today—also, for example, wholly incorrectly—determine the popular view of what political norms should obtain in South Africa. Mill would not have approved uncircumscribed universal suffrage, or lowering the vote to the preposterously juvenile age of 18. In the second paragraph of *On Liberty* he writes, ". . . this doctrine is meant to apply only to human beings in the maturity of their faculties." Liberty (and the notion derived therefrom of popular government) is not for children, not for innocents still living in a state of nature, not for those uneducated in the meaning and obligations of the concept. ("To the incontinent," warned Goethe, "knowledge brings no profit." The same goes for political freedom.) (Wing that one from the platform, and you know what your audience is going to hear? "From the incompetent," warned Gertie . . .) There can be no misunderstanding of the man. Mill hammers the point home. "Liberty, as a principle, has no application to any state of things anterior to the time when mankind have become capable of being improved by free and equal discussion." To adduce his authority for, let's say, abolishing all literacy requirements, can be dangerous.

Watching out for Received Wisdom

We take for granted what is dimly remembered from American History I or Economics II. What we have misunderstood from our school days. What—maybe—was ignorantly and wrongly told to us by our teachers. It is common to hear Adam Smith cited as an apostle of free trade, to take another example of accepted notions; and, indeed, he did fervently espouse free trade . . . circumstances excepting, which a bit of rummaging through the *Wealth of Nations* (book

4, chap. 2, pp. 430–31) reveals. Smith subordinated what he styled as the "opulence" that accrues to a people from untrammeled trade to considerations of defense, as in relation to the British Navigation Acts of his time, and when it "will be generally advantageous to lay some burden upon foreign, for the encouragement of domestic industry . . ." The greater good of national security in mind, he favored a policy of industrial self-sufficiency; and for the same compelling reasons reluctantly approved retaliatory duties in what came to be known as the tariff wars. These identical arguments, of course, are used by the American steel and textile and shoe industry lobbies. If you oppose the shortsighted punitive legislation against foreign competition being proposed in Congress by politicians like Jesse Helms (in the case of subsidies for American tobacco farmers) or Bob Dole (in the case of wheat subsidies), who are beholden to these special interests, do not at your peril fling Adam Smith at them, because they may fling him right back in your face. On the other hand, if you are Roger Milliken, debating William Simon on the need for some protections against "economic aggression" by the "slave-wage" textile mills of Korea and Taiwan, it would suit—and be piquant indeed—to claim precedent in Adam Smith.

Making Doubly Sure the Authority One Cites
Actually Supports One's Case

Well, if J. S. Mill was not the radical libertarian we had assumed, and Adam Smith not the uncompromising free trader, surely we can trust other received premises, such as what we have always known about the great Prussian Karl von Clausewitz's preference for offense in war over defense. This example is particularly interesting, for being so deceptive. Because: so much is true about Clausewitz. He did prefer a pugnacious attitude to a static attitude: nevertheless, it is more accurate to say that he favored an opportunistically offensive spirit while recognizing that the strategic advantages lie with the defense.

This is the kind of tangle speakers regularly trip their tootsies in. Almost nothing can be trusted to be as it seems, or as we are comfortably accustomed to assuming it is, and we are required again and again to verify even what we hold to be certitudes so consecrated by use that they sound platitudinous. Actual human blood may be spilled on account of such confusions. Clausewitz, we discover, would make a poor witness against the "Star Wars" interstellar defense initiative. He would have been appalled by the folly of the Light Brigade's charge, concurring with the French officer who commented that though it was *magnifique* it was not *la guerre.* (The French, notwithstanding, reacting to their humiliation by the Huns in 1870, and possibly misreading the great Prussian authority, thereafter schooled their officers in an ideological predilection for attack. This may also have been a hangover from the departed glories of Napoleonic times: Danton's ". . . l'audace, et toujours de l'audace"— with the result that they flung and flung and flung their armies at the entrenched German lines during World War I, bullheadedly accepting the most awful carnage to no end. See *The Price of Glory,* by Alistair Horne.)

Citations from Authority That Do Not Ring True

When *you* quote anybody, not only check to be positive that your citation is accurate, and that it fairly and completely represents the position of the source; try to make sure also that what you quote isn't rubbish. That is, that the great man you cite wasn't nodding. If, upon analysis, you personally decide—pay no attention to established opinion, or to what you think you *ought* to think—the generalization is stupid, or fatuous, or just wrong, you may wonder whether it is accurately attributed to the otherwise sensible fellow. For example, academic antagonists typically in my days on the stump made much pious and self-congratulatory crowd-pleasing hay from averring (with modest downcast eyes, and palms virtually, if not virtuously, on their breasts) that they, like Voltaire, might disagree with what I said, but would nevertheless fighttothedeathtodefendmyrighttospeak my vicious nonsense.

Apart from my certain knowledge that they would do no such thing (most of them couldn't have fought their way out of a paper bag, forensic or other); that, in fact, academics are past masters in the suppression of dissident views; it transpired, on investigation, that Voltaire never made such a half-witted statement. It was apocryphally attributed to him. It was beneath the great Frenchman, we might have guessed, the French being noted for their grasp of the realities; because, as the late, great polemicist Willmoore Kendall concluded about the proposition, having submitted it to analysis, it is utterly without sense.

Correct Fixed (Erroneous) Assumptions with Utmost Care

Now, François-Marie Arouet, Voltaire, was a scoundrel. He was a cynic. He was one of the mischievous eighteenth-century *philosophes* who have done untold damage to epistemology since the so-called Enlightenment. He couldn't be trusted intellectually, and improvised a "philosophy" of history (*La Philosophie de l'histoire*, 1765,) that was factitious rubbish and that he knew was rubbish. But he was no dope. Yet he is alleged to be seriously proposing: A. That his opinions and those of someone else have equal moral value— equal claim to truth. (That is, a person who advocates child-murder has as much right to be heard as the person who is against child-murder.) Therefore B: no opinions embody greater, or better, or morally preemptive rights over other opinions, which is a total relativism of conceptual values, and thus, admittedly, not uncongenial to the man. Therefore C: there is no objectively ascertainable Truth or Right. Therefore D—it follows—why fight to the death for anyone's right to speak his piece when the principle itself is relative, tendentious, merely arbitrary, of no discernible greater value than the opinion of, say, a Communist or Fascist that nobody but Communists or Fascists have any right at all to be heard.

It is crushing to lay oneself open to analysis of this obliterative kind by one's opponent; to have laid such large stock in some cliché that a little pondering upon would shortly have revealed to be empty. But if you yourself should have occasion thus to smash an opponent, watch out for analyses so logically tight, and thus so exacting of an audience's cognitive faculties—which are given no time to mull the various steps over, which must grasp each step thoroughly and instantly it is spoken—that people are bewildered. In affairs of the heart, it is unwise to put into writing everything that one says. From the podium one is better advised not to say everything that one might write. Professor Kendall's evisceration of the pseudo-Voltairian proposition is much tighter than the rendition of it above. But even my looser, more easily comprehended version had to be stated very slowly and part by part repeated. Despite which, I was not always sure I was getting it across to audiences, because it is passing difficult for even the most intelligent listener to follow subtle verbal logistical twists and turns. (I know I am unable to; I have to see it written.) Many speakers make the mistake believing that they have quite crushed their opponents after such an exercise, when they have accomplished no more than to bewilder the audience. Keep it simple.

Subtle Distinctions

Take Clausewitz's celebrated dictum: "War is nothing else than the continuation of state policy by different means." Do a job on that.

Once shot, twice warned. As the saying goes, there is no education in the second kick of a mule. You are wondering: OK, am I being set up again? Did Clausewitz make this statement, is it correctly quoted, and is its sense a fair representation of what he intended?

The answer to all three misdoubts: yes. You are not being sandbagged. (That's the correct sense of what Clausewitz wrote.) Nevertheless, the aphorism is frequently incorrectly interpreted that Clausewitz proposes war as an *extension* of policy. This imputed sense is false. Clausewitz wrote further on (in his magnum opus, *On War*), more elaborately, of his proposition, "War is nothing else than *a continuation* [emphasis added] of political transactions intermingled with different means. We say intermingled with different means in order to state at the same time that these political transactions are not stopped by the war itself, are not changed into something totally different but substantially continue, whatever the means applied may be. . . . How could it be otherwise?" he asks. "Do the political relations between different peoples and governments ever cease when the exchange of diplomatic notes has ceased? Is not war only a different method of expressing their thoughts, different in writing and language?"

He terminates with a memorable phrase: "War admittedly has its own grammar but not its own logic."

All of which is nice, and philosophically interesting in a very Germanic way; but the distinctions are next to impossible—in my opinion—to impress upon the comprehension of the run of American audiences; not, I once again hasten to add, because we are a dull-witted people, but because (a) Americans have not been trained to the fine distinctions, failing consequently to understand them when they are drawn, (b) in common with most other civilized folk, our capacity for audile understanding is not as keen as in (wholly) illiterate societies. When I stop to ask instructions of anyone about how to get someplace, I cock my ears, smile, thank the kind guide effusively, drive off . . . and promptly realize that I have failed to absorb what I was told. (Which tale anticipates the necessity of listening carefully.)

Collect pet dictums and aphorisms; be prepared to defend them; but don't let them dictate to you. They do not substitute for thought. To his credit, Mr. Valenti eschews the use of Bartlett. He considers such shortcuts "cheating"—*aperçus* cheaply come by. He claims more than passing acquaintance with the article or book that he adduces, or from which he culls a passage in support of his thesis. He is scrupulous to annote chapter and verse in his journal, and before using these quotations he looks them up, checking their accuracy and their appropriateness.

Oh, the woes I have suffered from not following this prescription! Do not thou, fair reader, thus err. Refresh thyself with the provenance and precision of what thou weenest most worshipfully engraven on thy soul. I really loved the trenchant "Magis magnus clericos non sunt magis magnus sapiens" (The most learned of scholars are not the wisest of men), from Seneca by way of Montaigne, which I used with withering effect on, oh, innumerable occasions. Then some joker complained it couldn't be Seneca who said that, because it was lousy Latin. I replied hotly that maybe Seneca, who hailed from the Spanish province of Cordova, spoke a corrupted tongue. Nettled, however, I looked it up, and saw almost at once that not only had my sloppy typing cut the tail off *sapientes,* ridiculously rendering it *sapiens,* which was thereupon logged into my word processor's memory bank, whence into my poor head, but that my even sloppier and errant recall had for some reason preferred the first-century Roman to the sixteenth-century French wit who was in fact the author of the aphorism. These two errors had set in my mind like concrete. (It's still lousy Latin, I suspect, but blame Rabelais, not me.)

Moses himself might have made a mishmash of the Ten Commandments if the Lord hadn't provided him with stone tablets, nicely chiseled. Check it, and doublecheck it. The basic evidentiary materials for almost any talk can be dug out of the relevant indexes in the library; but of themselves such source materials are unlikely to suggest those revealing insights—that original and captivating perspective—that will delight an audience and hold it.

Discovering and Using Fresh Ideas

There are folk who wouldn't recognize a fresh idea though it smacked them in the face. We are all obtuse in some areas (viz. Myers-Briggs), and we are therefore obliged to borrow what we cannot dredge up out of ourselves. The more one reads about anything the easier will one recognize the conventional arguments, on this side or the other, because they keep cropping up. When a person catches himself yawning, or getting impatient, he can be certain the argument is tired. He has by then also probably found it wanting, which signifies that he has advanced to a more sophisticated plane. One is gaining a mastery of one's subject. One is beginning to become formidable.

All this takes time—or a good researcher, if one is well-fixed enough to hire such. When a person does a lot of talking on any single subject, he discovers that relevant facts and arguments stick like burrs to the memory. I had no difficulty when arguing economics regurgitating stews of relevant statistics—unerringly—that I might have read that afternoon on the plane. It is a matter of attention, I guess. The mind fastens with a kind of ravenous eagerness on what is useful to it.

Astonishing is how serendipity operates. It's like discovering a new word: you may never have noticed it before, but almost from the day you look it up you encounter it everywhere. You may never have given much thought to the toxic effects of chemicals, but from the day one of the rigs in your trucking company skids on a highway and spills some noxious fume or other, you will find yourself assimilating knowledge about chemicals and their properties faster than ever you believed possible. You may never have had the remotest interest in louseworts, but the moment activists from the Sierra Club get an injunction against further work on the dam that threatens the weed's habitat, you, who supply the cement, will develop an overpowering interest in louseworts and milkworts and soapworts, and all other manner and kind of worts, and will absorb knowledge on the subject like a blotter soaks up ink or a government bureau tax money. Everything you read, you find, carries an article on, or reference to, or some useful revelation about worts. Your mother-in-law, by god, you discover, obtained an advanced degree from Cornell on worts. Your girlfriend has worts sprouting between the boards of her garden deck and can't get rid of them, your wife comes back from the Garden Club chattering enthusiastically about a slide show on worts, your daughter suddenly declares that she intends to give up creeps for worts, and your son comes down with them. As you stump from town hall, to court hearing, to chamber of commerce denouncing worts and all their works, which are a menace to civilization, to the virtue of American womanhood, and to the virility of American men, and also to your cement factory, you become in three months' time one of the nation's outstanding experts on worts, and you will probably be dropped by your girlfriend, deceived by your wife, and bitterly disappointed by your daughter, who has gone back to cultivating creeps, because you have become also the world's most dreadful bore on the subject of worts.

Indispensable General Culture: Works of the Imagination

Though a thorough knowledge of one's topic can be gleaned from library sources, and though one's general technical reading will replete one's dossier on louseworts, snaildarters, chemicals, or most anything else, that special fillip, that illuminating embellishment, that striking and intriguing analogy, that joyous metaphor that can transform a forgettable speech into something the audience will go home buzzing about are not likely to be found in the pedestrian pages of the *New York Times,* nor in the bureaucratese of the *Statistical Abstract of the United States Government.*

Every aspiring speaker should own at least one of the major encyclopedias and Mortimer Adler's *The Great Books.* This is an expensive proposition, but they are indispensable to have in the home not only for reference, but for nourishment. And that brings up—returns us to, I have suggested it above—a major problem for almost any American under sixty years of age who was not lucky in his or her family and educational background.

It is not our fault. We didn't ourselves destroy education in this country. Just the same:

Any born English-speaking Jew, and any English-speaking son or daughter of the Christian West, who has not savored, indeed, soaked him- or herself in the King James version of the Holy Bible is irreparably ignorant and culturally deprived. (If he has been schooled in the new Anglican or Catholic translations, he is no longer ignorant, but he has been culturally, irreparably done violence to, and should have resort in a court of law against the perpetrators of these tin-eared transmogrifications.)

That's for starters. Any Englishman or American who has not read his Greek and Roman myths, his Homer, the real legend of King Arthur, Dante, Chaucer, Milton, Cervantes, Shakespeare: oh, the lot! in this country up unto and through Hawthorne, Melville, and Faulkner, and in both England and the United States through Tolkien—is culturally a barbarian, unfitted and unequipped for civilized discourse, and therefore mortally handicapped if he (or she: please recall I am addressing both genders) hopes for high distinction as an orator.

Sorry to be so blunt, but having unfortunately brought the subject up myself, I can't duck it. I am treating realities. This is not a question of being some kind of snob; it is one of maintaining the dialogue of civilization down through the ages as well in one's own time. It is maintaining a communion of intellects and sensibilities the better to achieve a communion of souls.

Else one can become an OK talker on the utilitarian and vulgar political levels, but never more. When Commodore Vanderbilt steamed back into New York harbor from his extended European grand tour, there was bad news. He penned the following note to two of his partners, which I quote from memory:

Gentlemen:
    I find that you have been cheating me. I will not sue, because the law is too slow. I will ruin you.

Now, apart from the satisfaction of one's certainty that Vanderbilt kept his promise, remark on the hardfisted prose, punching out words of one syllable, the twin-voweled third exception to which, *ruin*, resonates; the compelling—the riveting—interior rhythm; and the stunning control of tone, the finality of which must have tolled like a mortuary bell in the hearts of the two rascals he addressed his missive to. This from a lowborn, semiliterate brawler in the rough and tumble of the nineteenth-century American business world. But he knew his Joel. He had obviously soaked himself in Nathan and Ezekiel. There is by contrast probably not a single utterance by any great modern "captain of industry" that has survived the annual stockholders' meeting, and that is because the great and lesser captains of industry today are culturally as the baboon on Petrus Camper's scale.[1] (I only just became aware of the existence of Camper, courtesy of Jay Stephen Gould—see below.) As a nation, we have become cultural boors, and it is now questionable—it is being questioned—whether it is taxonomically admissible to style ourselves a civilized people. It's quite tragic that until 1945 or 1950 one could assume that any American from the most basic literate background was versed in our cultural heritage, which nourished the imaginative faculties, because if not at school, he picked most of it up at home; and that until maybe as late as the early 1960s even illiterate households in this country were familiar with *the* fundamental document of our civilization.

This is no longer the case. And it's a crying shame, because for many of the more ambitious readers of this book—through no fault of their own—it necessitates a pile of catching up. Any person aspiring to become a speaker well furnished in his imagination simply must fill those gaps in his cultural knowledge that he may discover. Happily, the chore is pleasurable. A nice thing too is that since all of the foundation stones of our culture are universal in character, the reading of any one of them, say the *Iliad,* say *Hamlet,* say *Moby Dick,* will almost certainly provide the public speaker with insights for his very next talk, at the least aphorisms. The reading of a single great epic poem, or play, or novel will at once enrich the speaker's text. It will feed, and may even suggest, the next twenty. There are no shortcuts, however. Though T. H. White's King Arthur is terrific, Sir Thomas Malory's is the mother lode. Happily once again, it is never too late to start—and to get hooked on the reading. The true "mind-enhancing" drug that the generation of the 1960s, and those of the decades since, have been searching for is literature.

The Joys and Uses of Heterogeneous Reading

We've been talking about the basics. More is necessary. I browse book stalls and collect curiosities. *The History of Blown Glass,* for example. Or *Homesickness in Insects.* Or *Life with the Hottentots.*

1. This minute my barrister eldest son leans over my shoulder to remark, "Dad, the reason businessmen no longer write letters like that has nothing to do with culture. Their lawyers wouldn't let them."

I collect books on heraldry, Scottish tartans, wind instruments, shells, herpetology, numismatics, and sundry other exotic and arcane subjects. From an old engraving I learned that Louis XIV's bird dogs—Spanish setters—were Bonne, Ponne, and Nonne, which information has yet to be of use, though some day I am sanguine it will be. The works of fanatics about their obsessions are always fascinating. Almost any biography by a candidate for national office who lost is an example. One reads without believing. The sheer ego of some people is instructive and fertile with insights about the human species, at least for me. Theosophists, scientologists, and other votives of quack religions are good sources for insolent and eccentric and outrageous analogies, which can reduce opponents to quivering fury—as when one draws a mock-serious comparison between the tenets of Seventh Day Adventists and the latest macro-ecological projection of doom by Barry Commoner or some other guru of his sect. I regularly read such as *Natural History*, not only for the essays by Dr. Gould, but because I have discovered some of my favorite metaphors in those pages. Why are some thoughts born *precocial*, for example, and why are others so totally antithetical as to be *allopatric?* Anything that is odd, quirky, absurd, strange, and revolting in a fascinating way is a treasure.

Making Platitudes Palatable

Two springs back I was asked by a friend, John Lindsay, to stage a debate for the luncheon program of his Rotary Club in our small home town of Camden, South Carolina. I heard myself saying sure; and an opponent was promptly tapped—a young and attractive lawyer called Ken DuBose, who was running for County Council.

The topic was to be something Ken and I had heatedly (and amiably) discussed one night at a supper club we belong to. The Carolina Cup Steeplechase is an annual event, drawing tens of thousands of visitors. A noxious tradition has crept in, whereby local and state politicians are given free passes to the infield rail, at the finish line. I was grumbling about this perk, and Ken was boisterously defending it, when John Lindsay overheard us.

I regretted accepting the invitation almost before the word "Yes" had popped out of my mouth.

The obligation had me more on edge than if I'd been invited to illumine the College of Cardinals in the Sistine Chapel on the philosophical unicorn called "social justice," to whose mythical nonsense they are addicted. Our speaking school had just swung into high gear, and there had been copious publicity. Behind the goodwill of my audience—seventy or eighty tradesmen and professionals of my adopted home town, many of whom had known me since child-hood—steely-eyed assessment would be taking place. To wit: Is this guy as good as he's cracked up to be? I had never debated in Camden. There is, of course, no necessary connection between one's ability to perform and one's ability to teach; there are successful football coaches and baseball managers who were mediocre athletes on the field. Still . . .

"What can ail thee, knight at arms?" my wife, Tasa, asked me over lunch, quoting the divine Lope. I jogged my two miles that evening sockless in my espadrilles, taking on a cargo of fine sand and gravel that cut me across the bridge of my feet, but I did not notice. "Has sweet sleep not knit up thy ravelled sleave of care?" inquired Tasa next morning, quoting the sublime Calderon. The more I worried about the ridiculous gig I had let myself in for, the more I rued my inability to say no to almost anything. The construction of a case that did not languish from its own tedium was going to be difficult. The essence of my position was my antipathy to privilege. Having served up that sanctimonious sentiment, what else, other than an elabora-tion of platitudes, was there to say? Not much, I quickly discovered—sweating at my Kaypro, with a Buckley School seminar that very weekend and deadlines falling also for a column and a book review. Furthermore, to heap on politicians—they are such an easy mark—was not only too easy, it risked offending sensibilities. A third rule is never inadvertently, and only for the most profound reasons pur-posely, wound. There were city and county elections in the offing, and there would be local politicians, or relatives of local politicians, in the audience. How to make my points fun: barbed, yet innocent of venom?

I struggled. If there was nothing original to say, how could I make my conventional points *sound* original, or at least eccentric? In my summation, how could I repeat myself without giving away that I was in fact merely repeating myself—without boring the audience?

Well, at the risk of irremediably impoverishing the reader, I skip to that summation; because here is where my omnivorous and eso-teric reading paid off.

Several years ago I came across a revolting creature called a hagfish. I did not actually make its acquaintance, but I treasured it in my heart, and had used it in a novel I am at work on. It would do just fine for my summation, the object of which, you remember, was to reiterate my conventional position in a manner memorable enough to give it the semblance of originality.

I asked the Rotarians, who were happily digesting their Seafood Hut fare:

> "Do you know what a hagfish is?
>
> "A hagfish is a very disgusting creature. It is eel-like in appearance. It is kin to the lampreys, which feed upon fishes, boring into their bodies, usually by way of the anus, and devouring their viscera and flesh.
>
> "Hagfish are the lowest existing craniate vertebrates. Webster describes them thus: 'The mouth is round and surrounded by eight tentacles. The nostril is single, very large, and opens behind the pharynx. The tongue bears horny teeth, the roof of the mouth a single tooth. The eyes are rudimentary; the ear has but one semicircular canal; the skin is smooth and secretes a great quantity of slime.'"

"That's a hagfish," I continued, enjoying the rapt attention of everyone who had not turned bilious.

> "That is also a fair description of a politician, whose skin secretes a quantity of slime, whose tongue and other parts unmentionable grow keratoid at the prospect of power, who is certainly among the lowest existing craniate vertebrates, if he can be said to have a spine at all, and who, as the hagfish bores into fish to devour their viscera and flesh, bores into the body politic and gorges on its tender juices through unscrupulous use of the tax power. . . .
>
> "If there *must* be an enclave for politicians at the Carolina Cup [I concluded] for fear of the moral and goodness knows what other contagion they are liable to spread among the public, let it be situated somewhere to the rear, say between the hot dog stands and the latrines."[2]

A week or so later, I asked my good friend Jim Burns, who owns a hardware store, "Why haven't you come to my farm to try out the big pond? I'm getting tired of inviting you." He leered at me, saying, "I'm afraid I might catch a hagfish."

2. Ken DuBose's summation was a fine piece of fun at my expense: we had a good time, neither of us emerging bowed, and neither excessively bloody. He went on to win his election handily; but not before making me the solemn promise that never will he block my view of the finish line.

4

Sharpening the Wits

Delivering a speech and taking part in a debate are closely related activities that require different faculties.

The person who has learned to give a good talk can be confident about his opening statements. Unless that person has had ring experience in the rough and tumble of debate, however, he may not know how to deal with sharp refutations of his position after he has done. It is a sad spectacle to watch an intelligent person come apart under pressure when wrested from his prepared text.

We'll be continuing our discussion of the general principles that rule in constructing a good speech (last chapter: scrupulous accuracy in fact and citation, finding and using fresh material; to come: researching the case, logical construction, and the correct use of language), but here I want to extol the virtues of debate as an essential exercise for anyone who aspires to think and speak confidently under fire. I want also to address an apparent anomaly that may have been aggravating the reader.

You remember from Chapter 1 that the three bugaboos most often cited by people who attend our seminars are:

1. nerves,
2. the panic of stage fright,
3. lack of self-confidence.[1]

Notwithstanding, we have stressed the necessity of pouring grease—as it may seem—on a stove-top fire: of riling up the nervous

1. Close second concern: organization of materials.

temperament, which we contend (1) is essential for most personalities, (2) acts as an anodyne against stage fright.

That's sufficiently difficult to accept, though it boils down to substituting emotional responses (when a person is eager to speak his piece, fright is psychologically overwritten). But then we go and compound this apparent contradiction by asserting that the intellectual and emotional energies of debate steady nerves, and thus also help combat fright. How can both approaches avail?

Well, they do. Upland hunters for the explosive ruffed grouse and the heart-hammering southern bobwhite quail learn this from the time they are in knee pants (which dates me). The young shotgunner is told, "Shoot fast, and shoot slow." It is a puzzlement. Yet that is just exactly what he must do: be quick, waste no time getting his gun up and swinging on the bird; but also take his time concentrating on the one target out of the covey, on its speed and angle of flight, squeezing the trigger off at precisely the right moment.

The apprentice gunner is being told: trip your reflexes into action lightning-fast, for which the catalyst of excitement is necessary, but maintain cool concentration.

This is no paradox. In speaking as in gunning, it's mind over emotions, though absent the emotions, mind alone produces lean fare, and can even become the prey of regressive emotions. The aroused temperament keys a speaker up to his best performance; debating helps teach the speaker how to tap that state of nervous exaltation without succumbing to it. Debating builds up confidence. One may reel under adversity; one won't collapse.

It was, I think, at High Point College, in North Carolina, in the autumn of 1971, that a most awful, and in several respects instructive, vicissitude befell me.

'Twas late in the evening when my 15-year-old daughter Elizabeth and I flew into High Point from a contentious booking in Indiana. A student met us. Dumping us at a motel, he advised that we would be called for at 8:15 sharp on the morrow. We nodded wearily, tumbling into bed within minutes of his casual so long.

That morning was frantic. I had failed to leave a wake-up call, or set an alarm—rousing late, with scarce margin for coffee and a hasty review of my notes before the telephone announced that Professor Such-and-So was cooling his heels in the lobby. On stage, while the lecture hall was filling, a dangerous lassitude took hold. My mind wandered . . . How many bookings to go? Six. (Or was it seven?) How many more dreary motels to check in and out of? Five. (Or was it four?) The introduction, which was cursory, afforded me just enough time to extract from my briefcase the manila folder containing "Aristotle Didn't Swing," a saucy put-down of the inane youth movement that had the country in a kind of thrall for almost a decade.

I speak off a written text. There were long citations in this talk from Plato, Aristotle, Seneca, Augustine, Aquinas, Montaigne, Macaulay, Goethe, and I forget who else. Coming to the end of page 5, I flipped it over . . . to discover that page 6 belonged to a lecture called "Why Conservatives Can Be Progressive." So did page 7. So did the next fifteen pages.

For an instant, I froze. I am not precisely wedded to my texts—the talks are in the subconscious committed to memory—but they are my crutch, my lifelines. They are that from which I derive confidence. Where was dear Ari! Where had my security blanket gone! The briefcase rested on the platform, within reach; and though it would have been inelegant to excuse myself, go to it, and fish out the correct text, I now recalled that upon reviewing the lecture in the motel room I had hurriedly dumped all my talks out on the desk, and, when the desk clerk's call came, snatched up only the one folder.

Struggling to recover composure, I kept mouthing words, dissimulating as best I could by tone and expression the panic that threatened. My mind raced. I was thank God managing to dredge up from the subconscious connective tissue, but what was I to do about those long quotations? These I had purposely resisted pipping into my memory bank, because I feel it is more effective, when making a direct quotation of any length, to read it in deliberate manner, contrasting the author's style with one's own constructions.

Well, I winged it thirty-five minutes. It was excruciating, but I survived. So did the audience—I guess. I paraphrased where I could not recall exact language, freshly thinking through the sense of those passages I had culled. Even when my tongue knotted, my syntax becoming to my own ear impenetrable, I gazed blandly (idiotically?) out across the rows of two or three hundred students and faculty, as though what I had just said made perfect sense, speaking with an extemporaneous directness, whole passages from the text popping into my head in the nick of time.

Afterward, while we were waiting in the dressing room to be taken to lunch, Lizzie asked me, "Daddy, you're so pale. You're sweating. Why, you're trembling! Are you all right?" I was not all right. My teeth chattered. I shook from chill. Between spasms I tried to explain what had happened: I was succumbing that very moment to stage fright—now that the agony was over; after having probably ascribed to Hobbes what Hume had said, to Burke what de Maistre had said, to Mick Jagger what John Lennon had said. But she, dear heart, reassured me, crying, "I swear nobody knew the difference. Daddy, nobody could tell, truly, it all sounded perfectly normal."

Which was comforting, until I thought about it. (It occurs to me that I have not been invited back to High Point.)

I suffered another near calamity in Salt Lake City. I had been invited to address a convention of the Mormon Elders after their banquet. The table for sixty or more people was set up in the dining room of the wonderful old Utah Hotel. My speech would please, I was confident. It was an examination of the Wickedness of the Welfare State, the Materialistic Poverty of the Great Society, and the Deviousness and Corruption of its chief architect, Lyndon B. Johnson.

It was truly a philippic against the character and career of the ex-president, beginning with when he stole his first election to the Senate. I had labored long and hard over it.

This time the introduction was protracted, and too kind. The chairman was just turning to me, saying, "It is now my pleasure to present Mr. Buckley," when the hotel's public address system broke into the proceedings, declaring in solemn tones, "We regret to announce that ex-President Lyndon Baines Johnson has died of a heart attack."

What a sensation. There was probably not a Mormon at the table, nor maybe ten in Salt Lake City, nor a hundred in the state of Utah, who had anything except contempt for Mr. Johnson. The chairman nevertheless at once rose—as did we all—asked us to bow our heads, and intoned a homely *De Profundis* for the villain's soul, followed by the Lord's Prayer, in which I of course joined, though I choked on the amen. We sat down. "Now, Mr. Buckley," resumed the chairman, "would you be good enough to proceed with the interesting presentation I am sure you have brought us?" Why, sure.

A third and last example. At a convention banquet one evening the master of ceremonies turned unexpectedly to me, declaring, "Mr. Buckley will now kindly lead us in the Pledge of Allegiance to the Flag." I was thunderstruck. I had never learned the pledge. I had never spent sufficient time at an American school, at the grade level when one was drilled in such rotes. But as everybody rose, so did I: turning reverently to the flag, placing my right hand, palm open, across my breast, and intoning, "Our Father, Who art in heaven . . ." After a moment's astonished hesitation, the audience joined in. It was, after all, a pledge to a higher allegiance.

In the first of these illustrations I very nearly came a cropper from a combination of fatigue and relaxation that robbed me of my alertness. In the other two contretemps a sanguine self-satisfaction, which is also subversive of a speaker's edge, contributed to my discomfiture. Only long experience in the free-for-all of debate, where the unexpected is what one gets, saw me through these awful moments. In forensics, debate is combat duty—invaluable in helping a body steady his nerves and weather the unforeseen. *It is undesirable, nevertheless, wholly to suppress the tingle of incipient fear.* Apprehension must be excited if one's performance, whether jumping horses, or running the 440, or giving an important presentation to one's colleagues in a board room, or addressing thousands of people at a convention, stands a chance of succeeding. Public speaking is not a matter of popping to one's feet and sounding off. *It is a performance.* It is an acquirable skill, but it is also an art, for which a person must cultivate, if he does not have it to begin with, the temperament of an artist.

I hit this theme one last time because it is so critical, and because too many schools of speaking around the country preach to nonsensical excess the virtues of relaxation. There is—I admit—an element of risk in the state of nervous high gear I recommend, but it is also—I insist—by way of an inoculation against panic. As is the actor at the opening of a play, waiting for the curtain to go up, a person must be at once half scared to death and raring to go. With the increase of one's professionalism, a lessening of both sensations occurs. With time, there may be too little apprehension, to the detriment of performance. There are well-known pros—performers, comedians, talk show types—who lose their zing because they have so suppressed the nerves that a kind of ennui invades their act, sapping it.

I can testify, moreover—alas—that there is no absolute protection against attacks of stage fright; not years and years of experience on the platform will foolproof one to onslaughts of inexplicable terror. One late winter I was booked at the Women's Club in Louisville. I had been there before, and had enjoyed it. The people of Louisville (for that matter, of all Kentucky) are kind, and hospitable, and a special pleasure to be with. The members of the Women's Club were warmly appreciative, which always makes a speaker feel good. I lost my heart to one very ancient lady who hobbled down the aisle of the auditorium escorted and helped by two ladies who were less venerable only by comparison. They took seats front row center. When I had been introduced, and had pranced my way to the lectern, they beamed up at me, their hair and dentures brilliant in the noon light, nodding at me in encouragement. The eldest of the three, sitting between the other two, had an especially sweet smile, so it was to her that I privately dedicated my remarks. I hadn't got out ten words, however, when she dropped off to sleep, dozing peacefully through to the end of my talk. With my concluding words, her companions, the one to the right of her, the other to the left of her, dug their respective elbows into her ribs, startling her wide awake; whereupon all three raised their hands and enthusiastically clapped, beaming as before.

I was tickled to recognize these same ladies on my second booking at the club, two or three years later. They had changed not at all, hobbling slowly down the aisle to occupy the same center front row seats, their hair still snowy, their bright faces still rosy and darling with goodwill. It made me feel so at home; which, to a hobo of the lecture circuit, as to a wandering troubadour of old, is a dear and precious feeling. There was one mutation. As I launched into my first paragraph, all *three* ladies promptly dropped off to sleep! I couldn't have been more amused . . . and of a sudden felt fluids percolating into the joints of my knees, felt the knees grow weak, a chill in my vitals, a kind of seasickness, cold perspiration on my forehead, and a trembling in my legs and arms and hands that threatened to become violent. I was in the clutches of an acute attack of stage fright. As usual, I spoke from a prepared text that I had on the lectern before me, and I can recall turning the first page. After that, I do not remember a single thing. For half an hour, my mind was utterly blank.

I came out of it a few paragraphs before the end of the talk. I saw that I had been unconsciously flipping pages, because I had the last before me. My shirt was wet through, my tweed jacket was damp, and I had sweated heavily under the armpits. The other, awful sensations had vanished. Practice had apparently carried me through, because there were no bewildered expressions on the faces of the audience. I hastily concluded; and this time two other ladies book-ending the three ancient ones in the center nudged the outer two awake, who then elbowed the most venerable of the three awake, and, as before, they raised their faces at me with sweet glad smiles of appreciation, clapping with brio.

I have no explanation for what happened. I do hypothesize. I had been so relaxed by the familiarity of the three old ladies that I temporarily forgot I was giving a performance. That realization must suddenly have hit me as I raised my eyes from them to the crowd of two hundred or so women, who were all staring intently at me. Not having geared myself to perform, summoning and harnessing the necessary nerves, panic filled the vacuum.

Debate sharpens wits, tests logic, tries opinions in the hot forge of argumentation, and better than any other forensic exercise builds composure. What astonishes in this super high-tech civilization that depends more and more on the flow of accurate information and the ability of people and machines to communicate with one another is the little attention that is given to formal discourse and debate in most high schools and colleges—come to think of it, almost no attention is paid to dialectics in our schools—and also how little popular debating is as an intellectual exercise. Like millions of other Americans, I love watching sports, basketball and baseball excepted. A duel in tennis, or the matching of brawn and wit that can develop in memorable professional football games, excite me. The shoot-out in Super Bowl XIII between Terry Bradshaw of the Pittsburgh Steelers and Roger Staubach of the Dallas Cowboys was unforgettable. What are the elements that made it so, we may ask? The exclusively physical endowments of the athletes having become so extraordinary, quick thinking in the heat of action and what sports announcers call "momentum"—the psychological imposition of will by one player, or team, over another player, or team—count increasingly. We all understand this. How come in our intellectual preparation we nevertheless neglect that contest, trial, and tempering of wits in the open pit of debate before rowdy and irreverent student audiences whom the contestants from hard experience learn that they must sway as much with the heat of their will as with the felicity of their tongues?

Why, I wonder, don't the networks get smart and field cadres of professional gladiators during the dead hours of, say, Saturday afternoon, when, so desperate are they for programming, they run over-the-hill superjocks in tiddlywinks and alley-oop tourneys for fifty

thousand smackers first prize? *Madre mia!* Why aren't major corporations with a stake in American brainpower, like IBM and Xerox,
not funding snappy debates by crackling good pros—on prime time,
and else than in the wasteland of educational channels, to which
gravitate all those long-winded bores we endure else only on Sun-
days? Tell me ain't nobody going to tune in? Bosh! It hasn't been
tried: with the right format, under crisp control. And with megabuck
prizes—why not? Millions of Americans enjoy TV game shows, in
which, as well as luck, both quick-wittedness and aplomb, the key
ingredients of debate, are in one way or another featured. One ad-
mires the dame who in sixty seconds, an oversized clock clicking
them off, comes up with the correct synonyms for the ten words
barked at her, for which she wins, oh, a Lincoln Continental, a nigh-
tie from Frederick's of Hollywood, two tickets on a dirigible to
Borneo, a pool table, fifty bottles of Drano, ten thousand hand-baked
Mexican tiles to build a terrace to put the pool table on, a twenty-
eight-speed bike, a fifty thousand-gallon prefab kidney-shaped swimming pool to go with the terrace on which the pool table can be
displayed, a fur coat, a washer-dryer, and an International Harvester
bulldozer to dig the hole in which to place the fifty thousand-gallon
prefab kidney-shaped swimming pool beside the terrace on which
the pool table will be proudly displayed.

We enjoy smacking our lips over the loot; but we admire also the
composure and lively intelligence of the winners. Why not so on a
higher plane? Debates need not all be "heavy," remember. At the
Union in Cambridge, or at the Political Union in Yale, sly and amusing topics are often billed. People enjoy watching antagonists famed
for their wit, humor, cunning, and gall square off on talk shows. Why
then—the question nags—has the competitive intellectual game of
formal debate, for which one can assume there is a wide affinity in
the American character, not become a staple at schools and colleges,
at town auditoriums, and on television? Why have not corporations
and professional associations at the least promoted in-house debate
clubs, which would teach their members and executives so much of
value to them? I am amazed.

There do exist debating societies here and there across the country. If there is none in your community, organize one. A fast-paced
format under the iron control of a moderator is essential. I recommend the one developed by historian and political columnist Profes-

sor Max Lerner and myself over the decade when we were hot properties on the college circuit, and which has been widely copied since. It contains the formal structuring that keeps chitchat down to a minimum, it provides for sharp interaction between the principals, testing their mental footwork, and it brings the audience right into the fray. That format may be found in Appendix III.

In the meantime, be faster'n greased lightning reaching for your mind, but shoot your mouth off slo-o-w-ly.

5

How to Build a Formidable Case
(And Crush the Opposition)

> A thing is not truth till it is so strongly
> believed in that the believer is convinced that
> its existence does not depend upon him.
>
> —JOHN JAY CHAPMAN

Want to know how to crush the competition? Build yourself a formidable case.

That may be circular reasoning, begging the question, and a lot of other unmentionable faux pas in dialectics, but it is nevertheless the heart of the matter.

Speaking for myself, the entire Buckley bag of dirty tricks consists in hard work. If on any happy occasion the cogency of my arguments has been intrinsically more telling than that of my opponent, this was probably a matter of luck; but if my arguments have been more tellingly presented, more striking, and more plausible, that derived from long, long hours of research and reflection.

Mastering the Opponent's Case

There is always, somewhere, a faster gun. Folk who do a lot of public speaking will readily confess that rarely have they encountered an opponent whose intellect was not at least the equal of theirs, and whose knowledge of the topic was not often more extensive or more profound. The examination of issues from a public platform, however, infrequently penetrates beyond the second or third levels of complexity in which almost anyone can be competent. One does not have to be a genius, and omniscient, to hold one's own. I got along all right because usually I had *his* case down pat, so that I was able to counter my adversary's thrusts with refutations prepared well in advance and tested informally on friends.

(Everything I am saying in relation to public affairs applies as well to any activity that entails what is called—I detest these terms—the "decision-making process": the analysis and evaluation of marketing strategies by a corporation, the consideration of the pros and cons of a new educational facility by a school board. Whatever. Back to my bailiwick.)

Antoine-Henri de Jomini, the great Swiss martial theorist, wrote a treatise on the campaigns of Frederick the Great of Prussia that was brought to the attention of Napoleon. "Impressed with the author's intuitive understanding of the Napoleonic touch," I read in a source book,

> [Old Bony] had Jomini . . . report to him at Mainz in September, 1806.
>
> The campaign of Jena was brewing in Napoleon's mind. Jomini, at the end of the conference, asked if he might rejoin the emperor four days later in Bamberg.
>
> "Who told you that I am going to Bamberg?" asked the emperor—not, one assumes, without annoyance, for he supposed his destination a secret.
>
> "The map of Germany, Sire, and your campaigns of Marengo and Ulm."[1]

In just this manner—because he understood them so well—Lee was able to anticipate what new disaster "Little Mac" and his successors would bungle the Army of the Potomac into. I cheerfully admit that being a conservative in the 1970s had its forensic advantages. Until recently, it has not been easy for a person of liberal politics to master, and thus anticipate, the conservative argument. Since at least the Roosevelt revolution, books on current affairs, the scholarly and political journals, the popular press, novels, plays, and the very ethos propagandized the tenets and assumptions of liberalism. One was brought up sucking at the liberal teat. Almost everything one heard, and everything one read, expressed the liberal world view. To anticipate what the hive would decoct as the correct opinion about anything was, for a conservative, as simple as breathing.

Not so the reverse. The only brand of right-wing thought most liberals knew anything about was the stereotype contained in their text books and deplored by their teachers. The only right-wingers

1. Edward Mead Earle, ed., *Makers of Modern Strategy* (1943; reprint, Princeton: Princeton University Press, 1986), p. 81. The tale loses a little for being told by Jomini himself.

most liberals ever had personal acquaintance of were racists, anti-Semites, isolationists (pre–World War II), paranoiac anti-Communists (post–World War II), social snobs, Wall Streeters, proponents of privilege, Philistines, and ignoramuses. Thus, the complacent liberal of the decades 1950–1980 was unaware of new currents on the right, which often had the conservative championing positions (legalization of marijuana, for example) that took him by surprise. After seven years of the Reagan Administration, the shoe may be on the other foot: liberals have had their gizzards stuffed with conservative and neo-conservative rhetoric, which they can safely assume they have down pat, whereas conservatives may make the treacherous assumption that the liberal position has been frozen all this time.

Know Your Adversary

In my days as a loose cannon on the circuit, I collected the published work of people I was scheduled to debate, or whom I had already debated and was booked to oppose on a public platform again, where possible running their citations down to the source. I made copious notes during debates, perusing them later for the jab that had snapped my head back, for the statistic that had surprised me and controverted my evidence, and for the attributed opinion that seemed to me to be strange, or out of character, for the authority. Plenty of times I was corrected, which was salutary for my ego, and, on the whole, upon reflection, good for my position, obliging me to abandon a weak or false argument for a better one. Eat your crow like a man. (See further on this subject below.) When I met that opponent again I made a point of confessing, "The last time we clashed on this topic I said so-and-so, and you said to the contrary, such-and-such was the case, which at the time I did not believe: but you were right on that detail, I want to apologize to you. Would that the balance of your position were illumined with similar lucidity . . ."

Confronting Specialists in Their Field

Though any would-be polemicist must thoroughly acquaint himself with the opponent's ideological position successfully to brave him in debate (one must know whence he is coming), one need not oneself sport a Ph.D. in the other fellow's discipline. Let me explain that difference.

My lecture agency, concerned for the connotations of frivolity in the title "novelist," billed me as a "social critic," whatever that is. (Would an anti-social critic be a misanthrope?) I am unaware of any doctorate being offered in "social criticism." I have earned no such doctorate, nor, indeed, any other. The absence of suffixes after my name disconcerted some sponsors, who insisted on introducing me as "Dr. Buckley," or "Professor Buckley," though I politely and firmly declined the title. Only a certified economist—this primitive thinking holds—is capacitated by his technical background to assess the beneficence of the application of a given system of economics, not to speak of its theoretical validity; only a political "scientist" is able to assess the goodness and validity of a system of government.

Yet this is, we *should* know, quite false. Theory *qua* theory is one thing, and on such an esoteric plane I grant that it takes a professionally trained economist (quack *qua* quack?) to palaver intelligently with another economist, on the principle that one has to be at least half unhinged oneself to comprehend a creaking door. Applications of economic theory to the human condition in its political existence, however, reduce to a matter of performance, which can be objectively tested and appraised by anyone, or to values, which are subject to moral judgment. Regarding these last, we assume an inherent capacity in the common man to distinguish the good from the bad, the false from the true. In the realm of the intellect, admittedly when it comes to pure ratiocinative power, there are estates and dominions. (Let physicists talk to physicists—about physics.) There are soaring philosophic cadenzas that reach right up into the metaxy, the "in-between" realm of cognitive activity between God and man. Happily, we don't have to concern ourselves about that in debating whether municipal land should be set aside for a new park, or whether our business should pioneer a new technology, or whether supply-side economics alone should be trusted to bring down chronic federal budget deficits. Therefore, do not you be intimidated should you lack specific expertise on a subject: you can quick-study enough for the practical purposes of most occasions where you must defend or advance a point of view. Remember always: a leader asks his technicians (a prime minister his generals, a CEO his lawyers and accountants) whether something is within current systems capacity, not whether it ought to be done, or must be done, or is desirable. John Kennedy did not know how we were going to get to the moon; he just knew that we had to try.

Notwithstanding, the sound judgment of a generalist cannot always be relied upon to prevail over the specialist's vast knowledge of detail in one-on-one confrontations. What then? We are constrained to assume that the writer of this book did not disgrace himself when he clashed with professional sociologists, economists, and political scientists, as he was called to do. The question naturally occurs: How did he get away with it? How did he keep his scalp in place? Why was he not regularly cut to ribbons by his cathedratic foes? Well, this little chicken shook his head over the phenomenon often himself on the campaign trail: concluding that what his opponents most labored under, simply, was a lack of adequate preparation *detoxified of ideology.*

Putting Aside Ideological Blinkers; Avoiding Dangerous Assumptions

Whether in the board room or on a speakers' platform, one cannot afford complacency. One cannot blind oneself to concurrent possibilities and even concurrent, simultaneously viable, and equally defensible "truths" that in their logical extension appear to be incompatible. (The Bill of Rights provides vivid examples of this: almost any right enumerated in the first ten Amendments when pushed by fanatics to an extreme conflicts with some other right.) Just as in physics, where for every matter there is its conterminous negation, the antimatter, so in values there can be—this is *not* always the case—coexisting and competing values. A speaker must always assume that the other side has a much better case than one's initial prejudice about the matter inclines one to credit. (The obverse rule: always assume that your case is weaker than you suppose.) If one's attitude is, Can you believe So-and-So actually holds that sanctions are effective in imposing Nation A's policies on Nation B?—look out! That attitude is going to expose its holder to a bad time. Positions that are "beyond believing," or "incredible," or "lunatic fringe" may have a lot more riding for them than one suspects. Conservatives used to rant glibly—I ranted glibly—that "you can't legislate morals." It was an article of faith, first popularized in Barry Goldwater's *The Conscience of a Conservative,* and it became a slogan. If anything has been more redundantly demonstrated, however, it is that morals can be, and indeed continually are being, "legislated." The relevant Supreme Court decisions *(Plessy vs. Ferguson, Brown vs. Board of Edu-*

cation) and the several Civil Rights acts of the 1960s did not extirpate racism from every American heart, but they have revolutionized our society, to the effect that from kindergarten up children are being inculcated in the accepted public view that racism is without mitigation evil. Conversely, the Supreme Court decisions *(Roths-Albert, et al.)* rendering it next to impossible to combat obscenity and pornography, and subsequent legislation opening the floodgates of filth, have helped to rear two generations of Americans who tolerate almost no limits to the consensual exercising of their sexuality. A code of sexual morals extending back two thousand years and upheld by most of the established religions has been overturned, though such new venereal diseases as Herpes and the dread AID Syndrome have put a damper on what once (quaintly) was called promiscuity.

Ideological commitment can hobble the mind. Ideology is a devil that can obscure plain sense and obliterate from one's consciousness the most flagrant facts of a matter. An argument can bark its shins on the hardest evidence, ideology will not notice. I know. It was the instinctual conservative position that in no way could the publicized "rupture" (we thought of it in quotation marks) between Soviet Russia and Mao-tse-Tung's China be real. Why? What a question! It was ideologically impossible, that's why. A Commie was a Commie was a Commie. What we gullible Americans were being fed about territorial disputes and dialectical hair-splitting by the agitprop bureaus of our enemies was a deliberate Sino-Soviet ruse, or simply an exaggeration by our own (ever-idiot) press that never would prove of any political use or advantage to the West, and that could only lull us into complacency. That was the conservative credo on the matter, and *National Review* published a thick special issue—probably the only deadly dull issue in the magazine's history—in support. We were wrong. (And I have since been tempted to elevate into a law that Anything That is Dull is Probably Dumb.)

The position that to one's settled way of thinking seems most outrageous, if it is expounded by people who do not belong to the fever swamps of fanaticism, or whose sanity there is no reason otherwise to suspect, will have at least plausible arguments in its support. They may be factitious. They may be in addition meretricious. They may be based on misconstructions of historical events, or on misleading and invalid material evidence. But these blemishes are for the public speaker to discover by diligent research and tough analysis. *Never make the mistake of not taking your opponent's case seriously.*

And never take him lightly, or he may rise up like a rake whose prongs you step on, slamming you in the face with his staff.

A word of caution: not all that on the surface *seems outré* isn't *not* truly far-out, reprehensible, and to be rejected. Extreme positions will sometimes be supported by the most seductive arguments, these generally appealing to vice. Severe quotas on immigration from the Orient, couched piously in terms of protecting our working men and women from coolie labor, may mask, and precisely gain their support from the ulterior appeal to, racism. Righteous fulminations against any kind or species of censorship, couched in terms of defending freedom of expression, may mask the pecuniary greed of panderers of porn, or the lubricity of consumers of porn. During the early and mid 1960s, I wrote screen plays for a multinational production outfit that was closely associated with a major American movie company. That was the era of the "sexual revolution," when individual sexual mores were undergoing radical transformation, especially among the young, and when obscenity and sexual depravity were beginning to appear in films produced for mass audiences. I remember reading the testimony of slick and slimy Hollywood types before Congressional subcommittees that were investigating the matter. Oh, how they postured, standing for Art against Babbitt and Bowdler, defending the sacredness of the First Amendment, which if not constructed absolutely so as to permit them to shoot for public viewing whatever they pleased would bring down Night.

I was almost impressed. Then I received a form letter from the American producer. Really, it was a kind of imperial decree, which I paraphrase:

TO OUR SCREEN WRITERS.
    Research has shown that 75% of the movie audience is composed of young people from the ages of 17 to 25. *Therefore*, all scripts will contain a sexually explicit scene every twenty minutes of film time.

Oh, the scumbags!

Any position in which lies buried an appeal to base human instincts is validly suspect, until proven innocent, and if in support of a position some of the arguments contain this ulterior motive, which will be expressed typically in the most sanctimonious language, one can bet one's buttons that rank hypocrisy attaches. On the other hand (sorry), impugning motive does not necessarily impugn the argument. (See below.) Only the argument that advances the ulterior invalid or reprehensible design, and that carries in it no justification other than its root in that design, is to be rejected outright.

What to Do about Scoundrels

On occasion I discovered that the facts had been misconstrued by my (distinguished) opponent, the statistics he used outdated, or spurious, or even invented, and the citations taken radically out of context and either willfully or ignorantly abused. You heard right. Some people are hardened liars. Not all those liars were politicians, either, though politicians in other ways are the greasiest cats to skin, they have an answer for almost everything. Needless to say, I showed no mercy when I discovered that an opponent was deliberately falsifying. What malicious pleasure I experienced during our next debate hearing him launch into the disingenuous argument that he may have got away with last time we met, but that this night would bring him to his destruction; what delicious anticipation tensed the muscles of my thighs and calves as I waited for the opportunity to spring up and have at him! I shall suffer in Purgatory for it. The prospect of reducing a complacent opponent who is also a lying son of a bitch to a bowl of quaking jello, speechless with consternation at the unforeseen refutation of his case, is an unholy bliss for which I will apologize to my Creator but to no man. A warning for the here and now, however: a speaker must be sure to *affect* a becoming (albeit quite false) modesty in his triumph—though he is about to burst with sublime well-being and a raucous sense of exultation as the killer in him slakes his thirst on the pumping blood of the victim. Be a gallant loser, if lose one must (the aphorism for which I am expecting to be anthologized is this: *good losers have plenty of practice*); but in all happier occasions be a hypocritically humble winner.

What I wonder about is those folk I met on the debate platform who smiled serenely while I refuted their statistics, because they were demonstrably wrong, or pointedly reframed their quotation in its true context to show that it meant something else entirely; yet who, in their summations, proceeded to ignore that they had been utterly squelched—pickled in their pretensions, hoist on their petards, pinned by their poignards, not to mention plucked of every last quill in their quivers. One is left gasping. The reader will have had similar experience in a "business situation," when the head of a department simply ignores the facts that are inconvenient to his prejudices. One cannot credit one's ears. I have gaped at, and in a way admired, the gall of such folk; but what has not ceased to amaze is when in a third or even fourth contest they persist floating the very same fallacious arguments or cockeyed statements of fact that (a) they know are quite wrong (they had been told, after all) and (b) they can expect me promptly to tear into again. The reader has probably had this frustrating experience too, for which there is no recourse. More than to a fundamental intellectual dishonesty, I attribute such astonishing behavior to the swelled opinions of themselves that people of a certain eminence acquire, to their intellectual sloth, and, in one exasperating case, to their inability to listen to contrary opinion, endowing them with an impervious complacence.

What to Do When One Is Found Out

If one's dear assumptions are exploded on the stage, one's statistics debunked, one's lazy appeals to what is known as *argumentum ad populum* ("As everyone knows . . .") skewered ("*I* don't know, and in point of fact it's not so"), it is only in special circumstances permissible—it is human, and I guess on that account forgivable—to bluster through without admitting right then and there that one stands corrected, or in one's summation to affect a lordly indifference to correction. Sometimes this works. Audiences can be slow to understand that one has been dealt a mortal blow. One's opponent may fail to press his advantage. Debate under some auspices *can* be a game, from which this form of dialectical contest derives its unsavory reputation—a not altogether honest contest of wits, the rules of which allow for a certain bravado and insouciance. This would hold for an intrafraternity college debate, or maybe an appearance before the Cambridge Union, or at any time—say a "Roast"—when one is indeed expected to perform (*pace* Plato) for the eristic pleasure of the audience. But where the debate is *not* billed merely as an exhibition of dialectical cunning, in which the artfulness of the contestants more than the validity of their contentions are the criterion, but instead a serious examination of the merits and truth of a proposition, to persist in standing on arguments that have been disemboweled by one's opponent, to attempt to disparage by the authority of one's public position, or to ignore, and thus intend to bury, his valid contradictions of one's statements of fact, is absolutely dishonest and despicable. The graceful thing to do when an opponent demonstrates conclusively that one is guilty of some factual blunder or incorrect line of argument is, as suggested earlier, forthrightly to admit it, and then as adroitly as possible remove the debate to more favorable terrain. (But don't throw in the towel too precipitately—see Chapter 7.) The speaker thus put at bay may even turn his mistake into an advantage, because opponents who relish one's discomfiture too obviously, coming back again and again to mock a person for his error, will regret it.

Debate as a Means of Broadening Perspective

Debate practice helps ingrain the habit of according the opponent's position wary respect because the exercises often require a person to uphold the side he personally disapproves. In collegiate national competitions, the teams must dispute both the negative and the affirmative of an issue, sometimes within minutes of each other. This switching of sides has helped give debate a reputation for insincerity—and debaters a reputation for deviousness—but what we are talking about is merely an exercise, a testing of dialectical skills. The virtues are that being obliged to argue against the grain stretches one's imagination, subverts and helps overcome bias, and compels one to practice putting oneself in the other's skin. Researching both sides of a question cultivates the habit of looking for both sides of a question. It instills respect for the attractions of the side one personally may detest or disbelieve. Formal debate experience is of inestimable value in building a solid case, but if a person does not have the opportunity to engage in this exercise, he can practice its virtues in other ways. In the privacy of his soul, or of his bathroom (the context he feels more comfortable with), he can subject his own prejudices to stringent scourings and, mayhap, long overdue flushings. Meantime:

Having examined with the most rigorous thoroughness all those silly, absurd, wrongheaded, perverse, myopic, and totally unacceptable points one's opponent is likely to argue, find, wherever you can, valid refutations. First, though, play the Devil's advocate. See whether you cannot draw up a virtually irrefutable argument in your opponent's favor. Once one has thought through the very best case the opposition can bring forth, one should be able the better to counter it, or, at least, dull its impact. One is in any event prepared to absorb the heaviest guns in the enemy's arsenal.

The Law of Relative Preferences

Where research and reflection bring an honest body to the opinion that for a certain argument—an argument that is damaging, but not critical, to one's case—there is no conclusive refutation, he has two choices, the first being to hope the opponent somehow flubs, which is wishful on his part, the second being to apply what we might dub the Law of Relative Preferences. Thus: it may be true that obscene literature is material in bringing about a deterioration of public morality, and that a causal relationship can be established (I doubt it) between pornography and crimes of a violent and sexual nature; but these evils are not to be compared with what efforts to suppress, or censor, such emanations would bring, namely, a dangerous impairment of freedom of expression, entailing that precious right to the capricious judgment of sometimes narrow and ignorant local boards. And so forth. (I would knock those arguments into a cocked hat, but they suit for illustration.) Or: it may be so that in the United States nuclear power plants can be designed to be all but foolproof against a major escape of radiation; and it may be so that fossil fuels are inevitably going to run out, and that synthetic fuels, and solar energy, and the extraction of oil from shale are alternatives of a cost and complexity and technological limitations that render them impractical as an absolute substitute for oil and gas; still that outside possibility of a cataclysmic burn-down that will poison the atmosphere of half the world, killing millions outright and hundreds more millions derivatively, or even exterminating human life altogether from a greenhouse effect, is so terrible that no one of sound mind and good conscience can defend nuclear energy.

What has this speaker accomplished? He forthrightly admits that his opponent has compelling practical arguments in his favor, demonstrating to the audience that he, the opponent of nuclear energy, is neither ignorant of nor insensible to them, but the moral argument he adduces overwhelms all other considerations. This apparent candor produces the strongest positive vibes in an audience. "I am a reasonable man, aware of the merits of that other fellow's position, which I do not discount; nevertheless, were we to allow ourselves to be ruled by immediate practical expediencies in this matter (quite possibly) of human survival it would be unconscionable." Keep on the lookout for the preemptive moral position to which arguments can sometimes be reduced. They cut like a sword through a lot of persiflage. And be aware that an assault on the position you defend may similarly be mounted from the moral high ground. (See below.)

There is a third alternative for dealing with an argument for which one can construe no valid refutation, which is to agree with one's opponent. If you cannot construe a convincing answer to him, and if the Law of Relative Preferences gives you no relief, in the privacy of your heart (or water closet) leaving you unconvinced, then, friend, you face a battle with your conscience.

The Angle of Attack

The greatest of the Roman orators, Marcus Cato, said, "Grasp the material, and the words follow."[2] They do. There is no guarantee against their being dull, however. They may be uninspired. They may lack craft and cutting edge. Having researched the question as thoroughly as you have the time for, sit back to consider what is going to be your angle of attack.

I divide this consideration into two parts: first, the search for an original, interesting, or if neither the one nor greatly the other, at the least overridingly important overall view that provides your side of the case with a kind of moral imperative; second, the discovery, where it exists, of the hidden agenda of your opponent.

The Hidden Agenda

Taking the second first, you may conclude that implicit in the arguments to do with safety and ecological damage drummed up by opponents of nuclear energy, there is a pervading bias. Your opponent in particular, or the antinuclear lobby in general, you may decide from the reading you have done and your careful and unemotional consideration of their arguments (I can't stress enough the importance of keeping a clinical remove from your sentiments in this process of discovery) are the sort who oppose nuclear power not so

2. "Rem tene et verba sequentur," from Rollin G. Osterweis's monograph "American Oratory in Historical Perspective," courtesy of the Library of New Haven Colony Historical Society.

much because of the merits of their case against this particular expression of high technology but because of their aversion for and hostility to technological advances in most, if not absolutely all, their forms. You may conclude that these folk are a twentieth-century version of the Luddites of England, those fanatics who tried to put a stop to the Industrial Revolution in that country by smashing the looms of textile mills.

Your reading convinces you that, indeed, you have flushed out the hidden agenda in this controversy. These people are not striving to shut down Three Mile Island because of the concrete dangers in the construction of that plant, nor are they marching against, and protesting, and picketing, and obstructing the completion of Comanche Peak because of the peculiar and specific dangers of that nuclear plant to the ecology of the area, but because they are against nuclear power, period. They are against Palo Alto. They admit to no distinctions between the defective and archaic construction of Chernobyl and the safeguards imposed by the Nuclear Regulatory Commission in this country. You may discover that these same people oppose all offshore exploration for gas and oil, the drainage of all wetlands period, the lumbering of all forests no matter the human need and irrespective of the program for reforestation, all open pit mining, the damming of any stream, and the erection of any plant of any kind on the course of any river. In short, they would cry Halt! to the technological revolution and are against what others would style the imperative of human progress.

This is the hidden agenda; and you attack those who picket Seabrook No. 1 and No. 2 on the grounds that their opposition really has little to do with the putative deficiencies in the design or safeguards of the plants in question but with a bias against *any* use of thermonuclear energy; or you move to another level and blast those who agitate against the harnessing of the atom as reactionaries of the Luddite stamp who would obstruct all technological progress of whatever kind, irrespective of its utility, benefits, or safety. This is effective argumentation. The background of a generalized bias calls into question the sincerity (if not the fact) of the evidence adduced by your opponent against Seabrook No. 1 and No. 2. It is also a flagrant resort to the genetic fallacy and *argumentum ad hominem*, both being sins. You are attacking the good faith and candor of your opponent, not the validity of the design faults that he has charged against Seabrook. If you are not scrupulously careful in the wording of your argument, you may be smearing him for what may be the accidental, or merely coincidental, association with nuts and cranks, and in this relation bolts too. (Communists oblige all their subjects to be inoculated against smallpox; your opponent favors obligatory inoculation against smallpox; therefore your opponent is a Communist.) You are impeaching the validity of his argument in the concrete for its origins (wherein the genetic fallacy) in what you deem to be a fanatical lobby devoted to shutting off the lights all over the world. Yet even the Devil may be surprised speaking the truth. The habitual philanderer is capable of preaching a rip-snorting sermon against adultery. Would that all who raise their voices against sin were sinless, or all who attack the rhetorical abuses of others themselves blameless, and all who happen to be right about one thing right about everything else. (In this book, I will inveigh against logical fallacies and solecisms, yet inevitably myself commit them.) Barry Commoner may give me a very special pain, only exceeded by the self-righteousness of John Gardner of Common Cause and Ralph Nader; but Mr. Nader may be correct about unacceptable dangers to public safety of a given industrial design, Mr. Gardner may be correct about the peril to the probity of congressmen who accept excessive fees for services unconnected with their legislative duties, and Dr. Commoner may be dead right about the genetic pricelessness of the snail darter. Nevertheless, though it is technically invalid to go after one's opponents on the basis alone of what one discerns as their hidden agenda, *it is in addition to refutation of their arguments in the concrete* a devastating, and I think under these scrupulous circumstances licit, dialectical attack.

I have planted some digs at the ecological lobby in these pages, so that you may suspect where I stand personally. I am anti-conservation. I would like to build condominiums on the walls of the Grand Canyon—in impecable taste, understand, after the style of the Pueblo Indians, using gesso extrusion blowguns.

Well, not quite. I have been setting you up, which is my next lesson. I have been preparing to sandbag you.

I am by instinct a kind of Luddite myself. I do not necessarily fall on my knees in adoration of the bitch goddess Progress, under whose aegis some very great mischief has been perpetrated. My vitals cry out against the defacement of our land by telephone poles and high tension wires, by the endlessly proliferating highways, and by the strip civilization on the access roads of any American town or city, with their used car lots and fast food restaurants and shopping "malls."

But I would not go back to the horse.

I would not do without the telephone or electricity either, possibly because for months at a time I have lived deprived of both, and though candlelight has its charms, I can tell you it has also its inconveniences. I am nonetheless reflexively against the Army Corps of Engineers, which drains wetlands, and I loathe the genus, developer, known to good ole boys like Decimus Junius Juvenalis as *Aedificator horribilis.*

That is where I stand by preference: against anyone who would tamper with the ecology in ways either harmful to it or destructive of habitat and natural beauty. This is not simply a kind of eccentric finickiness, moreover. In the dry sandhills of South Carolina my wife and I have wrested 250 acres from the monoculture of pine forest to which they had been relegated for seventy years, transforming what was a virtual ecological desert into a place that is teeming with wildlife of every sort. This has been a hard labor of love one decade long, to which Tasa has sacrificed hands once smoother than poured cream, now permanently roughened and scarred, and I a left arm that hangs almost useless because of a painful "tennis elbow," which I contracted not, alas, from an excess of gentlemanly play on a suburban court, but from bucking too many logs with a twenty-pound Pioneer bow saw, and one-handed horsing of my tractor over too much rough ground while manipulating bush hog, blade, disk, and harrow.

So, OK, those are my credentials. I banded birds in boarding school; among my favorite authors was Joseph Wood Krutch, and Peter Matthiessen still is. I belong to the National Nature Conservancy, which buys up precious remaining wilderness to keep it from commercial depredations. I am a charter member of the Wilderness Society. And I am embarrassed by the fanaticism of so many of my natural allies, the biologists and ornithologists and ecologists who have fallen prey to zealotry, and who have called upon themselves the biting dismissal that they prefer gila monsters to human life.

You would not have suspected the complexity of my position, would you? 'Fess up. You would have likely assumed from the digs scattered through the preceding chapters that I am a stock right-

wing anti-conservationist. You would have placed me in the crowd
of anti-ecology Philistines, or ignoramuses. And you would have been
wrong.

The morals are two: first, anyone entering the public arena should
not only research and reflect on a case hard, he should make bloody
well sure he does not assume things about his opponent, or the
opposition, that happen to be untrue, or too simple. Differentiate.
Second, the reader of this book should apply the object lesson I have
just provided to the construction of his next case: *sandbag, by bait-
ing, the opposition.*

Ambushing the Opponent: The Unexpected Angle of Attack

We elide now from the construction of a case to tactics in the
deployment of material. A speaker must live up to the public persona
he has acquired; but if he can ascertain, or can safely guess, that he
is expected to say thus and so, he should strive somehow to orches-
trate the construction of his case so that he says something else. If he
is expected to defend a certain bunker, he should choose not to. He
should be elsewhere, attacking from the unexpected angle. In this
manner should he put together his speech, so that surprise is contained in almost every page of it, keeping the close attention of the
audience while perplexing opponents. To this purpose he needs the
fresh material that we discussed in the third chapter—the benefits of
omnivorous reading.

He should scatter into his remarks a trail, however. He should
entice his foes into ambush.

A most effective tactic for throwing opponents into disarray and
confusion is to plant in one's own remarks a suggestion that appears
to fall right into their greedy clutches; and then, at the time of the
rebuttal, when the opposition have spent valuable minutes deriding
what they believe to be one's blunder, come back with a smashing
refutation that leaves them gasping for air.

You, the reader of this book, will know how to do this—that is, you
will know just what suggestion appears to place you at the mercy of
the opposition—because you will have studied their case so dili-
gently. You will know what whets their appetite, what will make
them positively slobber in anticipation of the kill.

Take a common argument in favor of affirmative action. For years and years conventional plaint has held that black wage earners, on account of racial discrimination, have not kept up with, or advanced commensurately with, white wage earners over the past decade. The high hopes subsequent to the civil rights battles have been disappointed; consequently (the argument goes), affirmative action policies are essential for redressing the continuing injustice.

If one is inveighing against affirmative action, one might marshal evidence to show how black middle-income wages have increased 25 percent (I invent the figures; I am not far off) over the past decade. This will apparently be setting oneself up for the opposition, which will triumphantly rise to announce that you, sir, you, madam, are all wet. Though black *middle-income* wages have gone up 25 percent in this period, white middle-income wages have increased 37 percent, and wages for blacks of all economic levels when compared with wages for whites of all economic levels are lagging by 42 percent below the whites.

One's opponent will sit down, flushed with the confidence that he has destroyed one's fatuous case and permanently impaired one's credibility with the audience; when in fact, the Lord has delivered him into your hands, because you, sir, or you, madam, now rise for your closing statement to observe that one's good friend has apparently had time to make only a very superficial study of the question, in that the brilliant black economist Thomas Sowell has demonstrated through the most exhaustive analyses that non-whites have lagged behind whites in relative terms *not* on account of racism but precisely thanks to well-intentioned, ill-conceived welfare policies that have robbed blacks of incentives, and *also* thanks to affirmative action policies that, in cases, have advanced unqualified individuals to the impairment of the reputation of truly qualified blacks. And so forth.

I am not here weighing the merits of affirmative action, please understand: I am illustrating a point. You, the reader, dangled the bait, your opponent incautiously pounced on it (because *he* had not studied *your* case well enough, else he would have been more prudent), and you came back to roll right over him. This is in my opinion a legitimate ruse. Cases are not always won on their merits, and Truth does not always transpire through the candlepower of her virtue. When one's object is to persuade people of what one thinks right, it is legitimate for a person to employ all the powers of persuasion that God gave him, and, within honorable bounds, seek to discombobulate the opposition. In all forms of warfare, it is a time-honored strategy to draw one's foes into the canyon and there destroy them.

To this worthy end, it can be fun (debating should above all be fun), as well as infuriating to one's opponents, and clever, to prepare a carefully documented and convincing refutation of an obvious strong point on the opposition's side, but hold it in reserve. Let them keep popping up to complain, "Mr. X has not replied to our contention that all whales are blue. Mr. X and his partner, Mr. Y, have repeatedly refused to address themselves to our premise that all whales are blue." Do thou ignore them. Permit the audience to wonder whether you simply have no answer, or are stonewalling. At what you perceive to be the dramatic moment—when the other side is fuming, and the audience maybe murmuring uneasily—you at length rise to declare in a tone of the most disingenuous amazement, "We haven't talked about the silly assertion that all whales are blue because we have been flabbergasted that anyone should still believe that old wives' tale, when in fact most advanced studies show that this is an incorrect presumption. We have here from the U.S. Marine Resources Commission a paper written by Dr. Theodore Stoopinsky showing conclusively that a majority of whales are in fact purple . . ."

By withholding this refutation until the eleventh hour, the veteran polemicist accomplishes the following: (a) opponents become overconfident, presuming that he is poorly prepared; they may be encouraged to float some other shaky contentions, which will set them up; (b) opponents may assume that our hero is ducking the blue whale issue, and so spend a lot of valuable time heaping scorn on him on that account, to the end that when our hero does finally address it with smashing and conclusive evidence, they are left speechless, and the audience much amused by their disarray and his—your—aplomb.

One can elaborate on this strategy to one's heart's desire. Prepare for the poleaxing of the opposition by mentioning early in one's opening statement the "infantile notion that most whales are blue," leaving it at that: a fat catalpa grub for opponents to rise to. If subtly enough plopped into the waters, the other side is bound to jump up, declaring, "Infantile, is it! Why, studies have shown for the past quarter of century that . . ." To which one responds by declining to address whatever evidence they produce (which careful research has indicated is outdated, or mistaken) as to the blue color of whales, aggravating the opposition no end, instead obnoxiously repeating in connection with some other point that it is as "simpleminded" as the "common fallacy about the blue color of whales," goading the opponents into responding with a perfect tirade about the true cutaneous hue of whales, basing altogether too much of their case on this supposedly self-evident factor; at which delicious juncture one delivers the knockout of that government commission study.

Analogies between Military and Forensic Tactics: Advantages of the Affirmative Position; Assuming the High Ground; Compelling the Adversary to Come at One

Clausewitz's respect for the strength of the defensive position is worth noting if one is arguing the affirmative about anything, because that is generally to be defending the status quo. In a board meeting, the officer reporting on his company's last quarter performance bears the onus of justifying the results, yet his is nevertheless the advantage. He is the affirmative. He stands on proven ground, and that is the high ground in almost any engagement. It is those who find the results unsatisfactory who must show why, and that they can do better. They are the negative. They must risk more. The defense enjoys established position and what is cognate to military "interior lines," namely, the infrastructure of experience and tradition. The opponent must always be the aggressor, and if one is occupying the entrenched advantages of a defensive position, one can choose to lie back patiently, waiting for the enemy to expend his energies; at which time, according to Clausewitz, like Stonewall Jackson at First Manassas, or General George "The Rock" Thomas at Chickamauga, one counterattacks—the defense going over to the offensive.

It is worth brushing up on the masters of military strategy if one is to engage in polemical wars. At any meeting with one's peers that may turn testy, let *them* shoot off their mouths and expend their energies while you bide your time, conserving your ammunition, choosing the propitious moment to deliver a crushing counterblow. Many of the same cognitive principles apply in battle of tongue and intellect as in battle by tooth and claw. One seeks always for *the* "strategical initiative," as Jomini advised, keeping an opportunistic lookout also for *the* "supreme" value of surprise. One endeavors to strike always at the root of an opponent's case, utterly to destroy him, not waste one's resources on lesser targets. Clausewitz would designate this as discerning the "center of gravity" of the enemy's position. Oh, yes, you may say: and that—the center of gravity—is the enemy's forces in the field, because isn't it old Clausewitz who first defined the principal strategic goal as destroying the enemy's ability to fight, and doesn't that mean engaging and destroying his armies?

Well, that's true also, but there are exceptions, one discovers. (As, you will remember, there almost always are.) In *Makers of Modern Strategy,* H. Rothfels points out that if the enemy country is wracked by civil dissension, the "center of gravity" may be the capital. In our Civil War this was so of Washington, and was perceived as being so of Richmond, which amounted to the same thing. Public opinion—as in our Vietnam War, both militarily and polemically—can be the critical center. The critical center that one should plot one's strategies against can be the central assumption of the enemy—or the central operating concept—not the arguments they deploy to defend it. "Often," Clausewitz concludes, "all hangs on the silken thread of imagination." This is the key insight. This was in essence Napoleon's objection to Jomini's didacticism, wherein the art of war was reduced too much to a set of *a posteriori*ly-derived rules, allowing not enough importance to a commander's intuition. And this is irrefutable: in forensic as in military warfare, it is imagination that ultimately prevails. In any engagement, martial or forensic, academic injunctions are useful as general principles, but it is conditions on the field of battle that inspire the master tactical stroke.

The Moral Imperative

I mentioned searching out what I called clumsily the overridingly important overall view that endows one's position with a kind of moral imperative, and then left the subject dangling.

It was discussed by implication with reference to the hidden agenda and the moral position to which many arguments can be reduced, such as concerning the use of nuclear fission for energy. Moral content is implicit in almost any public issue that one will be asked to debate, because rarely is polemical heat generated without somewhere there being a moral animus. (This is not likely to be true in a discussion over whether a pharmaceutical company should develop a new toothpaste.) The steps to take are these. First, dig out the underlying moral issue. Second, establish that the concrete measure one is upholding or opposing accurately reflects that moral issue. Third, investigate whether the probable effects of the measure itself will be true to the morality that motivated it, or that is adduced in support of it, or in fact, contrary to expectations, be detrimental to it.

Invoking the moral issues in a debate over the use of nuclear fission, for example, especially if one opposes deriving energy by this means, can be powerful, and almost certainly will arouse visceral emotions in the audience favorable to one's position. "Can you give me the absolute assurance that nowhere in this world will a nuclear plant burn down in an unimaginable catastrophe causing the death of perhaps millions of human beings—as so nearly happened in Chernobyl, which was terrifying enough?" Woe to the poor sucker saddled with defending nuclear energy! Such an appeal to the emotions can only be defused by invoking the Law of Relative Preferences and circumscribing the debate to, say, plants built in the United States, subject to stringent U.S. government standards and periodic inspections by the Atomic Energy Commission. One is nevertheless at a rhetorical disadvantage. The moral high ground has been seized. It is like being called upon to counter the arguments of someone who has preempted that strategic position at the outset by defining his view of whatever is being discussed as the "compassionate" view. He who happens to disagree is thus rhetorically relegated to the low order of unreformed Ebenezer Scrooges. It's cute, and unfair, and very, very telling: and in the case of a topic that legitimately evokes visions of Armageddon, a tremendous test of a speaker's skill to turn.

The moral argument is naturally a favorite of those who so oppose nuclear weaponry that they would dump our arsenal of missiles into the sea, and hang the consequences—the "better Red than dead" school. "Can you tell this house with absolute certainty that an exchange of nuclear missiles between the Soviet Union and the United States—besides bringing instant death to tens of millions of Russians and Americans—will not expose the planet to the risk of a greenhouse effect that could suffocate us all, snuffing out life itself? *Will* you stand before this house and declare categorically that there is no risk at all of this happening? Mind you, I am not asking what in your estimation the probabilities are. I am asking you: Is there *no* risk of this happening?"

The Dread Dilemma, and How to Escape It

This is the rhetorical device of placing the opponent in an unanswerable dilemma: Can you assure us absolutely that if we do not change our way of doing business we will not lose market position? Or: Our choice is to go with Brand A or Brand B, there is no escaping it, we have to fish or cut bait. In most cases it ain't necessarily so; few choices in this world are truly either/or, and the dreadful consequences of a wrong decision are not likely ever to be quite so calamitous as projected. But continuing with our example of a debate over nuclear arms, where consequences of this calamitous nature are the fulcrum, such a charged question can only be deflected (1) by speaking in very careful specifics regarding the radiation that would be released in such a hypothetical exchange; (2) by bringing up an alternative moral argument (the Law of Relative Preferences), namely, there are things dearer than life, as in Give Me Liberty or Give Me Death; and (3) by contending that one's opponent's proposal (that the United States unilaterally disarm), seductive as it may sound, can only enhance, instead of reduce, the implicit consequence (threat of nuclear conflict), because it is the U.S. retaliatory capacity and the implied threat in the very existence of our nuclear arsenal that have so far discouraged a ruthless exercise of its military power by an enemy that is demonstrably without morals or mercy. And so on. (This counter argument is stronger if the opponent does not advocate unilateral disarmament.)

One must reject the dilemma as false by showing that its either/or construction does not necessarily follow, or that one refuses to accept the morality of the course being suggested by the dilemma. During the height of the protest against the Vietnam War, signs went up declaring, "Your country—Love it or leave it." The answer to such an inflicted dilemma is that one rejects the inanity of the proposition that because one criticizes a certain national policy, or because one exercises one's democratic right to dissent, or even because one personally finds the current *Zeitgeist* of one's country morally repugnant, one is some kind of traitor and under the obligation to quit the land.

Watch out for such false dilemmas, and for loaded terms that rhetorically label one in an unjustly pejorative way. These will be discussed in Chapter 7, "Spotting Errors in Logic."

Since the moral argument appeals to the emotions, it is forensically more effective than the intellectual argument. The man of cool, dry reason is always at a disadvantage when opposing a morally heated speaker or a demagogue. That's a fact of life. There is a wide difference in terms of worthiness between a calculating professional demagogue and someone in whom the wells of passion have genuinely been moved. Ever keep in mind when confronting an emotional adversary Felix Somary's dictum that the less well founded a position is, the more passionately will it be defended (viz. "The Social Laws of the Inverse Ratio," *Democracy at Bay,* 1952). Nevertheless, appeal to the moral emotions is legitimate. Building a case so that it climaxes in strongly grounded moral connections is an oratorical tradition that was much honored in the nineteenth century but that we tend to feel a little embarrassed about today. But: go ahead. If you have the temperament to get away with it. So long as the appeal to emotion is justifiable, generated naturally by the topic. There is more to this life than cold philosophy, wailed the lover in Keats's *Lamia,* who was bewitched by a serpent that had assumed female form.

> Do not all charms fly
> At the mere touch of cold philosophy?
> There was an awful rainbow once in heaven:
> We know her woof, her texture; she is given
> In the dull catalogue of common things.

Heuristic Argumentation

Related, because also carrying an emotional charge, and thus presuming a higher authority, is argumentation in what is known as the "heuristic" mode, which I situate here, under the moral imperative, instead of in the chapter on logic, because reasoning after this manner obeys sui generical rules.

It is a method—a tactic—more than it is a logic, defined by Webster as "serving to discover or reveal; applying to arguments and methods of demonstration that are persuasive rather than logically compelling, or which lead a person to find out for himself."

Heuristic argumentation is neither a debile dialectical mode, nor one to be ashamed of. It assumes a truth, or a reality, to which all subscribe; and that is a weakness only when, as when turning from one's opponent to appeal to the crowd in heuristic fashion, one discovers that one's assumption is not shared. Paul of Tarsus was unblushingly heuristic. "When I came among you," he told the Corinthians (1 Cor. 2:1–5), "it was in weakness and fear, and with much trepidation. My message and my preaching had none of the persuasive force of 'wise' argumentation, but the convincing power of the Spirit. As a consequence," however, he noted, "your faith rests not on the wisdom of men but on the power of God." Saint Paul did OK.

Upsetting the Moral Argument: A Warning

Nevertheless, watch out. The tables can sometimes be devastatingly turned on the moral argument, as in the example regarding affirmative action. Affirmative action is in essense an heuristic argument, having no basis in logic: it is proposed as a way of redressing past wrongs, which came about because of racial discrimination. The moral issue is the sinfulness of racial discrimination, which also crosses the grain of the equal protection clause of the Constitution. That is, the moral issue has been incorporated into the basic law of the land: the Constitution is officially color blind.

But that's the rub. Affirmative action can be attacked precisely on the grounds that the policy by definition is not color blind, and is therefore immoral; it can also be attacked in that its effects, the preferment of blacks, all circumstances supposedly being equal, over whites, have been shown to be pernicious by such authorities as Thomas Sowell, of unimpugnable integrity, in that in practice what happens is the advancement of inferiorly qualified blacks, which tends to give blacks *as a race* a bad reputation among white employers, thus paradoxically promoting racism.

Smugness

Reducing matters to the moral argument is recommended especially for summations, at which time such emotionally laden appeals work best. (Contrive to have your wattles shake with indignation, if you have wattles. If not, go out and buy some.) There are dangers always, not the least being smugness. The person who adopts a high moral tone in an argument can be taking the lazy way out of a good hard look at the concrete issues. Watch for that in opponents, particularly those whose official positions may be superior to one's own: the head of one's department, the president of a college, a minister, the governor of a state, one's post commander. To such people righteousness comes easily, and one notices that they are appealing over one's head to the audience, or to someone higher up in the chain of self-importance, or even to God. Be patient. Counter with concrete evidence, with unembellished yet trenchant statistics, with a remark recalling the pontificator to dry land, such as, "To get back to what we were talking about," or, "Returning to the here and now," or, "Those are wonderful sentiments, and if they had anything to do with the case I would be the first to second them . . . so to speak." Just don't be gulled by the facilely moralistic opponent, about whom we will have more in the next chapter, and do not yourself substitute smug self-righteousness or facile moralizing for the laborious business of compiling the evidentiary material that makes a solid case. Get the facts. Get them right. Get them down. Get the facts on both sides of an argument. Test the reasoning on both sides of the argument, and set that down. Reflect. Is Argument A persuasive, is Argument B convincing? Can you somehow make of Argument C, for which you have personal antipathy, an attractive brief? You can? There is something to be said for your opponent's point of view? Reflect some more. Decide what in the coldest, last analysis seems to be more reasonable, what has the more compelling evidence in support, what is ultimately cogent, and right. This is your case, in which you have taken nothing for granted, well thought through, proofed in the furnace of your analytical faculties.

How most effectively to serve that case up is a consideration that comes after.

6

Differentiate, Discriminate,
Draw the Relevant Distinctions

There is more to be said about building a formidable case and crushing the opposition.

You have heard about building houses on sand. One chill November evening my sons Hunt and Borja went duck hunting in a South Carolina oak and cypress swamp. They chose a half-submerged log to take their stands on. Which was fine, until it began swimming away.

In the South, this is known as a cock and gator story. Though it's true, and here pertinent. Whether setting up for ducks, or preparing to shoot off the mouth, be fastidious about underfooting. When it comes to winning arguments, keep present not only that any invoked principle must be superior to competing principles, but that factual support for the principle must be rockhard solid.

In addition, the speaker must be dead sure that what he adduces by way of fact or principle in support of his case has materially to do with it.

It's curious, but two kinds of people use irrelevancies when they speak: bores and comedians. Comedians do this to a purpose. Bores just naturally lapse into it, adducing anecdote after statistic after analogy that miss the point entirely, or have only passing acquaintance with it.

Talk to the Point

Be relevant. Speak to the point, and keep it lively to others, or shut up. As always, be self-critical. Is what you adduce, apart from pertaining to your case, material and substantial? The weight of your evidence must prevail, or the best you can hope for is a standoff. The old saw in constructing a speech runs: tell them what you are going to say, tell them, tell them again, and then tell them what you have told them. But don't bore the pants off them by simply reiterating your points in the same plodding way, and tell them no nonsense. Do not adduce to your support what upon repetition sounds sillier and sillier.

To avoid that, tell yourself what you are going to say, tell yourself, tell yourself again, tell yourself what you have told yourself, and then find someone from Missouri to tell it to all over again: and if you can bear it—if you are not yourself bored bug-eyed by the sound of your voice—and it still makes sense, you have probably roughed out in your mind a solid schema.

Pausing before the Leap

Unless you are certain that the principles to which you pledge your troth are valid, relevant, material, and supported by the evidence, keep your sword quiet in its scabbard. I have regretted guarding silence less often than I have regretted popping off. Grinding one's teeth while fools hold sway is no fun, but it's preferable to biting one's tongue. The brilliant idea that pops into the mind in the heat of discussion is to be resisted. Too often it is like those wonderful flashes that illuminate landscapes after the third bourbon on the rocks: no good when judged soberly in the dread light of day.

Inappropriate Levity

Similarly, people who are wont to enliven meetings with humorous flippancies can be out of order when the matter under discussion is deeply serious. Now, Heaven knows I am all for more humor in this world, but humor can be inappropriate, and the kind of remark I am talking about is generally impulsive, a little silly (it will be irrelevant), and interrupts to no purpose the person holding the floor. One can always tell a misfire. There follows a silence, describable as "deathly," relieved mayhap by a nervous giggle from the single person in the room one oneself deems a lightweight. The wisecrack earns a long penetrating gaze from the CEO, or commanding officer, or department head, in which one can see a radical withering of one's stock;

whereupon he (or she) says icily to the person who was interrupted, "Would you continue, Mrs. Harrison?"—or (worse) himself resumes the thread of his discourse.

Anyone with a sense of the ridiculous has shot his mouth off in this embarrassing manner at one time or other. It is hard to hold one's tongue if one's temperament is exuberant, and if the vanity of all things is lively in one's mind, rendering prolonged discussion of grave subjects, such as the closing of a plant, or the abandoning of an unsuccessful product, absurd. Think as much (Eccles. 1:2; 2:21–23 is on your side), but don't say it. The philosopher's vanity may be the practical man's life concern. What there is no excuse for is impetuously sounding off with an unsustainable argument, or espousing an untenable position, when one has five minutes to think the matter through.

Dialectical Precision

Choose with care the ground on which you mean to stand and fight. Differentiate. Discriminate. Draw the relevant distinctions. There is no better illustration today of the need for rigorous scrutiny of fact and principle than the outrage over South Africa's racial policies. Probably more people make bigger dunces of themselves on this than on any other issue, because the pitfalls are many, the complexities tortuous, the solutions not easily perceptible, if any there are, and the stakes tragic. The facetious remark in this connection is wildly inappropriate: human beings have died, human beings daily are being killed—beaten and tortured to death, or burned alive with the flaming necklace of a rubber tire around their necks—and, thanks in part to the loose thinking that informs what passes for World Opinion, many thousands more human beings are yet likely to lose their lives.

But where is the right? Are those apartheid policies, for example— out of hand—wholly condemnable? Do they contain no rationale over which folk of goodwill and reason can disagree, without, perhaps, assigning moral opprobrium?

Snap Judgments—The Self-Evident Fallacy

What seems self-evident sometimes doesn't stand up to scrutiny. We have indicated as much before, but it bears repeating and repeating and repeating. The popular and facile moral position—one that elicits mass approval—can be deceiving, and, as in the case of South Africa, simpleminded. Anytime one sees a mob thirsting for somebody's scalp, this is the signal to pause. Take fresh stock of the guilt or innocence of the intended victim. One may be surprised, or disturbed, by what one discovers. One may rescue oneself from the deep embarrassment of having snapped to a shallow judgment.

That the white supremacist government's policies of apartheid are utterly repulsive and revolting, expressive of a deep, dreadful, and wicked racism that should be abhorrent to every decent person is just such a self-righteously satisfying snap judgment. Moreover, there is truth in it. *There is a layer of truth almost always in the false self-evident proposition, which is why it so easily recommends itself.* The Irish are drunks. Black males are unable to control their violent impulses. But one must ask: is it the whole truth? Is it entirely fair? Is it historically educated? Are there no extenuations? Black males in the United States are charged with a disproportionate number of violent crimes, that's true, but there are cultural, sociological, and environmental factors that weigh against the judgment of an intrinsic susceptibility to passionate excess. As for all Irish being drunks: those who drink do seem to drink heavily, and the tendency apparently passes down in the genes even to sons and daughters of the Old Sod who have escaped the gloomy Irish climate; yet the epithet is of limited use, there are Irishmen who do not touch a drop. Are all Baptists dry, the French ingrate bastards, male homosexuals bitchy of tongue, Turks cruel, people who hold that abortion is a matter of choice murderers, Jews who feel sorry for the displaced Palestinians scum bags and scalawags, Shi'ite Moslems kidnappers and terrorists? Is terrorism all of one cloth, unmitigatedly evil? (What are Afghanistan resistance fighters waging when they mine a road or blow out of the skies a military plane carrying civilians, war or terrorism?) Are all terrorists, judged individually, nothing other than the cowards, murderers, and sadists once so roundly condemned by President Reagan, to be banished from civilized discourse? (What about Menachim Begin, a proud former "activist" in the cause of Zion? Should President Jimmy Carter never have invited him to Camp David? What about Oliver Tambo, chief of the African National Congress, who justifies terrorism by blacks in South Africa as the only riposte to the institutionalized terrorism of the white government—should Secretary of State George Shultz have granted him an official audience?) Finally, are South African white supremacists without distinction evil-hearted folk who seek to perpetuate an unrighteous situation by which they maintain themselves as the master race, subjugating blacks and "coloureds" with a kind of gratuitous fanaticism?

The South African Example—Self-Righteousness Gone Amuck

They are being treated by most of the world, including by the patently hypocritical totalitarian world, as though they were everything just said of them, yet the answer to that last question is: wrong, right, right, wrong.

People of the maturity and depth of understanding of Amy Carter prefer being arrested for obstructing the South African embassy in Washington, thus making public record of the superior purity of her soul, to examining the distinctions. But who will blame Miss Carter when she is endorsed in her moral posturing by an overwhelming majority in both houses of the Congress, which voted economic sanctions against that beleaguered land, never mind that South African blacks will bear the principal burden of this exercise in self-righteousness. (Oh, what fun it is to be self-righteous! To be righteous is another matter entirely, because this state of grace is earned by fasting, abnegations, scourgings, shipwreck, and threat of death.)

All this ooze of easy piety sits ill on the stomach. One may abominate the Jim Crow nastiness of apartheid—as I hasten to make clear that I do—but in thinking the South African tragedy through to oneself one has to begin with the proposition that the Afrikaners, far from being bad folk, are on the whole as good and decent and religiously minded a people as it is possible to meet. Boers may be dull, like most people of Teutonic, Dutch, Saxon, and Scandinavian stock—like Pennsylvanians, or Minnesotans, or South Dakotans, or, one dares venture, some folk even in the hinterlands of Georgia—but racial politics aside, Amy's mama and daddy would be quite comfortable with them.

Then what demon—the cautious person must ask himself—has provoked their hateful policies?

Well, not demon, it transpires upon reading a smidgin of South African history. God Almighty. In *their* view. God led them into the

Transvaal, it was with God that they made their prayerful covenant when they were besieged by blood-thirsty savages on all sides, God gave them victory in the desperate battle at Blood River, God delivered the promised land unto them. If South Africans are fanatical, they are no less fanatical than the Israelis who believe that Israel is the promised land of milk and honey bequeathed by Jehovah unto perpetuity to the descent of Abraham, which inheritance no one shall wrest from them. Just tell the Israelis that they ought to give up sole sovereignty over Jerusalem, no matter by how many Arabs they are outnumbered, and see how far you get. (About as far as Nixon, Carter, and Reagan together.)

To the Afrikaners, it is an article of faith that they were given the land in sole possession by On High. It was a land not running with milk and honey, moreover. It was a barren, desolate place. Whereas in ancient Israel, other Semitic tribes pastured their herds and sowed their wheat by the River Jordan before they were driven out or exterminated by the Hebrews, the territory across the River Vaal was totally empty. It was not the possession of Zulus, who were an *arriviste* nation out of the northeast, brutal and sanguinary invaders, from whose yoke the other black tribes begged the Afrikaners to deliver them. The Boers did not merely claim the land of the Transvaal by right of conquest, theirs until such time as they lack the strength to keep it (as, at just about the same historical period, did we in the West, like the Jews of old, slaughtering, subduing, or driving out former inhabitants); it was an empty space that the Boers filled, reserved unto them by Almighty God.

Doing the Opposition Justice

Hold on, reader. Don't give way to impatience. Don't skip these pages, or throw this book down, because what I have just set forth does violence to your deepest convictions regarding the white tyranny in that distant land. Remember: to argue well, to do justice to *our* side of an equation, we must do justice to *the other* side of the equation. We must place ourselves in the other person's skin. We must endeavor to comprehend for what reasons he holds his wrong, absurd, or, to our (enlightened) way of thinking, evil tenets. Whatever we may think of it, what I have described is the transcendental justification Afrikaners call to their witness. This is what *they* believe.

This is how *they* view matters. They are not being self-righteous in the sense that Miss Carter is susceptible to the accusation; they are basing their perpetual exclusionary right to the land they occupy and dominate on divine intervention, and thus on supreme authority. They may be as wrong as many would say the Latterday Saints are wrong in their conviction that the Book of Mormon was angelically handed to Joseph Smith on the hill anciently known as Cumorah, but they are not on that account—that *racist* account—"evil." They may be as subject to primitive superstitions as atheists take for granted all Christians and Muslims of any variety are, and their doctrine of racial superiority may be as mistaken and as opprobrious as almost everybody agrees today such doctrines are, but the Afrikaners, like the plantation Southerners of slavery times in the United States (read *Tombee*, by Theodore Rosengarten, William Morrow and Company, 1986), are not "evil." An assumed absolute right by black Africans to lay claim to all continental Africa below the Sahara is *in their view* an irrational superstition, unfounded on any rhyme or reason other than pure jingoistic black racism, irrelevant to the history of the Transvaal, and subordinate in any case to the preemptive claims of the myth (as others may deem it) that is their creed.

The Use of Telling Analogies—Reduction by Analogy

We have been examining this issue as a skilled speaker might from the platform. He is opposing the popular view, remember, which invites caution and necessitates a skillful turning of the moral tables. His opponent is probably languishing from the desire to storm up to the lectern, grab it, and denounce the speaker as an apologist for the most execrable racism since Adolph Hitler. That is the risk our hero runs. He is aware of it—oh, believe that he is! Standing up to a mob is perilous to one's health. Note, therefore, the dialectical thrusts in the preceding paragraphs—what some might label dialectical low blows. In exorcising the demon image of the Afrikaners, he has had the ill grace to draw a comparison between South Africa and Israel, a sacred cow for most Americans, created in its modern political existence just two generations ago, scooped out of territory that was arbitrarily seized from its inhabitants of two thousand years, like South Africa theocratic in its core, and like South Africa with respect to blacks and others, exclusionary in its policies toward the Palestinians, about which it is nevertheless an article of faith that the state, though we may deplore some of its policies, has an imperscriptible right to exist *as a Jewish state;* and the speaker has slyly, though not unfairly—what is sauce for the gander is sauce for the goose—drawn a comparison between the Afrikaners and our own nineteenth-century expansionist history, depending on the audience—you, the alert reader—to fill in the buried premise: is Amy Carter next going to sit on the Capitol steps until this same simpleton Congress votes to give the land west of the Mississippi—our Jordan, our Vaal—back to the Indians?

The Fallacy of Selective Indignation

By use of such analogies, the speaker has put the audience in white South African shoes, which should defuse some of the prejudice against him and his attempt to restore reason and moderation to the matter. Has he been harsh? Perhaps. Mean? Nasty? Not the least, given the provocation. This is a legitimate response—unsparing, nonetheless germane and justified. We can assume Miss Carter is well-meaning; she was notwithstanding plainly in the wrong when she blocked the steps of the South African embassy. She was playing dirty. Good Lord, she wouldn't have been aware of that, so carried away was she by her indignation against the white South African government. But it is illicit to cloak one's cause in moral righteousness when one is in reality practicing what Sir Arnold Lunn dubbed "selective indignation," and when one's testimony slurs over the distinctions, if any. If one detests authoritarianism, one detests it in all its guises, right or left. If Amnesty International excoriates cruelty and torture in Albania, it forfeits moral authority unless with equal vigor it also excoriates such revolting practices in, say, Paraguay and Chile. Miss Carter is egregious in her public manifestations against apartheid; does anyone recall similar public witness by her regarding Soviet persecution of the Jews, or for that matter with regard to the second-class-citizen status of Palestinians under Jewish suzerainty? A showy political act whose content, as in this case, boils down to moral sentimentality, is the exercising of a kind of terrorism on the rational faculties; and merciless critical riposte is justified. Because *giving quarter to moral mush is an abnegation of intellectual responsibility, indulged in at the price of intellectual integrity.* Yet, and yet, if one were debating Miss Carter at, let us assume, a college campus, would one lay into her in this fashion?

Let the question ride a few moments. Meanwhile:

Applying the Analytical Faculties

Differentiate. Draw the distinctions, and examine them, even when they lead you where you do not care to go. The vexed South African question gives one's critical faculties a good wringing out. Black South Africans perceive themselves as the aggrieved party, we can agree. But that is not enough. The claim of victim status must be scrutinized. What is the nature of their grievance? It falls into two parts, which have to be taken separately. There are, first, the insults to human dignity deriving from Jim Crow and other segregationist practices. There is also, as black Africans see it, and we Americans by empathy sense it, violation of a substantive political "right."

Differentiate. Discriminate. In what does this "right" consist? Well, in the mystical notion that "black" Africa belongs to black Africans, which the Boers score against when they say it is an exclusionary and racist idea, no more supportable than white South African racism. Or is what we are talking about the "right" of black South Africans to political equality in accordance with the democratic doctrine of majority will?

Narrowing the Argument—Searching for Its Crux

Here we may be on firmer footing. There are some four million white South Africans who run the country and subject to their sole political will some twenty-six million blacks and Asians and "coloureds." Asians and "coloureds" have recently gained a measure of representation in the political process, but blacks have been up to now steadfastly excluded. Protesting the racial policies of the Boers on these grounds appears to nudge the argument over from race to political systems of which we, in the West, happen to approve. Are we then now talking about democracy? That is, are we saying that it is wrong to exclude a majority, black or white, brown or yellow, or mixed from the political process? Or are we—is not Miss Carter— going one step further and talking about an absolutist construction of popular government—rule by the *demos,* with, in the light of recent African history, fugitive political safeguards for minorities within the society. The Soviet Union, one recalls, has a Constitution that on paper guarantees to Soviet subjects basic human and political rights, which are routinely violated.

The Perils of Radical Construction

This absolute political egalitarianism has been called unkind names, dictatorship by the rabble being one. It has only been approximated in the United States in the past decade, following on Supreme Court decisions and Congressional legislation, the Constitutionality and wisdom of which are still matters of impassioned debate.

The radical political egalitarianism that we now practice in the States can only properly be considered an experiment, one that may prove to be folly. The radical or extreme construction of an accepted general principle (the goodness of democracy as a political system) is always suspect even in those circumstances where the general principle has been in successful operation over time; its extrapolation and transplantation to circumstances wholly foreign, and in which the fundamental conditions themselves for the success of the general principle are absent (literacy, civility, historical ethnic tradition) is practical folly and polemical lunacy. The blacks of South Africa who will constitute 81 percent of the integrated state have no Magna Carta anywhere in their historical background. They have never practiced even the most limited popular government. Tolerance is nowhere in their historical tradition. Their history is characterized primarily by intertribal ferocity, whose law of tooth and claw signified for the conquered death or bondage. Still would we impose on South Africa a radical construction of popular government that horrified the ancient Greeks, that would cause J. S. Mill himself to blanch, summed up in the slogan "One man, one vote," which has been corrected in the context of post–World War II African experience to "One man, one vote, one time." All black African territories that have achieved nationhood and black majority rule, without exception, have succumbed at best to one-party rule, at worst to the most ferocious tyrannies. Promises to the contrary. Lofty statements of principle in charters or constitutions notwithstanding. Are white South Africans "evil" or even paranoiac because they fear such an outcome in their own country, with the history of Rhodesia so fresh in their minds, and so dismally instructive? Are Afrikaners unreasonable when they react with horror and anger to the childish textbook prescriptions that the Amy Carters of this world seek to ram down their throats?

Argumentation from the Known to the Proposed, with the Object of Ridiculing the Proposed

This is the kind of stringent pathological examination to which all controversies—especially ones emotionally so highly charged—must be subjected to. One must be relentless. Have those Americans who by their public action would bring down the white South African state this redhot instant given no thought to the political consequences of their protest? Who, one must ask, will benefit primarily from the civil wars that are bound to ensue, from the turmoil and anarchy? Deducing from past, analogous experience—it is fair and appropriate to deduce from it—the slaughter will be resolved in a Marxist or quasi-Marxist dictatorship of despotic character and in Third World service of Soviet ends. This is conjecture, of course. Are we eager to test the odds?

Weighing Arguments in the Hierarchy of Values

The answer to that can be perhaps, adducing the Principle of Relative Preferences. Is apartheid such an offense against the decencies, so heinous, so categorically immoral, that it becomes our duty here in the United States, in conscience, in the name of our common humanity, to strive heart and soul for its overthrow, no matter what may ensue?

Having Isolated, Examining the Core of an Argument— Drawing Relevant Distinctions

Could be. But we must first learn more about the policy of apartheid. Having swept persiflage away, we must concentrate on, and split, the atom. All arguments must be reduced to their core, the core itself examined and attacked.

In what exactly does apartheid consist? (Differentiate. Draw the relevant distinctions.) It comes in two parts. There is what South Africans denominate "petty" apartheid, and "grand" apartheid. The second is the "separate homelands" concept, wherein chunks of territory within South Africa's political boundaries are given over to black tribes that supposedly originated there, or near there. These—

well, these reservations—are designated by the South African government nation states: leetle nation states, deprived of an independent foreign policy, but sovereign in most other respects. Let's put "grand" apartheid on hold for just a moment.

"Petty" apartheid is probably what shocks the visitor to South Africa most, especially the American over forty years of age, who, when he sees gas stations, stores, water fountains, and toilets segregated into separate services for blacks and whites, suffers a kind of guilty warp in time from the forcible reminder of what obtained in the South through the middle 1960s—just twenty years ago. (It is like a nightmare to revisit our own ugly racist past.) Jim Crow is a redhot iron that sears forever into the conscience: it is an inexcusable affront to the created dignity of black South Africans—no matter what unreconstructed Afrikaners may think about the subject. (In this *they* are wrong, as the good white Christians of the slave South were wrong: morally and theologically in error.) The "influx control" laws under which blacks are restricted to seventy-two hours only in white urban areas outside their "homelands" are abhorrent; and though similar laws restrict freedom of movement in Ethiopia, Kenya, Mozambique, Rwanda, Somalia, Sudan, Tanzania, and Zaire; and though such as Ethiopians, Mozambicans, Rwandans, and Zairians must carry work and residence permits and cannot move without the permission of the government; on the principle that two wrongs a right do not make doesn't excuse the South African oppressions, though under the principle of similar cases, as it is called, does permit one to ask such as Miss Carter why they pick on South Africa alone? Why not other African states? Why not states closer to home, such as Cuba, Nicaragua, and Chile, or Israel, Syria, Iran, and all the Soviet satellites—oh, there are so many who trample under human dignity!

Apartheid is some forty years old. It has been resisted and fought by many heroes and heroines, and the universal repugnance for "petty" apartheid has slowly and surely had effect. The government of President P. W. Botha is a reformist government. Over the years, plank after odious plank in the "petty" apartheid edifice has been dismantled. Why is not Amy Carter giving at least grudging recognition of this progress? Because it is all hypocritical window dressing on the Botha government's part, or because outright abolishment of these insults to black human dignity is not the issue? One suspects the latter. "Grand" not "petty" apartheid is the bone in the throat.

We come to the end of our examination. I have met white South

Africans who are themselves embarrassed by the extension and quality of the territories that have been designated homelands. The soil is too dry and too poor, the boundaries too parsimonious. I have talked to white South Africans who simply despair of the solution itself, as being politically unattainable in a hostile world. Other white South Africans deplore "grand" apartheid on principle. They favor a single, multiracial state with protections for the white, Asian, and "coloured" minorities. But none of these noncolored critics (I don't say there aren't others) viewed the separate homelands proposal as inherently outrageous. Unjustly apportioned, unworkable, inexpedient, unwise, or undesirable, but not wicked.

Testing the Validity of the Opponent's Animus: Does It Justify the Reform?

Should we? The three major nationalities that make up the Swiss Confederation, with its twenty-three cantons, nearly three thousand communes, and four linguistic areas have for over four hundred years got along famously under a kind of "grand" apartheid arrangement. The reservations we in the United States established for our Indians are "homelands" (except for the tragic Creeks and Cherokees, who were removed thousands of miles to Oklahoma from their native Florida and Carolinas), though with nothing approaching the political sovereignty vouchsafed by the South African government. Do black Africans themselves view the desire by a ruling caste to preserve an ethnic homogeneity as untoward? The Ivory Coast expelled sixteen thousand Beninese during the mid-1960s, Ghana expelled five hundred thousand "aliens" in 1969, Zambia expelled all its "aliens" in 1971, Uganda expelled fifty thousand Asians in 1972, ten years later kicking out thousands more Banyarwandas—and so on. Other dominant African tribes have elected the expedient of slaughtering the minorities, with the intention of wiping them out entirely, which is a very permanent kind of apartheid indeed.

Summing Up

Always conclude with an encapsulation of your argument that neatly reduces it for audience comprehension.

Where are we at? If common sense and the history of Africa below the Sahara instruct us that (a) any guarantees for the white population are destined to be tossed into a cocked hat and sailed out the smoke hole within two years after *uhuru,* (b) following the surrender of political equality to the black population the black tribes at once engage in the most savage and merciless intertribal warfare, (c) the economy goes to hell, with famine and disease afflicting almost all the population, (d) a one-party, dominant-tribe state emerges from the bloodletting, subjugating the other tribes, black or white or "coloured," relegating them at best to "second-class" status: in short, a reversal of the present situation, a black elite lording it over whites and "coloureds" and Asians and other blacks, which one assumes is morally no more acceptable to Miss Carter or the Congress of the United States, (e) the ravished economy is shackled to some form or other of socialism, guaranteeing impoverishment of the new nation as far as the ken of man can project human affairs, (f) the foreign policy of the new black nation becomes Third World, which is short-hand for a kind of self-servicing idiocy fueled by envy, and (g) a neo-Marxist supreme leader, or succession of neo-Marxist supreme leaders, takes the helm, indulging in plunder and nepotism at best (Kenyatta, Nyerere, Mobutu), wholesale butchery at worst (Idi Amin)—then what alternative have responsible white South Africans other than attempting to sell some form of "grand" apartheid to the black population, and to what ruin and destruction and slaughter is Amy Carter seeking to condemn them by her moral posturing?

The Role of Tact: The Speaker's Objective

Thus should go any careful person's analysis of emotional stands on public issues. What solution one might propose for the South African tragedy-in-the-making is immaterial to this book. (I do have a proposal.) The exhaustive analysis that must be conducted by anyone who would take a stand for or against a controversial issue, especially in public, is the important thing here.

Antagonizing the Audience

I dealt roughly with Miss Carter in my analysis of the uncritical sentimentalism and irresponsibility of her public protest. Never mind that she asked for it: it's likely to have upset some readers, causing them to ask, "Is this the right way to respond from a speakers' platform?" (even though moral sentimentality, because it brings disrepute on truly moral outrage, must never—at least theoretically—be spared).

The answer is a qualified no. I would have made approximately the same points had I been engaging in debate with Miss Carter personally, or at some gathering of young people, but in greatly modulated manner. No way would I have sought to humiliate her. Different would be the case were I testifying before a Congressional subcommittee, however. Since it is a fair assumption that moral hypocrisy reigned supreme in House and Senate votes on sanctions, one should have no qualms about blistering such hides. They are thick enough. The same goes when dealing in any public forum with corporate pullouts from South Africa. Take Coca-Cola. There is as little moral substance to its symbolic gesture as to Miss Carter's protest, but in Coke's case cheap commercial politics were being played. The company is in the meantime busy expanding its activities in Russia and Red China, whose combined 1.25 billion subjects might go mad for joy were they to receive any of the rights and immunities guaranteed to South Africa's blacks by the Botha government. Coke's Roberto Goizueta deserves nothing less than scorn from the speakers' platform. Had I heaped on Miss Carter in public as I have in these pages, however, I'd have antagonized the audience more than I may have antagonized the reader, because it is one thing to tear into someone at the remove of print, it is another to do so in person. We may like to see a pompous windbag perforated in a public forum; we do not like to watch the humiliation of earnest young folk who believe with all their hearts that they are doing the right thing.

A speaker must ask himself sometimes what contents him: to win the intellectual argument or win the audience. Demagogues and politicians (assuming that a distinction can be drawn between the two) typically care all for the popular vote, nil for the esteem of the judicious few. Intellectuals may feel an elitist thrill from winning the argument, and even prefer to lose in the popular mind, about which they are snobs.

The ideal situation is when one can do both: prevail intellectually and win the election. Sometimes this is not possible. Very often it is not easy. Honorable folk will never sacrifice the first for the second. And on the whole, there is, I think, a kind of poetic justice in this cynical world. Lincoln probably lost to Douglas in the second (and most important) of their famous debates that summer of 1858, at

Freeport, Illinois, but was vindicated by his election to the presidency two years later.[1] If one is convinced of the cogency of what may be an unpopular idea and keeps pounding on it, eventually it is going to prevail. An evil idea may also prevail when it is repeated often enough by what we mistakenly dub a "charismatic" personality (the word actually means full of grace), such as Adolph Hitler (who was full of the Devil). The moral: Immediate historical gratification does not signify that over long historical perspective our cause will be judged right or good.

The Limited Power of Oratory

A splendid oration can serve to electrify the world with a novel idea. It can make the speaker's career. Generally the idea must be one in which optimism and good cheer prevail—one that is filled with possibilities, inflating hopes. We human beings react positively to the upbeat. We are half convinced of what we hunger to hear. One can rarely hope to convince a hostile audience by a public address, however. Quiet diplomacy, person-to-person lobbying, is ten times more effective. The able president invites leaders of the Congress, including opponents, to the White House for private talks before delivering his address on nationwide television. Effrontery on the part of a speaker is a poor tactic. There is the rare exception. That poet, skewed genius, and inveterate controversialist Hilaire Belloc stood for Parliament in 1905 in a staunchly anti-Papist district and recommended himself to the assembled voters in this belligerent fashion:

> Gentlemen, I am a Catholic. As far as possible, I go to Mass every day. This [taking a rosary out of his pocket] is a rosary. As far as possible, I kneel down and tell these beads every day. If you reject me on account of my religion, I shall thank God that He has spared me the indignity of being your representative!

A. N. Wilson, who tells the story in his 1984 biography of this impossible man, writes: "After a shocked silence, there was a thunderclap of applause."

1. "Looking at the Freeport debate, from the vantage point of time, one must conclude that while Douglas had the better of it for the purposes of the Senatorial campaign of 1858, Lincoln had planted certain seeds in the public mind, which would grow to large proportions by the time of the Presidential campaign of 1860." Rollin G. Osterweis, "American Oratory in Historical Perspective."

The Perils of Arrogance

Unless one is as gifted as Hilaire Belloc, however, one should be wary of emulating his gall. I never adopted a hectoring or superior attitude when I addressed college students. Never. Arrogance is only a lesser sin than condescension. In almost all circumstances it is politic to proceed to the destruction of an opponent's position with humility, which the wise person never permits to stray far from his consciousness, and which the fool will soon be impressed with his dire need of. There are folk who become mightily fussed when they are pressed by questions from the floor. They do not win adherents. They do not advance their cause. I do everything in my power to protect the self-esteem even of hecklers. (Just about the worst punishment one can mete hecklers is to consider their jibes and insults and obscenities with all apparent seriousness, which makes mockery of them.) It was not my purpose to "demolish the opposition simply as a logical exercise," as William Rusher puts it. I wasn't content to win the intellectual argument: throughout the late 1960s and 1970s I was campaigning to unsettle those political assumptions in which college students had been reared, to correct the impression that (all) right-wingers are cranks, reactionaries, or Fascists, and to intrigue them with the sense and (for students at the time) the originality of the conservative view. I was evangelizing. I was, if you like, "selling" a philosophical view. I was consciously attempting to do my bit to throw a hard right rudder on the political course of the United States, which meant assaulting and occupying the intellectual high ground.

Spreading the Word: How Best to Sell One's Case

This was in the late 1960s, the early and middle 1970s—dangerous, exciting, polemically explosive years! My purpose was long term: where I was able, to inoculate students against the demogoguery of the opposition; but there were occasions when I wanted to persuade at least some in the audience from a politically popular action that in its symbological content was as fuzzy as Miss Carter's protest.

The Moratorium, many of you will remember, was the apogee of the protest against the war in Vietnam, and, in retrospect, was also the apogee of the "counterculture." It was the big blowout for The

Kids. Organized by twenty-six-year-old Sam Brown, it came in two parts. First, on 15 October 1969, designated the day of the Vietnam Moratorium, an estimated one million Americans across the land in one way or another manifested their loathing of the war; and then, in mid-November, tens of thousands, mostly young people, gathered in Washington for a forty-hour demonstration called the "March against Death."

Come, Let Us Reason Together

I sought in most of my lectures at colleges that fall to persuade students against lending their support to this second demonstration. I did so not by mocking the noble intentions of the organizers, nor even by defending the war (whose prosecution had by that time so disgusted me that I was half convinced there could be no solution other than Vietnamization of the conflict, as it was called, accompanied by our withdrawal), but by asking students to apply to their antiwar convictions the critical principles that I applied to Miss Carter's protest: to differentiate, draw the relevant distinctions, and discriminate.

Given that an estimated 250,000 young people jammed the Mall in Washington, it hardly appears that I was successful. I like to think, however, that there would have been 250,400, or 250,600, without my labors. At one college in Ohio—maybe it was Nebraska—I gathered after my formal lecture with several dozen students and student leaders, asking them one by one to explain to me their motives for attending the march. It was sometimes not easy digging these motives out. That was not a verbal generation, you will remember. It was vociferous, but it was well, like, ya know: not rationalized. To be charitable. After a lot of patient mining, however, it became apparent—to the astonished students themselves, often—that their motives were (a) not thoroughly thought out, and in part even internally loggerheaded, (b) so diverse as to be contradictory of one another.

There were students who had once supported the war in Vietnam but who, like me, had soured on it for a variety of reasons, including fear of being called up. There were students who had been sickened and revolted by horrifying television coverage, and who just wanted it somehow all to stop. There were those who thought it was immoral per se, we had no business getting involved in the first place, and there were students who thought that since we would not win it, we could not win it, and therefore to prosecute the war further had become immoral. There were pacifists. There were pacifists, however, who were pacifists only about immoral wars, straddling uncomfortably, when pushed to it, the position that some wars, such as World War II, the Spanish Civil War (against Franco), our Civil War, and our Revolutionary War, were in their opinion just. There were Socialists and Communists, and these divided into those who were abject to the Soviet Union and those who followed a rebellious and generally extreme Maoist-Guevara line. I don't recall, but there were probably Trotskyites as well. I do know that there were anarchists who discovered to their shock that in this issue they were aligned with libertarians.

In bringing these shades of political opinion out into the open, it transpired to the students that their perceptions of the Moratorium could not all be similar. The ends they wanted to effect were different. The degree of their protest, and its political content, differed. I asked them: what was the message that the Moratorium was expected to send to the United States and the world? What moral and political lessons were to be drawn from the Moratorium?

They could not decide. They fell to disputing among themselves. What had begun as a cool exercise of analysis heated up. Finally some of the students were shouting at others, "Well, if you think I'm taking five days off to drive all the way to Washington just to give *that* impression of why I hate the goddam war and what I think about it, you're nutty," or, "That's not what I want to be there for at all! I'm not a goddam Commie," or, "It's *all* wars I'm against, not just this one," or, "That's crazy. Wars of liberation are OK, it's this effen imperialist war I'm protesting against." After listening to them a while, I asked whether those who objected to the Vietnam War on specific grounds wanted to express their philosophical solidarity with those who objected to the war on quite different, even opposing, grounds. I asked them, Was not the Moratorium bound to be a statement of the most awful philosophical and political confusion, where people of quite different and even opposing opinions were being gulled into marching under the same banner? What kind of statement was that? Were they not being used, and were they willing to lend their presence to what could only be a falsification—maybe even a deliberate and cynical falsification—of their ardor?

Relevance and Timeliness in Arguing from Principle

The method of the Socratic dialogue is effective. We should apply it at all times to our own opinions, subjecting them continually to differentiation and discrimination.

One can win arguments or advance one's point of view by deductive or inductive reasoning, or both. One is correspondingly vulnerable on both levels. Relevance—as we've indicated—is the criterion. When a speaker draws up his case, he must make sure (1) that his facts are in order, (2) that his operating principle is valid, and (3) that it applies to the situation. It was on this third ground that I attacked the Moratorium. I attacked Miss Carter on all three grounds: on her ignorance of the situation (the facts she churned up such moral fervor regarding were incompletely known by her), on the desirability of her egalitarian majoritarianism per se, and on the propriety of applying that principle to the situation in South Africa.

Arguments from principle are vulnerable also to the timeliness of the principle. What held in the past does not necessarily hold now. "Separate but equal" was a canon in deciding the Constitutionality of segregationist policies until the Brown decision in 1954; it is no longer valid or applicable. An unimaginative application of principle that may be valid for one concrete historical situation but not for another can be ridiculed by showing that it can bring about the reverse of what is ideologically desired—as in suggesting that overthrow of the white supremacist rule in South Africa (unlike, say, the defeat of the slave South) will most probably result in black supremacism, between which first and last states no moral distinction can be drawn. Democracy works for a civilized and literate society with a political tradition of tolerance of nonconformity; it is a disaster when planted on societies that do not share either these traditions or conditions. One must make sure that in one's ardent devotion to the principle that alcohol in moderation can be a good thing one does not plan setting up a distillery in Baghdad.

Taking Dead Aim: Identifying the Target

When a speaker rolls up his heavy artillery and trains it on an opponent, he must make certain of his target. I mentioned our farm in the Carolina sandhills. Our labors have brought their reward in songbirds, small game of most descriptions, and snakes.

We had a nine-foot bull gator in the big pond, also, but it's the snakes that—though they prey on mice, rats, pine voles, toads, and other pernicious or uncaptivating critters, but which prey also on baby quail, bunnies, and flying squirrels—do not enrapture my wife Tasa.

We have most kinds. Pretty little green grass snakes. Shy blue-bellied racers. Watersnakes. Coachwhips, garters, and large pugnacious redbellied moccasins, that look as though they ought to be venomous, but aren't. The blacksnakes, rippling across our sandy lanes like ribbons of patent leather, come seven and eight feet long. They are mean, flattening their heads when cornered, coiling, and striking viciously. But they do help control rodents, and a relished part of their diet is other snakes, including the poisonous varieties.

There was a granddaddy of a rattlesnake living under the lightwood flooring of the old homestead when we first took over the farm. We had to tear the cabin down, because it was falling apart, and when we did he skedaddled across the road into the bamboo and honeysuckle of the branch leading into our small fish pond, where he took up his abode. We leave him be there, and so far he has let us be, which is satisfactory to both parties.

One afternoon five years ago, however, when Tasa was mowing fairways through our characteristically unkempt lawn, Johnny, our towheaded youngest son, then seven, shouted, "Mamá, cuidado! Serpiente!" He had to run up to her and shout in her ear, because she could not hear well from the noise of the Ariens rider mower—pointing excitedly, face screwed up with anxiety—yelling, "Look out! Snake! Snake!"

Tasa stopped the machine, staring fixedly ahead to where Johnny was pointing. There, half-concealed in the tall grasses and coreopsis stalks, she spotted the unmistakable thick, sluggish, mottled, rusty-iron form of a cottonmouth moccasin.

We respect the rattlesnake, and we have nothing in particular against the copperhead. But we do not like the cottonmouth. I know nobody who does. They're ugly. They're bad tempered all the time, not just when they are gravid with young, or have first come out of their holes in the spring.

This was a big specimen—maybe four inches in diameter, as best Tasa could judge. "Quick, Johnny, fetch my pistol." Johnny raced to the cabin we have built in a patch of pine woods, running up the steps and into the screened porch. Out he came running with Tasa's gunbelt and holster. Never letting her eyes off the snake— which she would have run over had Johnny not spotted it—Tasa loaded five cartridges into the drum of her Ruger .22 "Peace-maker," then carefully raised the pistol by its graceful handle, clasping it in best Angie Dickinson style in both her hands, sighting along the ribbed plane of the barrel and *bam-bam-bam-bam-bam*—letting the moccasin have it with the five blunt-headed bul-lets in her cylinder, Johnny yelling proudly and triumphantly the while, "You got it, Mamá! You got it! You got it with every shot! I can see the holes! It hasn't even moved!"

Which, as Tasa lowered the pistol, struck her as curious. She had aimed at what she could see of the snake: its thick midsection. Shouldn't it have whipped about on it, striking in its death throes? Hushing Johnny, she approached a cautious step. Then another. (One can never be too careful: a black man we knew well picked up what he thought was a dead rattler by the tail, got struck twice, and died.) Then Tasa stooped, lifting her target by one end. She had got it all right. She had perforated it with all five shots. It was a bent exhaust pipe.

Rhetorical Questions

Do not spend good ammunition on the wrong target, but decoy your opponent, when you can, into unloading *his* magazine on tar-gets you float for that sole purpose. Rhetorical questions, put sarcasti-cally, are a good device to this end. "Does Mr. Blackwell truly believe that we are all going to be blown up as the result of an arms race that is largely the product of his imagination?" Mr. Blackwell will jump right up to declare, darned tootin' he believes it, and the arms race is no product of his imagination! One then has at him, beginning with the observation that a race implies at least two contestants, whereas the record of the past decade has been the Soviet Union increasing its arsenal of ICBMs by eight thousand, whereas we in the same period of time have reduced our supply of intercontinental missiles by approximately the same number; and so on. There are few advan-tages more devoutly to be wished than the hot temper of an oppo-nent. The seemingly fatuous rhetorical question will cause him to flare up every time, presenting one with a target that can be gunned down at one's leisure.

Loaded Language

Continue to be wary of the rhetorical coloration of positions, however. Is "Ending the Arms Race" shorthand for unilateral disarmament? Is "Keeping up Our Guard" a mask for bellicosity and an excuse for adventurism? Do not permit opponents to get away with it.

Say It Your Own Way; Restate the Proposition in a Manner Rhetorically More Favorable to Your Stand

Rephrase arguments so that they are more palatable. If a speaker is defending nuclear power plants, for example, which always raises the spectre of a burn-down, he should steal a march on the opposition by pointing out that the choice is not between safety and danger, but between systems for the extraction of energy none of which is absolutely safe.[2] Hydroelectric dams burst. The gases in deep underground coal mine shafts explode. Offshore oil rigs capsize. Comparing the loss in human life attributable to nuclear plants and conventional energy sources permits a speaker to draw the overwhelming conclusion that, on the record, atomic power is safer. Should his opponent counter (as I would be tempted to do) that "the past record of plain good luck does not bear on the possible, even probable, catastrophe to which we are inevitably being impelled in the future," our champion must reach high to defend himself. It is always difficult to argue against hypotheses, particularly if they are emotive. Anticipate these blows in the process of constructing the case. When one is placed in such a rhetorical tight corner, be ready, appeal to common sense. Put things in perspective: "Really, it strains credulity to ask us to believe that if we press a blob of shaving cream from a can onto our faces mornings to shave with, or spray our pet petunias against mealie bugs once a month, we're going to destroy the ozone." That, in fact, multiplied by millions and millions of people using aerosol cans every day, may be just the risk, but one does what one is able to ridicule the contention of one's opponent by

2. I am indebted to William Rusher for suggesting this example.

reductio ad absurdum. One carries his logic to ludicrous extremes, or one paints it as extremist. But if you want to convince people, or carry an audience against an opponent, never ridicule him, never permit yourself to humiliate an opponent, and never be satisfied with having got the best of the intellectual argument.

Persuasion is an art that begins in charity, not in righteousness.

7

Spotting Errors in Logic

Right now make yourself the solemn promise that you will acquire the two essential habits for becoming a good speaker, defending your interests (with the bite of a badger its hole), and advancing your point of view.

The first? *Learn to listen.* Learn to listen to yourself; and to your associates or adversaries.

Come to think of it, listening is also the second essential habit for becoming a good speaker. Listen for: telltale inflections. Subtle stops or shifts in the adversary's argument. Nuances slippery in their intent, slick in their delivery. The nervousness that betrays disingenuous purpose, and that should alert one to dubious logical progressions.

I remember as far back as boyhood my father lamenting that the art of conversation had been totally lost in our country. He was right. His analysis of the reason for this sad state of affairs was also correct. We Americans do not listen to anybody.

Simple courtesy should dictate otherwise. But we are so anxious to get in our two bits that we do not even pause to evaluate the berserk notions that may be hatching in our minds before we sound off, so that when we speak we are at a double disadvantage and doubly liable to make fools of ourselves: often not only unconscious of the points the other fellow has raised, and what may be the misinformation he has slyly insinuated, but blasting off with half-baked brainstorms whose contradictions we have failed to iron out. Our tongues run away with us—to our confusion; to everybody's embarrassment.

Listening in Order to Survive

A reason for acquiring the habit of listening to others more telling than courtesy in this unforgiving world is survival. Permit me to illustrate.

Years ago I founded a real estate syndicate in Madrid. One of my American principals was the late John Murchison, son of old Clint, who, along with the other investors, had to put up three million pesetas—about $50,000—by a certain date to lock in an important option.

John was a gentleman, and became a friend. But one evening a functionary from the Murchison Brothers headquarters in Dallas—he may have been a lawyer—telephoned. "Tell me more about this payment you have written Mr. Murchison about," he said shortly. I began explaining. He hadn't the patience to hear me through, however, advising me in supercilious fashion that the Murchison account would open up an irrevocable letter of credit to my name at the Bank of London and South America against a copy of the signed option, duly notarized. The connection over the transatlantic cable was poor, but something I understood the man to say prompted me to ask, "Are you sure?" He cut me off, telling me icily, "Mr. Buckley, of course we are sure. This is the way we do things, and that's that."

Well, the great day came; and the Bank of London and South America sent along an advice that indeed a letter of credit from Murchison Brothers had come into their possession, to the amount of three million *dollars.*

The functionary had not listened very well. He hadn't read my letter to his boss with more than passing attention, either. Under the terms of an irrevocable letter of credit, you understand, that money, less the three million pesetas owed to the owner of the property, was mine to do with as I pleased: $2,950,000. Oh, John Murchison could have sued to get it back, but for him to recover would have been a major legal undertaking, requiring months and maybe even years, if ever.

I had a Portuguese secretary at the time of whom I was greatly fond—a tall, gloomy, correct, and almost humorless lady called Miss Sequeira, who stuttered quite badly under stress. "M-M-Mr. B-B-Buckley, wha-at are you going to do?" "Miss Sequeira," I said, "we are going to mail the Murchison letter of credit back to Dallas, but meanwhile send the following telegram: Dear John, overwhelmed by your confidence and generosity. Oh, and Miss Sequeira, this is Friday. I expect you will be hearing from Dallas on Monday or Tuesday at the latest. When they telephone, just tell them that I've gone off somewhere, maybe Brazil, and you haven't the least idea when I'll be back."

Listening in Order to Catch Dissonances in Logical Construction

Pay close attention to what others say. And keep your ears pricked for inconsistencies, contradictions, exaggerations, strained logical connections, errors, and examples that are not altogether convincing. Be alert for conclusions that do not quite follow from the premises, or that, though they follow, do not inevitably, or exclusively, follow. On my very first lecture tour I remember reading in some local Midwest newspaper a statement by Robert Kennedy on the Viet Cong that stuck like a cocklebur in my mind, because something was wrong with it, though what for some reason I could not fathom.

This was 1966. He was speaking at Portland State College, in a fieldhouse that, according to the report, was jammed with two thousand students, hundreds more spilling over. Robert Kennedy was on his way to the White House. What he said anywhere, about anything, people listened closely to. The item went:

> The Viet Cong, the New York senator said, "have committed acts of brutal terrorism." But, he said, "they are part of South Vietnam and cannot be eliminated or excluded from its political life."

Now, I'll be discussing the seeming inability of reporters accurately to quote, or represent, any speaker; but taking this statement on its face, it was, I sensed, wholly perverse.

On the jet, it worried me. Any reader under forty may have difficulty comprehending all that Bobby Kennedy meant to The Kids. (Anyone who has been deprived of personal acquaintance with the Kennedys cannot fully comprehend the charm and magnetism of the clan.) The ground Robert Kennedy walked was not worshiped, I guess, but his least remark was as Scripture to a generation that felt so bitterly betrayed by history, so destitute of ideals, and that hungered so desperately for a hero. Sure as shooting, I would have his statement flung at me by the college audience that night, or the next.

I had stupidly left the newspaper at the breakfast table, but at the first stop, I bought others, locating the story. During the long wait for the next flight, I worried it in my mind over and over. What was wrong with it!?

My capacity for obtuseness is never exhausted. Not until that evening, at supper, while reading something else, did the simple logical sin, and Kennedy's philosophical confusion, flash into my mind.

There was, first, the ethical sloppiness of the proposition. They have committed brutal terrorism *but* they cannot be excluded from South Vietnam's political life. Quite the contrary is indicated by the premise: *therefore* they should never be included in South Vietnam's political life. In the first part of Senator Kennedy's statement there was an incontestable point of fact—the brutality of the Viet Cong— with deep moral implications. The second half might be a correct, pragmatical measure: that is, it might be so politically that it was unavoidable to include the Viet Cong in any settlement of the war (in fact, the Viet Cong vanished as a political entity the moment South Vietnam was conquered); but at least as reported, Kennedy joined two wholly different propositions by a conjunction, which was a syntactical lapse as well as a logical error suggesting (to me) basic philosophical problems. A conjunction is supposed to join only propositions of qualitative parity. Yet Robert Kennedy followed a statement of fact containing moral implications with a statement of purely pragmatic content.

Had he said—or had he been reported as saying—"The Viet Cong have committed acts of brutal terrorism, *despite which* they are part of South Vietnam and cannot be eliminated or excluded from its political life, this would have been a very different thing. Kennedy would then have been in the position of, in the first place, acknowledging the moral implications of admitting into political life a terrorist organization, and, in the second place, telling his public that from a practical point of view there was no help for it: which is the position, I concluded, that he intended to plead—political expediency in the Viet Cong's case overriding what was morally repugnant.

It is not merely fastidious to insist on correct syntax and syllogistic purity. These matters are not picayune. A person's style betrays his manner of thinking—and this man was running for the presidency of the United States. Basic confusion between the moral and the practical worlds transpired in his style, expediency in this sorry case taking precedence. And as in all cases where expediency does take precedence, the ravages wreaked in the moral realm reflect in the material realm. Because if one followed Mr. Kennedy's logic as reported, what he was doing was urging a *philosophy* of expedience on his audience of two thousand and more students. That's a poor vantage from which to begin assessing public or private policy. One may be obliged, as a practical matter, to fall back on the expedient course of action; one should never like it, nor propose expediency as virtuous. One should to the contrary publicly detest it, though swallowing one's sentiments *force majeure*. Robert Kennedy might as well have said to the students, "Since Murder Incorporated, morally repugnant, has proved ineradicable despite our best efforts, then we ought to come to terms with reality and invite a Mafia representative into the cabinet of the President of the United States."

Please note: this is different from saying, "Since we have proved incapable of eradicating Murder Incorporated, the astute course of action is to seek to take the profit out of their operations, by, for example, in a very carefully circumscribed way, legalizing the sale of hard drugs."

Telltale Signs of Bad Argument: A Litany of Formal Logical Sins

Listen. Listen to the internal rhythms and to external conjugations. Be alert for the speaker whose tone of voice becomes shrill, or whiny, whose forehead suddenly glistens, whose lips twitch in an anxious smile when making a statement or asking the audience to agree with his thesis, or who in other ways, by wandering eye or facial tic, betrays *or* the nervous habits that he must correct if he is to gain the trust of the audience, *or* the dubiousness of what he is trying to put across.

Aristotle is ever the master, but to sharpen your analytical faculties, get yourself a trot on the principles of formal logic. At the Buckley School we distribute a list of books that we recommend in the eternal chore of invigilating one's logic and the logic of others, which can be found in Appendix 1. Professor Max Black's 1946 *Critical Thinking,* published by Prentice-Hall, is comprehensive, if one can find it, and Professor Soper's *Basic Public Speaking* has a useful chapter on syllogisms and logical fallacies. My favorite is *How to Win an Argument,* by Michael A. Gilbert, because it's fun! Learn what an "undistributed middle" is, and don't confuse it for the weight you

meant to take off last winter by jogging, but didn't; become aware
that if you don't watch your undistributed middles you will end up
with such preposterous propositions as that because all men are mortal, and because all women are mortal, ergo some women are men.
That is only so in exceptional cases. Learn what it is to *beg a question,*
which hasn't a thing to do with politeness, but can with deviousness
("The filthy rotten capitalist system should be discarded because it
has long outlived its historical time," for example); what *heuristic,*
eristic, and *paraliptic* argumentation is all about (see Appendixes I
and II), and why you had better not; what dangers *denying the*
antecedent can get you into, and that it has nothing to do with your
father and mother, though it does tell you that if you are a Chinaman,
you are human, it does not follow that if you are human, you are
necessarily a Chinaman, and though it may be true that if you are a
jogger, you are nevertheless a rational being, it is not necessarily
exclusively inevitable that if you are a rational being you must cheerfully suffer corns, blisters, bone spurs, sprung tendons, sprained ankles, shinsplints, and the company of other fitness freaks; that the
fallacy of *ignoratio elenchi* does not signify running afoul of the law
for pleading ignorance of a lynching, wicked as that would be, but
that you have fouled up your presentation by coming to a conclusion
other than the one you set out to prove; how utterly primitive it is
to employ *post hoc, ergo propter hoc* reasoning, otherwise known as
the *fallacy of the false cause,* namely, of arguing from mere tempo-
ral sequence to cause and effect relationship—you know, if a black
cat crosses your path one day and the next you fall into a well, it was
the cat what dug it for you. That sort of thing. Setting your course
by this pernicious fallacy can have you asserting that because the
train did not leave on time, trains do not leave on time, which may
be true in fact, but you got there by invalid logic and so you should
take no comfort in your good fortune.

As in love, it is admittedly difficult to test for syllogistic soundness
in an extended argument. Whole chapters may separate premise
from premise, and chapters more pile up before the illicit or fallacious conclusion is drawn. It's like a heavy meal. One has to push back
from the table, so to speak—ruminate on the fare, burp discreetly,
savoring perhaps less the bouquet of what it truly is the author hopes
one will swallow (this metaphor is getting rapidly out of hand)—and
wonder whether it digests into as savoury a thesis as the diversions
and embellishments contrive to make one fancy. It is almost as dif-

ficult to spot and identify the logical sins in a rapid verbal exchange—when one is in a board room, or in conference with one's peers and superiors. Even folk whose brains mesh with machine tool precision rarely give vent to their thoughts with the same tidiness. We tend to elide critical connective tissue; we jump to intuitively arrived at conclusions (they may be correct), or skip about, arguing sometimes from what is called the *principle of similar cases* (if what's sauce for a gander isn't—*mon foie!*—also sauce for the goose, the burden of proof is on the naysayer), but other times from *imperfect analogy,* extrapolating in ways that in the moment of their utterance seem plausible though they do not scan. In conversation, *circular reasoning*—begging the question—seems to come naturally: " 'R'-rated movies are dreadful because of the violence and carnality they exploit." Right. Which is why they are rated "R." In heated debate, just about everyone falls into the *fallacy of common practice* ("All the kids in my class are shaving their heads like Iroquois braves and dyeing their scalplocks purple, so why shouldn't I!"), *argumentum ad hominem* (aspersions of an invidious character, for example, "You jerk, just because your old lady sucks gin through a straw at breakfast doesn't mean we gotta ban beer at the church picnic!"—which, come to think of it, actually protests *ad hominem* argument), and even *argumentum ad baculum,* which is resorting to brass knuckles, such as, "Smith, your opinions are greatly appreciated, let me assure you. Now, you damn well do it my way, or you're fired!" The questions to keep ever alive in one's mind are: does the analogy fit; does the example follow from the premise, and does it truly develop from it; and is the indicated consequence truly inevitable?

Formal Syllogistic Analysis

It's interesting (how different men can be!) that President Jimmy Carter was to err in an opposed direction from Robert Kennedy, his moralism overwhelming the political realities of an imperfect world, to wit his alienation of many important longtime allies, such as Brazil, because he could not restrain himself from scolding them for their suppression of political dissent. Reducing this to a syllogistic schema, his argument ran thisaway:

> First premise: Democracy is the only decent government.
> Second premise: The U.S. should not associate with indecent governments.

Third premise: Freedom of expression is vital to democratic government, without which it cannot be said to be democratic.
Therefore: Any government under which political dissent is suppressed is unfit for the U.S. to associate with.

The rule governing the validity of arguments is this: An argument
may be fallacious in three ways: (1) in its material content, through
a misstatement of the facts, (2) in its wording, through an incorrect
use of terms, or (3) in its structure, that is, form, through the use of
improper processes of inference.

Applying these criteria to Jimmy Carter's reasoning, the first
premise is false in its material content, because there are many forms
of good government, one being monarchical, for example, always
given that the king is a good man. (Plato sniffed a long nose at
republics, saying of them that they are the worst of good forms of
government, and only the best of worst forms of government.) The
second premise is also guilty of false material content, in that we deal,
though we may not like it, with indecent governments all the time,
as in fact President Carter prominently did in his overtures to the
Soviet Union. The third premise falls into the same error, in that in
no government, not even our own, is freedom of expression absolute.
Mr. Carter was attaching an extreme construction to this right, promoting a rigid standard that did not allow for local traditions and
concrete local situations (the *fallacy of accident,* see below), such as
terrorist activities in a country or acts of insurrection. The premises
are all three so shaky and disputable, not to mention wrong, that any
inferences drawn from them are at best arbitrary.

The careful listener must keep cocked ears for the two kinds of
fallacies. These are "verbal" and "formal." A typical formal fallacy
is that of the *illicit premise,* where the terminology is not consistent, the major and minor terms not being distributed in the premise. A common example is: Some tax auditors are not friendly. In
this premise, apart from its being guilty of a crashing understatement, reference is to all things friendly but not to all tax auditors,
which makes an uneven foundation from which to infer any conclusion. In verbal fallacies, definitions are muddied and switched, as
for example:

That dog-bit man is mad.
Mad people belong in institutions.
Dog-bit men should be impounded.

Now this might follow if by "mad" one had established that the dog-bit man was crazy, not just merely angry, but it would hardly be persuasive unless one had in addition established that the guilty dog was rabid.

My friend and colleague Richard Quinn, an author, editor, and publicist, deals on a quotidian basis with so many aspiring pols, incumbent pols, and desperate suspiring pols that he has become hyperallergic to formal logical fallacies. As other folk break out in hives, he breaks out in undistributed premises, occluded antecedents, and obnubilated inductions, not to mention broken promises. His syllogistic reduction of President Carter's position is different from mine, and doubtless better:

> First premise: The U.S. believes that free expression and self-determination are basic goals of our foreign policy.
>
> Second premise: Any country that suppresses free expression and self-determination violates a basic principle of American foreign policy.
>
> Third premise: Free expression and self-determination are axiomatic only in a democratic form of government.
>
> Therefore: Nondemocratic governments (i.e., those governments that suppress free expression and self-determination) are evil and unfit to be associated with by the U.S. government.

The problems with this logic, he points out, are multiple. Among the material fallacies:

> *Secundum Quid* (the *Fallacy of Accident*), which consists in applying a general rule to a particular case while ignoring the circumstances (or accidents) that make the rule inapplicable. (This is when a general proposition is used without paying attention to the qualifications that govern it and may invalidate its application to the matter at hand.)
>
> *Ad Populum*, which consists in an appeal to vulgar attitudes rather than logical reasons.

A glaring formal fallacy is that of the illicit premise, mentioned above in connection with tax auditors and things friendly, which violates the rule of equable distribution. Concepts like "evil" and "unfit," which are judgments distributed in the conclusion, are undistributed in the premises. Expressed in terms closer to the processes of Mr. Carter's logic, we have this: Democratic governments encourage free expression and self-determination. The government of Brazil is not a democratic government. Therefore, the government of Brazil is evil and unfit.

The destruction of the Reagan presidency, by contrast, has followed on an ill-advised attempt to split the difference between Robert Kennedy's amoral pragmatism and a righteousness (speaking of Reagan) regarding terrorists every bit as strict as Jimmy Carter's in his obsession with the democratic purity of our allies—that is, though the entire government of Iran under the Ayatollah Khomeini is a terrorist organization, given the geostrategic realities the U.S. must seek somehow to enter into dialogue with what may be a moderate element there.

This was a hoop no creditable foreign policy could be made to jump through. White House confusion and ineptness aside, the opening to Iran managed with a kind of perverse brilliance at one and the same time to offend the deep resentment of the American people against that rabid country and make incomprehensible hash of Administration policy regarding terrorists, while achieving no practical advantages whatever. This is in the way of not having one's cake and getting acid indigestion just the same, permitting one to wonder whether Tip O'Neill in his most lubricious reveries ever could have devised anything so dumb for the Reagan Administration to flounder into.

Richard Quinn adds that Reagan's ill-starred policies "have been based on two syllogisms the conclusions of which conflict without any apparent conflict among the premises." Thus, Syllogism No. I:

> First premise: Iran is a government known to train terrorists and to promote international terrorism.
> Second premise: Terrorists kill and take hostages in order to make demands and to enhance their cause.
> Third premise: The act of dealing or negotiating with terrorists shows them that their bloody tactics are effective, and this encourages more terrorism.
> Therefore: To discourage future terrorism, one must never deal or negotiate with terrorists or terrorist governments like Iran.

Syllogism No. II:

> First premise: Khomeini is a very old and sick man.
>
> Second premise: Intelligence reports indicate that there are people in the Khomeini government less radical than he who may be willing to free American hostages in exchange for an arms deal with Iran.
>
> Third premise: Supporting these more moderate elements may destabilize Khomeini's regime or at least give us allies in the power structure that will emerge after Khomeini's death, thus enhancing our ability to persuade Iran to get out of the terrorism business.
>
> Fourth Premise: When Americans are held hostage anywhere in the world it is the President's duty to do everything reasonable to free them.
>
> Therefore: To discourage future terrorism, and to gain freedom for American hostages in Iran, the U.S. should negotiate an arms deal with certain factions in the Iranian government.

Comments Quinn:

> Now, obviously Syllogism No. I collides with Syllogism No. II. Yet it does so without any apparent conflicts among the premises of No. I and No. II. The premises are all consistent with a sincere desire to resist international terrorism—a point that President Reagan in vain has endeavored to make allies and his fellow citizens comprehend.
>
> The trouble is that both syllogisms are fallacious, in that No. I applies a general rule to a particular case, ignoring special conditions (*secundum quid*), while No. II runs afoul of *the logic of knowing* (that is to say, a claim to knowledge must be withdrawn if the premise is based on tacit knowledge or belief rather than actual, overt knowledge). All of which is to say that our President gambled and lost.

And how.

President Reagan tempted the Fates with a schizophrenic policy, one moralistic, the other pragmatic. But to have hoped to get away with it, he had been advised to prepare the ground by drawing necessary distinctions, as in the preceding chapter. He should have noted in a public address devoted exclusively to the subject that (1) all acts of terrorism are savage and brutal and beyond the bounds of civilized tolerance, (2) terrorism as a policy is cruel and uncivilized, (3) distinctions have to be made among (a) terrorist governments, such as those of Libya, Syria, and Iran, (b) terrorist quasi-governmental organizations, such as the PLO, and maybe the IRA of Northern Ireland, and (c) terrorist individuals or semi-anarchical terrorist groups, such as the Islamic Jihad (allied with the Lebanese Shi'ite Hizballah), or the Party of God (which is said to be controlled by Iran), the German Baader-Meinhof, the Basque ETA, not to mention our very own Black Panthers. Reaffirming in this same speech that he has nothing but contempt for terrorism as a policy, whether carried on by rabid individuals or rabid governments, (4) one may be obliged despite one's desires to deal with the mad dog government, or even the quasi-governmental mad dog terrorist organization, though one would hope never in such way as to appease their demands or appear to countenance their actions, whereas (5) it is folly under any circumstances to attempt to deal with the other species of terrorist, which rise to the surface, do their bloody deeds, and then sink back down in the bog like vile bubbles of methane gas. This may not be the stance one would personally choose—he might have reiterated—but as the chief executive of our government it is the unsatisfactory general policy forced upon one.

The wonders of hindsight! Such a statement would not have made all the attending sins of the Iran affair right, but the American public and American allies would have been spared the shock and bitter disappointment.

The Sophistical Refutations

The reader who wishes to pursue formal logical analysis further can go to the horse's mouth, namely Aristotle. One should begin with his reflections on prior and posterior analytics, proceeding to his treatise *On Sophistical Refutations.* The Philosopher, as Thomas Aquinas always referred to Aristotle, bestowing on him this supreme title uniquely, ticks off a lot of folk we know well, maybe even as well as ourselves, when he notes: "Now for some people it is better worthwhile to seem to be wise, than to be wise without seeming to be (for the art of the sophist is the semblance of wisdom without the reality, and the sophist is one who makes money from apparent but unreal wisdom)." One learns from Aristotle that there are four classes of argument in dialogue: the didactic, the dialectical, what he calls "examination-arguments," and "contentious" arguments. The last are those that "reason or appear to reason to a conclusion from premises that appear to be generally accepted but are not so." These are the fallacious arguments that we most often encounter in our daily lives, in business, and on the stump.

Aristotle is a funny old bird. He tells us that among the first things one must do is to grasp the aims of those "who argue as competitors and rivals to the death." This may be one's professional or business rival, one's sibling, or one's spouse. The aims are five in number, he tells us: "refutation, fallacy, paradox, solecism, and fifthly to reduce the opponent . . . to babbling." Ah! How devoutly to be wished! The first aim is achieved by (for example) demonstrating that an opponent plain has his facts wrong, and that his entire case falls therewith, which is ever one's hope that one will be able to do; the second by demonstrating to the audience that the opponent is using fallacious arguments; the third by leading the unwary opponent into paradox (or, as we discussed briefly in the last chapter, and will be discussing more fully below, into dilemma, which can be real or false, and should be real if one is honest); the fourth by so disconcerting the opponent that, "in consequence of the argument," he is tripped into grammatical error (the perils of which will be discussed in the next chapter); and the fifth by going to bed with this book at night and rising with it in the morning.

Aristotle examines each of these polemical goals, commencing with refutation, which he reduces to two styles, the first depending on "the language used, the second independent of language." The first of these styles of refutation he then subdivides into six tactics (the reader will note how relentlessly this master of argument splits cognitive hairs), they being ambiguity, amphiboly (the distinction between *amphiboly* and *ambiguity* is now virtually lost), combination, division of words, accent, and form of expression. Taking ambiguity first, he gives examples: "Those learn who know: for it is those who know their letters who learn the letters dictated to them." This is nonsense, because "to learn" is ambiguous: it can mean both " 'to understand' by the use of knowledge, and also 'to acquire knowledge,' " such as T. S. Eliot's famed lament,

> Where is the wisdom we have lost in knowledge?
> Where is the knowledge we have lost in information?

Another (dilly of an) example of linguistic ambiguity is: " 'Evils are good, for what needs to be is good, and evils must needs be.' " This consummate piece of sophistry is more common than at first one might believe; but the reader will note how closely it treads on the faulted reasoning of Robert Kennedy regarding the Viet Cong. The linguistic fallacy here lies in "what needs to be," because the meaning contained in this phrase is double: "what is inevitable, as often is the case with evils, too (for evil of some kind is inevitable), while on the other hand we say of good things as well that they 'need to be.'" I can't resist one more: "What you profess to-be, that you profess-to-be: you profess a stone to-be: *ergo* you profess-to-be a stone." Substitute for *stone* Montaigne's blockhead, and one converts an amphibolic sophistry into the oh-so-true of the oh-so-many.

Skipping to fallacies that are independent of language, Aristotle finds seven, of which a ubiquitous fault is the fourth—"that which depends upon the consequent." People lapse into this when, supposing A is, B necessarily is, "they then suppose also that if B is, A necessarily is." They are given to such as: since we must suppose that it is useless to cry over spilt milk, when we see that milk has been spilt, we may suppose that no rational creature has spilled tears. These same folk are guilty of putting carts before horses, which is most awfully strenuous on the horse, and for that matter of locking barn doors after horse and cart are gone, because they assume that if one supposes shut barn doors necessarily imply that horse and buggy are safely inside, shutting barn doors will put both back.

Aristotle would despair of the writer of this book, so we will not linger with him (Ari) much longer; except to make note for the reader that he is there, and that perusing him is profitable; and except to cull some fallacies that apply to the confusions we have been studying. The study of formal logic is of inestimable value, and the ability to reduce an argument to syllogistic form is a tremendous advantage when one is called upon right then and there to rebut somebody's verbose sophistical nonsense; but inferences and conclusions—depending on how attentively one has schooled oneself to listen—can sound fishy, alerting us to logical fault, whether we are able to keep pace with Aristotle or not, and whether or not we retain in our memories the label for the exact logical gaffe being committed.

Dumb Logic Can Sound Dumb: Reading Aloud to Oneself

Is it necessary to repeat: one should be at least as severe with one's own constructions as we have been here with Kennedy, Carter, and Reagan? Take to heart the preceding chapter. Madam, think your thoughts through. Sir, read what you write a second, a third, a fourth, a fifth time, not for the pleasure of authorship, but with the purpose of making mincemeat of your own arguments. As you read, mouth the words. (When I am composing, I grunt and groan so much that often I have a sore throat at the end of the day, and once a landlady in Rome rapped peremptorily on my door because she suspected that Something Not Permitted in Her Decent Establishment was going on.) (I was writing a love scene.) Sometimes when one utters the words, weaknesses in one's argument that the eye skipped over spring to notice, because not infrequently—the relationship between thinking, composing on paper, and speaking is so intimate—what is illogical, or unconvincing, or incoherent, or inherently incorrect *sounds* wrong; sounds, when it is spoken, dubious, contrived, or untenable. The reader will be doing himself a favor, because this habit of rigorous self-criticism in turn instills the habit of speaking cautiously, of modifying, or suitably qualifying, one's statements. Remember, simple use of a conjunction does not necessarily establish an organic connection between thoughts, nor does use of a conjunction guarantee that there is a valid progression from premise to conclusion. "The kitchen door was wide open, and the cat drank the cream." "The hair dryer shorted out, so Ellen had tea with her classmates." Maybe the most infuriating example from popular culture of this fallacy is the ad featuring a bland young man who says, "I am not a doctor, but I play one on TV," whereupon proceeding to give the audience—us—medical advice! Nor does the use of "therefore," or "thus we see," or "consequently" work alchemy on conclusions that in fact, upon analysis, do not follow. "Sales are dropping rapidly, therefore we must cut production costs." "Our snake oil is 10 percent richer in calcium than the leading snake oil, consequently women with osteoporosis are bound to prefer it." Of which one can say, "It ain't necessarily so."

Sneaky Statistics

Watch especially for misleading statistics, such as that automotive production last year went up 100 percent in Sri Lanka, which may indicate no more than that two buggies were built instead of one. And do not swallow uncritically congenial or convenient statistics originating in a source that you have reason to suspect is biased toward the opinion you prefer. If Heaven has so withheld its grace from you that you are a Democrat, for example, check with *U. S. News and World Report,* or the *National Review,* or the *Wall Street Journal* to make doubly sure that Senator Teddy Kennedy's latest fulmination against the ills and perils of our existential condition mobilizes the empirical evidence accurately and draws valid conclusions from same. Have you, on the other hand, been numbered among the saints, do the opposite: test Ronald Reagan's latest exercise in angelic reasoning against those defamations that are sure to appear in *Newsweek,* or the *Washington Post,* or the *New Republic,* and so what if he couldn't remember? If anyone spiels statistics without stating their source, challenge him. And beware of ambiguous terms.

Question the deceitful averaging of statistics purporting to show an equality of condition that does not in truth exist. For example, "It's poppycock to suggest that executive remuneration at Chrysler Corporation is extravagant, when last year it averaged $29,000!" This statement may conceal that the salaries of low-paid stenographers were lumped into "executive" rank with Lee Iacocca's $8 million bonus. *Statistical averages must derive from equally weighted raw material to mean anything.* If too broadly based, they may distort reality. If not broadly enough based, they can be wildly misleading— as in batting averages the first week of baseball season. Also: be aware of the difference between an *average* and a *median.* An average is an arithmetical mean; a median is merely a point in any series at which half the numbers are on one side, half on the other. If five five-pound sacks of Idaho potatoes contain, respectively, five, six, eight, eleven, and fifteen spuds, the median is eight, the average nine. The ones to the right of the median are probably a disgrace to the state of Idaho.

Stuffed Shirts, Blowhards, Prevaricators, and Other Scurvy Characters

Accomplished liars, pompous folk who are not used to having their pronouncements challenged, and politicians make the most outrageous statements and claims with the greatest aplomb. When you hear these glabrous, unctuous, oily-toned speakers tell you the way it is, let your system fly red flags of warning. Pay closest attention. Doubt and scrutinize everything. And for pity's sake do not thee become like that. Challenge your most cherished convictions almost every day; when you speak or write something that you have long assumed is self-evident, or fact, that's just the time to go back to the books and verify it—or to think it out yet once again, because time has a habit of subtly transforming into dogma what one began by proposing only as a hypothesis. A gentleman in my small city of Camden who is greatly impressed with his acumen and importance enjoyed holding forth on the inevitable appreciation of real estate. "Yes, sir," he liked to say, digging a thumb into the proximate armpit, "a person can't go wrong investing in land in this county. No way won't the value go up." I held my tongue: but I was sorely tempted to remind him that in the spring of 1860 agricultural land these parts was worth one hundred gold dollars an acre, and that following Fort Sumter it wasn't again worth a nominal paper dollar the acre until the 1940s. The 1985–86 crash in the value of farmland, along with the glut in office space, have since muted this self-important individual on the subject of real estate, but he will likely find some other pony to pontificate on with the same air of absolute certitude.

The Dialectical Vice of Self-Satisfaction

Watch for the bland, smooth assurance in speakers who exude self-satisfaction. They beg for the ice pick that will punch holes in the full sail of their vanity. Any member of the Establishment, whatever it is, adopts this tone with the object of derogating criticism as nit-picking of a low order, beneath dignity. Watch for that fellow! He is trying to get away with murder; he is covering up; he will not address criticisms, rather will he seek to roll over them under a weight of unsupported assertions. Do not let him get away with it! And keep an eye out for those vices in yourself.

A public speaker should avoid endeavoring to impress the audience with the high esteem he may have of himself. His rhetoric will become flabby, his constructions loose, his assertions broad and hollow. Be truly humble. Treat every audience as though it were your first, and every man and woman in that audience as the jury over your conscience, for whose approbation you will expend your last energies demonstrating the validity and justice of your case. This will chastise excesses in your thought and help keep order in your logic.

Believe Nothing, Be Surprised at Nothing, Test Everything

Cultivating a skeptical attitude of mind does help one spot logical blunders, or sneaky illicit propositions, because one takes
nothing for granted. "What's white on the outside, green on the
inside, and hops?" The answer is a frog sandwich, of course. Children's riddles are good practice. A fellow walks into a bar and asks
for a glass of water. The bartender grabs a loaded revolver and
points it at the man, who thereupon says "Thank you," walking out.
(He had hiccups.) Another fellow with an apartment on the seventh
floor of a building always rides the perfectly functioning elevator
down to street level when he goes to work in the morning, but
always, upon returning from work in the evening, gets out of the
elevator on the third floor, trudging up the rest of the four stories
to his apartment. He doesn't need the exercise, so why this routine?
(He is a midget.)

Such pastimes help. Cultivate the habit of stepping back and
looking at matters from a different angle, especially one not suggested by one's adversary, or one that one's adversary claims is illicit or impossible. The happy reader of this book, having been
filled with propaedeutic wisdom, is primed for identifying logical
inconsistencies in himself and others because he has so scrupulously
studied the pros and cons of his position, as well as the faults and
merits of his opponent's position, that he is prepared for (a) the
logical pitfalls into which he is likely to tumble, (b) the fallacious
traps his opponent may be setting for him, (c) the meretricious reasoning that his opponent may likely employ. When one has famil-
iarized oneself with a topic, one is prepared to scent out at once
incorrect syllogistic gambits. If one happens to be on a school
board, for example, almost inevitably will the question come up
whether to expand facilities, and when to do so. Someone is bound
to argue, "At current rates of annual enrollment, we are going to
run out of classroom space by 1992." Cast a catawampus eye on
dramatic assertions of this sort. They are engendered by extrapolations from past performance, of which it can be said that the record
of the past is the God's truth only of the past, and is no more than
suggestively applicable to the future. From statistical trends it is
hopeless and even hubristic to predict human behavior, which is
why economists can almost never prophesy the course of the econ-

omy over the next twelve months, in that what obtained yesterday will not obtain tomorrow in exactly the same way, or to the same degree, and may even be reversed. That false fell sense of inevitability about demographic explosions has brought more than one school board to grief and more than one school system to bankruptcy. Whenever the inevitability of something is expressed, as in an ever-rising statistical curve, cry halt. The West is filled with ghost towns whose glorious future was certain.

Arguing tendentiously from trends is a close cousin of the fallacy of the false cause, to which people of the same temperament as that pompous character in Camden are prone. One hears it all the time in advertisements. Gilbert uses the example of an illicit correlation between the consumption of vegetable fat and the incidence of heart disease. At the same time that the latter went up, our use of animal fat dropped by 11 percent while consumption of vegetable fat climbed 74 percent. Ah-hah! went a lobbyist for the beef industry: this all goes to show that the increase in heart disease was brought about by an increase in the use of vegetable fats. Which, as Professor Gilbert says, is "a classic example of false cause: the simple correlation of two statistics . . . is far from sufficing as evidence for one's causing the other."

The increasing use of brittle plastics in automobiles is sold to the public in this deceiving manner. They are billed as lighter, and therefore as "fuel efficient," which the public has been conditioned to think of as good. The true reason is that they are cheaper. The buyer is being sold a bill of goods occulting bloated wages at the blue collar level and excessive bonuses in the executive suite.

A last classic example of the false cause fallacy is the assertion heard and read everywhere that, for example, smoking pot leads in a slippery slope sort of way to heroin. The argument goes typically like this: a recent study of heroin addicts finds that 85 percent professed to have started with marijuana. Therefore it is established what every parent has long feared and suspected: that pot precedes, and will ineluctably lead to, hard drugs. The argument doesn't hold water, however. All the study tells us is about the habits of users of heroin. No information is given about potheads who did not go on to heroin. In fact, it has since been determined that the vast majority of pot smokers never do get hooked on the hard stuff. All that study demonstrated is that if one happens to be hung out on heroin one likely began with marijuana.

A speaker must never permit himself to be trapped by the fallacy of the false dilemma, which we have mentioned in connection with putting together a strong case. There is something tremendously alluring about reducing matters to such pithy alternatives. Love it or leave it; fish or cut bait; put up or shut up; the language is so wonderfully pungent, and so American in its earthiness, in its toughness and crudity. Perdicaris alive or Raisuli dead: this is hero talk. Unless the alternatives are truly as implacably indisputable as Teddy Roosevelt (whose feelings on the matter were translated in John Hay's famous ultimatum) convinced that petty Berber pirate they were, don't pull this fast one in argument, it's bad manners, and don't let that sucker pull it on you. If some fanatic thrusts a petition in your face calling for the impeachment of the House and Senate Democratic leadership on the grounds that their agenda regarding key issues of foreign policy, defense, and arms control is indistinguishable from that of the Soviet Politburo, shouting, when you refuse to put your name to it, "What are you—a stinking Commie?" don't let yourself be bullied. You may cede the coincidence without imputing disloyalty to the Democratic leadership; your refusal to brand them as traitors does not diminish your opposition to their policies, nor signify that you have sold yourself to the Devil. Don't be intimidated by an either/ or.

When the dilemma is valid, however, reducing arguments in this way can be a crushing stratagem. One cannot both be and not be at the same time. One cannot deplore the quality of public education in America and at the same time declare against subjecting teachers to some kind of objective evaluation of competency. One cannot bewail the low ethical and moral tenor of our society, yet ignore that inculcation in values has been excluded from the curriculum of our schools. In the first instance it need not follow that one must agree to a written test for teachers (there are other means of evaluation), nor in the second instance that one must necessarily agitate for beginning the school day with a prayer (there are alternate means of teaching children right behavior). Nevertheless, he who says A, must say B; the speaker may not lightly subscribe to A without giving careful consideration to A's logical consequences, in the event that B is repugnant to him. It is fair to pin a speaker to this wall.

Arguments That Reduce to Opinion

Never, however, when it is you who are impaled on the stake of
your logic, admit defeat unless you are absolutely convinced of the
greater cogency of the other side. *In the vast majority of cases what
is being disputed is a matter of opinion, not fact.*

If your facts are controverted, by all means throw in the towel,
acknowledge your mistake. The conclusions you have drawn from
erroneous evidence can be fatally compromised. The conclusions we
draw from irrefutable fact are another matter. There can be as many
judgments from the same evidence as there are people. Everything
depends on the powers of penetration of one's ratiocinative faculties,
or on their cunning. It depends on one's skill at inductive logic (check
your aptitudes in Myers-Briggs), or on slant, or perspective, or bad
or good experience. We are all afflicted with tunnel vision in some
respects. If the sky is half filled with clouds, it's a matter of opinion,
or temperament, whether it's a sunny or cloudy day. When I was
nineteen I managed the well-nigh incredible feat of reading Gogol's
Dead Souls right through without cracking a smile. I read it again
when I was thirty-two and cracked my ribs. We must keep in mind
that in controversies arising from the interpretation of evidence, two
opposing opinions can be right, unlike the philosophical proposition
that something cannot both be and not be, or the physical principle
that no two objects can occupy the same space at the same time. If
one is momentarily baffled by an argument drawn from evidence,
the reason is either that one's opponent is a sharp fellow indeed, or
that—I'd bet on this, the old sin—one hasn't studied up enough. But
don't in either case give up. Try to turn the course of the debate or
discussion to other matters—while you cudgel your brains furiously
and hard. It is a rare occasion when some fresh angle does not reveal
itself, casting an entirely new light on the matter in dispute, and
sometimes happily inverting the logic to your favor, and even the
evidence, that was trotted out against you. One drear afternoon
during the first week of January my banker in Hartford telephoned
me (I was still living in Madrid) to say, "Reid, do you realize that for
thirteen out of the past thirty-one days your checking account has
been overdrawn?" I was appalled, until inspiration came to my suc-
cor. "By the same token, Ted," I replied, "do you realize that for
eighteen out of the past thirty-one days I had more money in that
account than I needed?"

Finally . . .

LISTEN. The bore never listens. To be a bore is first among mortal sins after the absence of charity. Dante missed it, but in the coldest core of Hell there is a ring reserved for those otherwise virtuous folk who have bored their Creator, or who, because the Creator somehow loves us all and wants us to love one another as He loves us, have offended Him by having bored other people during their term on earth. Not listening will get a body into a heap of trouble in the board room, or debating: one doesn't know what the other fellow has just said, and one is at a loss to answer him. But the worst punishment is nicely put by Mr. Gilbert. "The true non-listener suffers a lonely fate: no-one wants to talk to him."

When one is truly listening, he will be sensitive to revealing slips, or to the choice of language that discloses something about one's opponent or something about his argument.

The debate regarding abortion, for example, boils down to whether a fetus is a human being, and not just a physiological appendage of the mother, and therefore an act of murder to destroy. The discomfort that some "pro-choice" advocates may be feeling is betrayed by their awkward circumlocutions of the word "kill." They speak of "interrupting" the pregnancy, of "not letting it come to full term." They do not like to use *kill*. One does not kill an appendix, or a spleen, or a kidney. One does not kill the arm or leg one amputates. The fetus, on the other hand, is definitely *killed*, implicit in the meaning of which word is the termination of life, in turn implicit in which is the proposition of an independent existence, else the mother would die too. If one is debating this issue, it is proper to ask one's opponent, "Miss Steinem, why don't you just say 'kill' the fetus? Why do you avoid that word? What fears has it for you, or are you hiding from yourself sensations of guilt?" Getting personal, imputing motive to the opponent, are technical faults; nevertheless be alert for those opportunities. A slip of the tongue can signal tectonic plates deep inside a person grinding uneasily against a fault in their thinking.

Beware also, however, those rhetorical fallacies by sole virtue of which (if the word can be used in this connection) the noose can be slipped around one's neck. The tip-off is often that the person assumes a high tone by definition for which he does not deign to provide any substantiation in logic or evidence. It happens all the time, and it is a pet peeve, which suffers irritation almost daily when I read the newspapers—most often in the context of passionate public controversies, such as, once again, abortion.

Which may turn out to be the great polemical confrontation of totally opposed and mutually exclusive world views. Like slavery, abortion is a moral issue, and like all moral issues, it fires the passions. The label that people who favor allowing abortion at the impregnated woman's will adopt for themselves, "pro-choice," is a piece of rhetorical usurpation of the high moral ground, because their opponents must naturally be "anti-choice," and that invites images of zealots who would trample under the Bill of Rights. The dialectical terms are fuzzed up, besides. Is "choice" the issue? (The fetus, for one, never gets asked.) The question surely rests in whether abortion constitutes homicide—whether the fetus is a tiny human being (just as Roo in the marsupial pouch is a tiny Kanga, never mind that he is blind and naked), in which case "choice" is as irrelevant as it is in the cases of suicide and murder.

Equally guilty of insouciance, however, is the anti-abortion movement in adopting the "Right-to-Life" label. Are those who may tolerate abortion in cases of rape or incest, or when the mother's life is in jeopardy, *against* life? Are libertarians who uphold a person's option to choose abortion inimical to the sanctity of life? They may unintentionally undermine that sanctity, but it goes beyond the bounds of rhetorical propriety to imply in them a Hitlerian contempt for personhood. It is as spurious to aver that holocausts follow from catheters as that alcoholism follows from a Millertime or two.

Don't permit yourself to be sandbagged by a planted inference from an opponent's righteous self-definition. Challenge it at once. Let "Right-to-Lifers" call themselves, simply, anti-abortionists; and let those "pro-choicers" call themselves anti the antis. Which may be inelegant, but who said dialectical precision is always pretty?

Listen. Listen carefully, with full critical attention. Be tough on your rivals or opponents; be tougher on yourself.

8

How to Stop Slaughtering the English Language

Almost nothing discredits a speaker so totally as abuse of basic grammar.

To fastidious ears, a glaring grammatical lapse is no less offensive than an obscenity. Sure, Will Rogers told his jokes and spun his yarns in the southwestern knuckle-cracking idiom that was perfectly suited to the material, and if one is blessed with his talent, one needs no instruction from anyone. All a body's circumstances not being equal to Will Rogers, however, the public speaker addressing a sophisticated audience of his peers is expected to exhibit a certain formal elegance in syntax and construction. He isn't playing the role of some half-educated coach on one of those awful pre-game shows, where the same stridulous clichés are grunted season in and season out in atrociously illiterate language that has become conventional. (I mean, just as Yasir Arafat, and now Don Johnson, shave with razor-blades that have all been clipped a quarter inch short, so coaches, sports announcers, and professional athletes consistently use *good* for *well* and *like* for *as,* which betrays this sort of thing as an affectation.)

Correct use of the English language at once distinguishes the speaker who is comfortable in classy company from one who is not. It's as plain as that. Language differentiates between the big time and the boondocks. Grammatical gaffes and stylistic infelicities can alienate the respect of an audience at the lowest educational rung. A person *is* often judged by the clothes he wears; the intellectual category of a speaker, as well as the validity of his case, are commonly—invalidly—judged by his style of address.

The accent in which one is raised, along with the peculiar rhythms and metaphors of one's regional idiom, assuming they are literate, one should by all means retain. Do not try to be a chameleon, ever. Do not try to deny or occult your antecedents. There can be no greater mistake. Is there an American intonation more euphonic than what philologists call upper Mississippi Valley? If you were born to it, thank your stars! Our country is blessed in the variety of its speech, which is so distinctive and filled with such character. Many years ago, when Tangiers was still a free port, I dropped in on a raffish bar where one might have expected to meet Claude Rains or Peter Lorre, but where there were mostly down-at-the-heel polyglots of no particular interest sipping their sad, wasted lives away. The owner— a tall, lean, deeply tanned man in his early forties—lounged beside the bar, talking to a customer. He wore sandals, tennis shorts, and a khaki shirt open down to the sternum, where gold and ivory ornaments dangled from a gold chain. I took him to be English, possibly French—until I heard in French the unmistakable charred oak tones of his voice. I called to him, "You're from Lexington, aren't you?" "No," he shot back, "Louisville."

Regional inflections impart great charm to anyone's speech. What would John Wayne have been without his not hardly's, or James Stewart without his adenoids? But this is not the same thing as being outright illiterate. Just as one should never try to affect some flavorless mid-Atlantic speech—the kind of English spoken by TV anchor folk—one shouldn't out of desire to ingratiate, make the mistake of affecting a down-homey style of language when giving a formal address. Save that for "Hee-Haw."

The ability to use language can make or break a person. This can be terribly unjust. I had a commanding general in the air force who was a first-rate professional. But he was incapable of articulating his thoughts in acceptable language, and he was aware of it. His poor English embarrassed him. It was a pitiful thing. He simply did not know how to express the exhaustive knowledge he had of his responsibilities, least of all to expound and defend the sound judgment that went into his decisions, in such fashion as not to sound like someone who never made it through the third grade.

The consequences were tragic for him. A posse of congressmen descended on our base one weekend. They were led by a very shallow staff that would never learn the half about running the Air Materiel Command that my CO had forgot; yet how pathetic it was to listen to his halting explications in language that had everyone wincing as he doubled up on his negatives and attached singular verbs to plural subjects.

He retired not long after in his permanent rank of brigadier general. He was maybe JCS potential, but he knew he would never rise higher, because sheer professional competence sometimes isn't enough.

Common Grammatical Errors

For the love of God and Prosody, and if you have love for yourself and your reputation when you mount the platform to deliver an address, do not commit the following egregious grammatical goofs.

Good vs. Well

Learn the difference between *good* and *well.* The first is an adjective, the second an adverb. A man who has been sick is now feeling well, not good. A man plays baseball well, not good. There seems to be an unholy passion for proletarianizing English, and it is the pits. It is not macho, nor showing the common touch, to murder the language, or to be inelegant in its use; it is to the contrary ignorant, or condescending, which is worse. Bad grammar, incorrect usage, muddies meaning. If a man is feeling good, he may be on his way to sanctification, a state of grace few of us, alas, can boast; if he is feeling well, on the other hand, you may be able to touch him for a loan. The technical term for this sort of thing is *amphilogism,* which means an ambiguity of speech, or an equivocation, brought on by grammatical fault. (Recall Aristotle's *amphiboly?* Curious, isn't it?) Now that you know the term, forget it. Never use it. I spoke of amphilogisms once, and at the end of the lecture I discovered that people thought I was talking about a strange new species of pond inhabitant, something between a salamander and a fish.

None of Them *Is*

Another of the more awful sins is to pluralize the singular or collective, like my poor general. *None of them are* is simply ignorant, despite *Time* magazine's acceptance of the barbarism. *Time* has lately been guilty of many sins against form and clarity.

While/Whereas

Don't you, however, mix up *while* with *though*, or *because*, or *whereas*. *While* implies that two or more things are going on, or being done, or felt, or perceived, or thought and spoken, at the same time. "I toasted the bread while she fried the eggs." "She filled the gas tank while I checked the oil." But never say, "While I thought she had a point, I did not agree with her conclusion." Say, "Whereas I thought she had a point," or "Though I thought she had a point," whether you are being sincere or not.

Which Witch Wrought That Havoc?

Time has also misplaced the difference in meaning between *that* and *which*. "The horse which kicked the boy is in the stable" tells you only where the horse is that kicked the boy, not *which* one. "The horse that is in the stable kicked the boy," on the other hand, tells you that one particular horse—the one in the stable, not the bay in the corral, nor the bobtailed mare over there tied to the hitching post—kicked the boy. And a good thing, too. "The lawn mower that is broken is in the garage" tells which one; "the lawn mower, which is broken, is in the garage" adds a fact about the only mower in question. Keep this in mind: *which*, unless it is preceded by a preposition, must *always* be preceded by a comma. If a comma doesn't make sense, use *that*. Read James Thurber on the "Whichmire."

The Human What?

Maybe the sin for which the current editors of *Time* will have to pay most in Purgatory is their illicit use of *human*, an adjective, for *human being*. This is to strip Man of his created dignity; it is ultimately to dehumanize us. One may well conjecture that the brutalities of this half century and the manifold ills of the spirit from which we are suffering relate to this search of the human adjective for its lost noun, but we shan't get into that, shall we?

Had Oughter/Did Good/Hopefully

Avoid regional grammatical liberties that are idiosyncratic of the uneducated classes unless for ironical effect. For example, the Southern "like ought to," or the Southern "I feel like we should," or "more better," or "had oughter." Eschew also jockstrap lingo, such as "He's got good quickness," or "He did good," or "We hope to do as best we can," and even worse, "We feel like we can do as good as we can ... hopefully." Abolish *hopefully* improperly used as an adverb from your vocabulary. I know I know I know: it is almost useless to inveigh against a pernicious linguistic vice, and such exquisite practitioners of English prose as James Jackson Kilpatrick have tossed in the towel on this one. I understand also that we have in our language no equivalent for the Arabic *In-shallah*, or the Spanish (derived from the Arabic) *ojalá* (*so be it* does not do the job), and the use of *hopefully* in this sense has arisen to supply the want of our growing ontological despair.[1] Nevertheless, ixnay. The integrity of meaning at all costs must be preserved. One grieves for the word *gay*, which has been brutally appropriated and pillaged of its irreplaceable, centuries-old meaning. *Hopefully* means full of hope, and only that, not it is to be hoped or one hopes.

He Hitteth Her: Pronouns

Prepositions are pesky little words that can bring a sentence to no end of grief, though I once knew a gal who never in her life left one dangling, nor for that matter turned one down, which did nothing for her reputation that *I* could judge; so don't fret yourself overly anent. But for pity's sake straighten out your pronouns, *he* is the subject, *him* is the object, *she* is the subject, *her* is the object, *I* is the subject, *me* is the object. "It was *he*," not *him*. "It is *I*," not *me*. Him and me did not go to the ball game; him and me went straight to Hell, where he and I deserved richly to go for committing a mortal grammatical sin like that. Him and I went to the ball game is even more— yet—deserving of perdition for mixing up subject and object, which is like topping ice cream with a pickle. And don't try to fudge (oh!) matters by using *himself*, or *herself*, or *myself*, as in "He and myself went bananas," which is the future I promise for anyone guilty of that solecism.

1. I don't recall the thudding misuse of this word before Vietnam, when the U.S. finally met defeat. Vietnam was the tree of knowledge for us. The myths of our invincibility and purity fell, and we joined the rest of the nations of the globe in history. The expression is fatalistic; it is a worldly wise ejaculation, at bottom a disillusioned ejaculation. *Hopefully* as construed today contains very little of hope, much of weariness and dejection.

Syntax

Practice constructing straightforward declarative sentences: you know, those lovely, simple, uncomplected sentences that begin with a subject, progress with a snappy verb, and conclude in a short predicate. Do not try to say too much in a single sentence. Chop it up. Snip it into two or three parts, each a sentence. There are dillies in this book of latinate construction, begging for editorial scissors—I know. He who doeth not what he preacheth apologizes for a Baroque temperament that he cannot at this late date reform, nor wishes to. He severely disciplines that temperament when drafting a speech.

Lean, Clean, and Mean

Keep your sentence structure uncongested. Relative clauses are to be used sparingly. Semicolons can be lifesavers, giving the reader the chance to come up for air, but they are sirens sweetly summoning the public speaker to destruction. Anything that in prose writing might append itself to the main thought of a sentence in the form of a semicolonar development should be uttered from the platform with the pause accorded to a new sentence—often, the audience should be reminded of the principal thought, or the subject, by a repetition of it. This takes longer. It is discursive. A speech cannot cover the same ground as an essay in anything like the same period of time, which one must keep present in preparing the text for a talk. Let's try an example requiring close attention from the audience—one that cannot be put simply.

> *Written:*
> "Brain can be weighed and measured, a material organic substance that is subject to laboratory analysis; the synaptic leaps that constitute the imaginative daring of mind, however, are beyond quantification, the process by which they occur being susceptible to description only, the phenomenon that actually takes place remaining beyond empirical understanding."
> *Spoken:*
> "The brain can be weighed and measured [use both hands, palms up and cupped, fingers slightly furled—figuratively weighing the gray matter], a material organic substance that is subject to laboratory analysis. What goes on in the brain [point index finger at side of head, just above ear, cocking thumb in pistol manner], however, when thought occurs—the electro-

magnetic synaptic leaps we make when we jump from one thought to another [pause], when we deduce from observed data [pause], or when our minds suddenly go *click!* [snap fingers of one hand] with an inductive perception—these [quotidian? tempting in an essay, given the distribution of alliterative syllables in the balance of the sentence, *nyet* in a speech] little mental miracles are beyond quantification. That is, though our laboratory instruments can record the brain's mechanical activity, the conceptual processes—how suddenly a genius like Albert Einstein leaps from what is known by the physics of his day to a theory of relativity never before conceived—is beyond scientific ken."

The audience will better absorb this much longer version of the same major thought than the tighter version, which is why speeches rarely read well.

The Use of Redundancies (in Moderation)

If good writing is lean writing, a good speech is even more severely to be trimmed of fat, but not necessarily of redundancies. Filling the spoken sentence with too many adjectives and adverbial phrases muddies the message, wearies the tongue, and stuffs the auricular passages of the audience with wax. On the other hand, though never to be treated as dumb, audiences can be assumed deaf. The message must be repeated, not larded. To this end, qualify thoughts sparingly, but do not stint on mnemonic rhythms and quasi-soritical (see below) constructions: "What this country yearns for is an ideal; and the ideal this country so desperately desires is not romantic, not vainglorious, nor inflated [use *hubristic* at your peril]—beyond our reach. To the contrary! The ideal this country demands, and can attain, and that tonight I propose to you, my fellow citizens, is . . ." This may sound like the exordium of a perfectly excruciating political pitch. I agree, but it illustrates what I am getting at. (See below.)

One Thought to the Sentence

Just as sentences must not be stuffed like sausages, full of indigestible suet, do not jumble different thoughts within the same sentence. "The reason traffic in drugs is so difficult to suppress, apart from a demand that grows exponentially with the degree of addiction, and the malignant influence of acid rock music on our young people, which is far from being a thing of the past, not to mention their rebelliousness and the peer pressure they may be feeling the weight of . . ." Do you know where this speaker is going? The audience becomes pent with a kind of breathless despair, hoping the fellow up there will get back on track, miserably suspecting that the entire talk will be much the same, its major themes, if any exist, impossible to extricate from the disorganization.

Ridding the Text of Dead Wood

Straighten out the syntax, clean each sentence of nonessential modifiers, establish the pecking order of thought, containing each in its separate sentence, and jettison useless baggage. Verbal excess baggage. Never say, "The question as to whether," say plain "Whether"; never say, "There is no doubt but that," say plain "No doubt" or "Doubtless"; never say, "used for fuel purposes," say plain "used for fuel"; never say, "He is a man who," say plain "He"; never say, "in a hasty manner," say plain "hastily"; never say, "This is a subject that," say plain "This subject"; never say, "His story is a strange one," say plain "His story is strange." What this boils down to is: don't be rhetorically pompous, be simple. And pull the plug on sententious fillers, like "the fact that." Just don't use that awful phrase. Instead of "owing to the fact that," say "since," or "because." Instead of "I'd like to call your attention to the fact that," say, "I'd like to remind you." Instead of "The fact that he fell is immaterial," say "His falling is immaterial."

Rhetorical Weapons

There are rhetorical devices (see Appendix III) that help to illuminate a point and lodge it in the audience's memory. *Litotes* are understatements the absurdity of which enhance the effect one is after. "Oliver North did not suffer from onerous supervision of his activities." Or: "Nobody has accused Dolly Parton of failing to fill a bill when she slips on a sweater." I don't much like litotes. There is something coy about them. There is a yuk-yuk, slap-the-knee quality about them. They pall, like Bob Dole's one-liners in his calamitous 1976 debate with Mondale, or like Bob Hope's predictable wisecracks when he introduces the current All-American football players. Litotes are not *oxymorons,* which can be a cute kind of double negative: "That dame with the rocks pulling her ear lobes out of shape is not unwealthy." That's an oxymoron—as ugly a word as the construction it defines is precious. Avoid them too, unless the circumstances really suit, as in "O, Susanna," which is built on—get this!—oxymoronic incongruities: "The day I left / It rained all night / The weather it was dry / Sun so hot / I froze to death / Susanna don't you cry!"

Similes and *metaphors* can make vivid impressions, but watch out for the mixed metaphor (suffering the slings and arrows of outrageous fortune is painful enough without being obliged to arm oneself against a sea of troubles, to cite the most famous of them), and be resolute against the overly extended metaphor. "The speaker revved up like a dragster at Darlington, accelerating his speech patterns so fast he burned rubber from the start and put out the Christmas lights at the finish. Why, he had to pop an extra chute to slow himself down." Ugh! Farfetched. There are, on the other hand, beauties, as in my recollection of this marvelous opening sentence by a writer for *Field and Stream:* "The Irish snipe is a very small bird with lots of sky around it." Volumes are spoken!

Paralipsis, of which the snipe metaphor is an example, almost never fails. This is to pass over a subject with brief mention in such manner as to emphasize the suggestiveness of what one omits. "My purpose in addressing you tonight is not to discuss the inadequate city reservoirs but to point out how the shortfall in precipitation since the month of January has severely restricted irrigation of our parks." (As the speaker goes on to describe how thousands of dollars of newly planted shrubs and trees are withering away, the need for more capacious storage against drought yawns greater and greater in the minds of the audience.) Or: "If one put her thinking in a nutshell, it would not overflow." Paralipses can be mean; they are immensely effective when well chosen.

Synecdoches can be useful. These occur when a part is made to represent the whole ("blocking and tackling are the ball game"), or the whole a part ("football is defense"), or a species a genus ("the Rasputins of court politics"), or a genus a species (an illustration of which totally escapes me). Of particular use to a public speaker is what might be dubbed "rhetorical *sorites.*" In the Aristotelian sense this describes an abridged form of stating a series of syllogisms, wherein the predicate of the first becomes the subject of the second, the predicate of the second the subject of the third, and so on, the

conclusion uniting the subject of the first proposition with the predicate of the last proposition. (There is a reversed form named after the
sixteenth-century philosopher Goclenius, who was chiefly famous for
being next to godliness.) From this there has evolved a second meaning—a collection, a series gathered together, an aggregation of matters more or less related. Rhetorically this is the way the psalms are
built, as in Psalm 6:

> O Lord! rebuke me not in Thy indignation,
> nor chastise me in Thy wrath.
> Have mercy on me, O Lord! for I am weak;
> heal me, O Lord! for all my bones are troubled.

Or take another of the penitential group, Psalm 101, *Domine, exaudi:*

> Hear, O Lord! my prayer, and let my cry come to Thee.
> Turn not away Thy face from me;
> in the day when I am in trouble,
> incline Thine ear to me.

The psalms are tongue-and-grooved; thematically, imagistically, and
rhetorically they are an organic extrusion, block building on block,
rhetorical echoes compounding in a powerful dramatic impetus
whose antiphons fasten mnemonically on the subconscious. These
are the rhythms and elocutionary practices typical of Southern black
preachers, and that white evangelists have adopted in almost the
same intensity. Spend an hour one evening listening to Billy Graham;
if you live in the South, Sunday mornings turn on to the Reverend
Jimmy Swaggart, or the Reverend Kenneth Copeland, who may be
the best of them. Such speakers can mesmerize tens of thousands in
open stadiums. Their object is more than supplying audiences with
emotional catharsis: they want their words to stick in the mind. They
therefore deliver them after the Old Testament manner. The Reverend Jesse Jackson has developed a pungent aphoristic style. "From
the outhouse to the White House" can irritate with repetition, but
once heard it is almost impossible to dislodge from the skull. The
same goes for other Jackson sayings. "We've got to get the dope out
of our veins and hope into our brains," or, "Nobody can save us from
us but us." These simplifications serve their purpose, which will not
be everybody's; but all who would like to have audiences carry away
something in their heads when the speech is over shouldn't scorn

such reductions, nor the succinctness of language that gives them effect. They are soritical in nature, providing listeners with the rhetorical symmetry in which the human ear delights, and from which poetry derives.

Finally, there are *plays on words*. Of the pun no more need be said than that it is a poor weapon to rely upon.

9

The Silver Tongue

Don't let on to the military, or to the gummint, or to the gnomes who write instructions for computer programs, but the purpose of language is communication. The elementary condition of communication is precision. This is why there are grammatical rules. And this is why words mean what they mean, and should be used with care and respect. Learn to watch your language.[1]

Keep It Simple

Fancy, sesquipedalian words—like the six-shooter I've just fired off—should be avoided by speakers on nine out of ten occasions. (The tenth occasion is when one has acquired a foot and a half in one's mouth.) This is a member of the Buckley clan telling you to keep your vocabulary simple *when you are delivering a talk.*

Every speaker is inherently in the business of education, true, but the field is not semantics, nor philology, nor etymology. Leave that to literary types. You want to be down to earth. You want your audience to understand just exactly what it is you wish to put across. This does not require you to be banal, or plebeian, or dull; it does not proscribe you from those grace notes that lift your talk from the pedestrian level. But when it comes to words, even when you may boast an intimidating magazine of exotic language that pains beyond mortal ken to keep to yourself, short, pithy, homespun vocabulary should be your choice. If there are two words that will do the job,

1. For good grammatical reference works, see Appendix 1.

strike out the longer one. Had President Roosevelt on that solemn occasion told the American people that we had nothing to fear but phobophobia, would he have carried half the country? If your option is between a word derived from the Latin, or more immediately from the Romance languages, and one derived from the Anglo-Saxon, use the second word, it is almost bound to be shorter and pack more punch. On the other hand, avoid slang.

Foreign Languages

As a general rule, resolutely reject phrases in foreign languages. This is a good idea for prose writing, too. If you feel you *must* use the French term for women's underwear, for heaven's sake learn to pronounce it properly. It is not *"lon*gerie," as one hears snooty sales-dames in every semi-swank Manhattan department store say, with withering scorn for the customer's uncouthness in asking for the bra-and-panties counter; it is "la-*a*-ngerie." It is not *"buff*-et, which is the blow one might be tempted to deal an obnoxious headwaiter, but bee-u-[not boo-]*fai,* which is what one selects from when one is directed to the salad bar for lack of a liquor license. A buffoon not to be endeavor with all thy might always. What old Louis said was, "Après moi, *le* déluge."

We all make mistakes, but the rule is: it is not what goes into a man's mouth that condemns him, it is what stumbles incontinently out. When speaking formally in public, or at a conference, or in a board room, don't permit to escape a syllable that you haven't first checked in a dictionary for correct pronunciation and meaning. If one is not oneself fluent in a foreign language, one should refrain from silting one's talk up with phrases in French or Spanish or German, which will in any case accomplish little more than to mystify the audience.

There are exceptions to this rule. Spanish idioms can go over big in Miami, San Antonio, or Santa Fe; Cherman is OK in Milwaukee; Yiddish in Bedford-Stuyvesant; Polish in upstate New York; and so forth. Sometimes there is no word in English that quite carries the impact of the foreign term. There is no equivalent for the Spanish *macho* or *querencia,* for example, and these have passed into our language. What can be *schmuckier* than a *schmuck,* unless it's a *ganseh schmuck? Joy of life* simply doesn't cut it when compared with *joie de vivre,* and we have no word that does the job of the

German *Zeitgeist,* nor anything that sounds so peachy as *Weltan-schauung.* (That really is a baked Alaska of a word!) For stylistic reasons one may feel impelled to use the unnaturalized *bon mot,* but it is probably a good idea to work in a paraphrase of its meaning.

Exceptions to the Simple Word Rule

Similarly, sometimes the common word will not do. One may incline toward a latinate synonym, either for rhetorical reasons or because of the richness of connotation that one may desire. Sometimes *eradicating* fancy expressions from one's style, and *extirpating* ponderous words from one's *lexicon,* is more expressive than merely cutting it out. In all cases be careful, and try to avoid some of the more common pitfalls that sloppy use of our language has dug in the path of speakers.

Knowing One's Verbal Oats

Do not use words you are not thoroughly familiar with, and don't take words for granted, because they can bite you. For this reason, never use a thesaurus. It promotes bad habits. It encourages one to employ words with which one has had no previous acquaintance, which means that one is likely to use them incorrectly. Words are like a well-beloved tool, or a shotgun, or that putter you've had since you were twelve years old that you can't face the links without; they must become old friends before they are well handled. Whole worlds of difference, for instance, lie between *meritorious* and *meretricious,* between *factual* and *factitious,* between *official* and *officious* (as in, "That fat federal gummint functionary fouled up the official report through his fanatical officiousness"—the fink), between *beautiful* and *beauteous,* between *credible* and *creditable,* between *dominating* and *domineering,* between *assiduous* and *acidulous* (as well as between those two words and *sedulous*), between *militate* and *mitigate,* between *liable* and *likely,* between *infer* and *imply* (from which one does the first), between a *donkey* and an *ass,* between *addled* and *muddled,* between a *ship* and a *boat* (or a *yacht* and a *boat,* which is the difference between a poor man and a rich man, or a fool and his money).

Less but nevertheless important differences exist between *adverse to* and *averse to,* between *turgid* and *turbid,* between *admission* and *admittance,* between *asseverate* and *assert.* Do not confuse *alternately* with *alternatively, decimate,* which means the eradication or killing of one tenth of a given number of things or creatures, and no more, with total slaughter.

Whenever you use a ten-dollar word, check it with an authority. Take heart: it is often more important to be aware that there are subtle or radical differences of meaning between certain words than to recall exactly what those differences are; so long as you are on the watch for tricky nuances, you will not blunder, because you will have the good sense to look them up (see Appendix III) once again before choosing them to use in a speech or report. Won't you?

Developing a Sensuous Love of Language

From the Bahamas to New Wales, our English language is rich in its many accents, inflections, and syntactical patterns. Nevertheless, there are standards that the public speaker should observe, and that, if one was reared in Brooklyn, or the Ozarks, or in Cajun country, one must develop a consciousness about. Correct diction and pronunciation can be learned by paying attention to words and respecting them each as a distillation of human genius; as, in fáct, that faculty of the soul by which alone we may be distinguished from beasts.

Pronownsing Words Correckly: When Not To

Phonetics is today rarely taught, which is not only a shame, it quite hobbles the person who would like to improve his speech. Whether the vowel is correctly spoken flat or long, however, can be deduced from other known vowel sounds in familiar words, though it takes longer. Ruth Gallagher and James Colvin's *Words Most Often Misspelled and Mispronounced* is pocket size, and handy compilations of words that people tend to massacre can be found elsewhere, such as in Professor Soper's book.

Standard English usage is good to know, but I find from the floor that exceptions to the correct pronunciation are sometimes obligatory. Anyone who mentions the *era* of King Philip of Spain, for example, pronouncing the word according to the book, will assuredly convey the impression that he is alluding to the dreadful mistake of the Armada, and if he should mention that we are all in thrall to our *era,* yet another *error* in communication is assured (I use *ih-ruh*). The proper articulation of *combatant* is *"com*batant," true, not "com*bat*-ant," but nine gets you ten that if you utter the word as it ought to be uttered the audience will hear *competent.* (As in: "That bunch of noncompetent troops stood by while the battle raged.") There aren't ten people in a thousand who will comprehend a speaker unless he screws his features into an unsightly knot when he speaks of a "gri*mass,*" and since Daffy Duck in the famous cartoon found Bugs Bunny "des*pic*able! this is the emphasis of syllables people both prefer and comprehend. Perhaps that shouldn't be so, but it is ex*pli*cable, and it would be im*pi*ous to set oneself against the popular will. I know a circuit court judge who in charging juries never uses the word *credibility* (worthy of belief), because somehow they hear *creditability* (i.e., 1. worthy of having commercial credit, 2. deserving of judicious praise; as, born of *creditable* parents), and their minds leap from a combination of those nuances to entirely different considerations of the accused's credit standing. Maybe that's because the teaching of good English in our schools has fallen into de*cay*dence.[2]

Diction

Next to knowing how words are supposed to be pronounced, and when the rules may have to be bent, what any speaker must practice is his diction.

Some people are born with tin ears. They simply do not hear themselves murder the English language. Using *don't* for *doesn't* and *ain't* for *is not* can be a matter of the economic and social class in which one was reared, though snobbishness plays a part in the acceptability of such usages. I remember clearly an octogenarian single lady I used to visit when I was a boy, in Camden—a Miss Virginia Wallace, originally of the Bronx, I do believe (her family summered in Saratoga), all white lace and cameo brooch at the throat, who affected *don't*s and *ain't*s because that kind of linguistic condescension had been the fashion in her salad days sixty years before (she had met Melville). It must have been daring in the 1870s, sort of a vicarious slumming it by language, but it had stuck to become natural to her.

2. *Decalogue* derives (through French) from the Greek word *dekalogos,* which combines *deka,* ten, with *logos,* speech. *Decadent* spins off from the word *decay,* both words deriving from the French *decadence,* and that from the Latin *de+cadere,* to fall.

Though it isn't easy to shuck either fashion or class, the speaker must make an effort to break out. He should listen to any recordings he can lay his hands on of Gielgud or Olivier, of Judith Anderson or Claudette Colbert. He must consciously ar-tic-u-late ev-ery syl-la-ble, *pi*ckling *ev*ery *pe*pper in *Pe*ter's *peck,* paying es-pe-cial attention to the vowels and consonants that tend to get swalludup, and to *ed* and *ing* endings. "I was go'un out, cause I cuhnt fine nothin' t'eat in the fri-gater." That exaggerates. But I know a most entrancing girl, a spellbinding girl—a sweet, lovely, glowingly beautiful young ma-tron—who appalls almost every time she parts her seductive lips to speak. I find myself flattening the back of my tongue against the roof of my mouth, silently uttering *-ing* for her every *-in* or *-un,* anguish-ing as I hear her begin a participle, wondering whether she never listened to the tintinnabulation of the bells, and shuddering to imag-ine her reciting the poem. It is such a pity. When someone gets up before an audience and in this manner dumbfounds standard pro-nunciation, it is a disaster.

There seems to be an almost total loss of love in this country for one of the glories of human history, which is the English language. Can't recall when last I ran across a reviewer in a newspaper or popular magazine who paid more than cursory attention to *the En-glish* of the author—how well or ill the book was written, not just whether it told a good story, or had something to say worth shelling out twenty bucks for. There are passing references to "serviceable" or "pedestrian" or "clumsy" or "academic" prose, but few apprecia-tive examinations of the loving care—and, oh! the desperate strug-gles—with which many of our contemporary novelists and essayists have hammered out their style. How bitter is their private satisfac-tion. But language is what ultimately counts in a writer: the yoking together in perfect tandem of function and form, of sound, sense, and suggestion. Hemingway at his best is Hemingway in his best form, and that's his prose, not his moral insights, which were juvenile. Faulkner *is* his language, without which all the magic of Yok-napatawpha County vanishes.

Excellence in Public Speaking

The great orator, similarly, must be a great stylist. (Why not aspire to this estate? Less is meanspirited.) He must in particular love words, our American English words, and glory in them, pronouncing each with eximious attention, deriving from juicy vowels and hard rock candy tooth-cracking consonants a sensuous joy that communicates itself to the audience. This is not to become enamored of the sound of oneself: it is to exploit the language for all it is worth, and if one was endowed with leather bellows for lungs, and a bronze bell for a voice, all the better.

But it is words that make the difference. In choosing the raw, short, pithy, crude, image-rich Anglo-Saxon words over latinate synonyms, the speaker ensures that his text will be filled with vigor. Old Testament cadences must ring in his skull. He must read poetry, and derive voluptuous pleasure from "But ah, but thou terrible, why wouldst thou rude on me / Thy wringworldrightfootrock?" or, "Come you spirits / That tend on mortal thoughts, unsex me here, / And fill me from the crown to the toe top-full / Of direst cruelty! Make thick my blood; / Stop up the access and passage to remorse, / That no compunctious visitings of nature / Shake my fell purpose, nor keep peace between / The effect and it!" He must school himself to these rushes, and regularly read them half out loud, mouthing the words, his own tongue rolling them over, the tip rubbing sensually against the backs of the canines and incisors, saliva spurting astringently from the tongue's sides to gather in slick squirty pools in those pits at the base of the molars. Oh, yes: as an oenophilist becomes a connoisseur of wines, the public speaker must endeavor to become a connoisseur of words, to develop perfect pitch, so that he eschews such monstrosities as *tergiversation* or *asseveration,* the utility of their denotational precision notwithstanding; preferring in the last extremity sounds to sense in the resignation of his knowledge that whereas a perfection of sound can be achieved, a perfection in sense is an illusion. Which is why exactly we must try so very hard indeed to approximate precision in meaning by observing the grammatical rules—knowing, however, that words contain their own grammar. They are their own authority. Words are after all symbols. Cym . . . bals.

Know your tools. If you are not proficient in the use of the tools of language, you can't hope to give a good talk.

10

Into the Tank, My Bullies!:
A Grab Bag of Useful Tips

In the 1940s and 1950s, Yale had a legendary swimming coach who during his long tenure shattered intercollegiate records, compiling the longest number of consecutive dual meet wins—eighty, or ninety, if recollection serves—in the history of the sport.

We lucky freshmen of the class of 1952 who were recruited to swim for the greater glory of Eli under the fabulous Bob Kiphuth were honored indeed. We flocked excitedly to Silliman Gym, trunks in hand, ready to thrash our chlorinated way to fame: to discover that Coach Kiphuth hewed to the belief that no swimmer ever amounted to a mouthful of bubbles in the tank who had not first strengthened and made supple his body by undergoing six weeks of the most fiendish calisthenics to have been devised this side of Gehenna.

When the great day came, and we were at last told to put on our bathing trunks, it wasn't to swim. Goodness, no! We were assigned floats of balsam wood which we were instructed to grasp by the stern, reaching out until the small of our backs ached, and shove ahead of us by the impulsion of our mightily kicking legs, lap after lap, mile after mile—the great Kipputh himself wielding a long, flexible cane rod from the sides with which he stung our backsides if they protruded more than the permissible inch above the surface, exhorting us to greater efforts in language that, gentle reader, you will be spared.

We are at that same moment in our preparations for the fiery world of forensics. We have learned: that we must somehow contrive to tap our nervous temperament in order to inject passion into our delivery; that we must simultaneously determine to what personality type we belong, exploiting its strengths while doing battle against its weaknesses; where to look for sources and material; the practical uses of an omnivorous curiosity, and how a skewed perspective or unusual analogy can illuminate a point; how to construct arguments; how to stretch the muscles of our minds; how to subject positions to the stiffest analytical tests; how to sniff out logical error; the importance of correct grammatical constructions; and how to use the basic tools—words—with loving respect. Now we are ready to wet our feet.

I. Getting the Act Together

A few last considerations pend, however. First is a matter of courtesy, or consideration. And of hard sense. Who is it that one is addressing?

Knowing—and Working—the Audience

We haven't sufficiently emphasized tailoring one's talk to the situation. The jargon phrase "target audience" is expressive. Always keep present (a) whom you are talking to, and (b) what reaction it is that you seek from your audience: what it is you want your audience to get up and do about a situation when your spiel is through.

Back in the first chapter we used the illustration of an official delivering a report on his corporation's faltering financial health. Nobody likes telling bad news. One can become associated with it, as messengers in antiquity too often discovered. (The true reason why poor Sir Walter lost his head is not that the cloak he cast before the lady's feet leaked, as foolish historians have it, but because he confided to Bess that snuff is carcinogenic.)

What if such were your duty? How would you go about discharging it? Well, it depends on who is sitting out there, and on the environment.

If one is addressing the high executive command of a corporation in a board room, one need not shilly-shally getting to the (dismal) point. One will proceed to extrapolate from the deteriorating trend to demonstrate what effect it may have, if unduly prolonged, on the value of corporate equity and on the rating of corporate paper, and how—down the line—this is certain to hamstring the company should it decide to retool, expand, or diversify. No need for anecdotes. No gilding. Extrapolations from past data about a future course of affairs are a fine way for people to behead themselves, so prudence must be exercised; but what one is saying is of maximum inherent interest to professional managers, and they will be attentive to every word of a presentation that, as the speaker contrives to make clear, could profoundly affect their careers.

Before such an audience it would be inappropriate and unnecessary to pound tables. The energy with which the presentation has been invested must still be perceptible, but is better downplayed. It is well kept just beneath the surface. ("Joe is bringing to our attention a very serious matter, but dammy! is he cool, is he collected!") Everyone must judge appropriate tone for himself, but in such circumstances as I describe, an address on the diffident side is probably recommendable, well modulated, undramatic, the diction precise, the sentences as short as they should be lapidary. The executives at that meeting, never fear, understand full well what hard and unwelcome things it is they are being told they must do. They are going to have to reassess those ambitious plans announced at the previous stockholders' meeting, and probably shelve them, swallowing pride; they are going to have to become more efficient, cut payrolls, stabilize wages, maybe even—horror of horrors!—slash executive salaries.

In this case the audience is relatively intimate, sophisticated, and knowledgeable, and should be addressed on that elevated plane by the speaker.

Assume, on the other hand, that one is the chief financial officer, or even the CEO, of a utility company, and that one has the unpleasant obligation of relating the bad news about return on investment to a general meeting of the stockholders. Assume that "populist" candidates have recently been elected to the State Utilities Rate Commission, providing good reason to suspect that the pending request for an increase is going to be turned down.

What do you want to accomplish by your pitch to the stockholders? You are not speaking to a gathering of security analysts, or to savvy, hard-eyed bankers, to whom you would present the news in professional terms. You are addressing a large and motley crowd in a gymnasium the size of the lobby of Grand Central Station in New York City. They are pensioners and widows. They are the guardians of orphans and the managers of union pension funds. You want to galvanize them into taking action (in which course shifting some of the blame). You want them to marshal their political influence. To such folk, one would endeavor to explain in simplest terms the importance of an inadequate return on investment, and one would spend less time on such (to this audience) nebulous matters as the damage a diminished return is bound to wreak on some future issue of company debt. (As a rule, never talk about incurring debt to stockholders: the very word is enough to panic them.) What one would choose to emphasize is the immediate consequences of an adverse ruling by the rates commission on the value of the stock and on current and future dividends. "This is your capital and your income we're talking about," one might declare. Maybe one's dignity won't permit one to thunder, but one would speak in a strong, loud voice, and one just might allow the heel of a clenched fist to thump the lectern. "If the State Utilities Commission does not grant your company the rate increase we believe is warranted—indeed, that the facts and figures indisputably demonstrate is necessary—further weakening return on investment, you may see the value of your stock fall 5 percent, or 10 percent, or much . . . much more—*how* much no one can predict—and though it is among our first concerns as your managers to protect the dividend, we won't be able to guarantee that, and we cannot of course hold out any hope for an increase."

And do not let it hang there when you are addressing two or three thousand people. The larger the audience, the slower it is to comprehend. Nail down the response you want—always. End: "But this need not happen. You shareholders of Public Services of New Caledonia can make your feelings known to your representatives in the legislature, to the state house, to your neighbors, to your local newspapers, maybe even to members of the commission themselves. The future of this company is in a very real way your future, and it is in your hands."

When you are asked to speak by an organization, inquire about its membership. Get a handle on who they are, what their preoccupations, and what local or national issues may be of moment to them. If you are invited to a small town, pick up a local newspaper: the intellectual level and the tone of the community are reflected in the lead stories, a football win, a marching band contest, the closing of a textile factory. Take your cue from these items, editing or embellishing your remarks appropriately. Your courtesy is appreciated. Boners you may avoid. Did you hear what happened to the speaker who sneered at the Green Bay Packers when holding forth in Fond du Lac? That is where his remains are to be found.

A second pending consideration is this: not when to start talking, but when to shut up.

The Length of the Talk

Keep it short.

Keep it shorter than you might think proper.

We have on the authority of Saint Ambrose: "Let us have a reason for beginning and let our end be within due limits. For a speech that is wearisome only stirs anger."

Saints are not in all things infallible. A speech that is wearisome puts people to sleep even before their anger is stirred. There was a handbook of homilies for Catholic priests when I was a child called *Five Minute Sermons,* which was governed by the principle that no soul got saved from the pulpit after that length of time. Would that this book were in circulation among the good servants of Holy Mother Church today!

Audiences, unlike churchgoers, are not bound to their pews by religious respect. They have the option of getting up and leaving, one that college students in particular exercise with sovereign frequency. I surely wouldn't have wanted to sit through the five full hours (split between two days) of Henry Clay's great oration on his Compromise Proposals in February of 1850, nor even through the long hour of John Calhoun's brilliant "Fourth of March" rebuttal. Our patience is shorter. And yet . . . and yet . . .

Friend or foe, who was not riveted to his radio in 1951 listening to General Douglas MacArthur's emotional oration before the two houses of the Congress after his dismissal by President Truman? It lasted forty-five minutes. I have listened long periods to orators who gripped my attention from first to last, in chambers where one could have heard a double chin drop, so spellbound were the audiences, and we have the example of Billy Graham and other evangelists we've mentioned, who speak lengthily, yet who move the spirit.

Suiting Length to Situation

The exceptions notwithstanding, brevity suits the modern temperament. I've noted that colleges want a full forty-five minutes for their money, though some are content with thirty-five minutes followed by ten to fifteen minutes of questions and answers; which—in the first instance—requires that one take extra pains to keep it interesting, exhausting all available means of building into the talk visual and eurythmic dynamics. One must for this reason among so many others never forget to keep the audience in mind. Is it heterogeneous, cutting across all intellectual and economic levels? Are they primarily farmers and their wives out there, or are they small town tradesmen? Is one addressing a convocation of hotshot IBM executives, who can be presumed of an exceptional braininess, and who will accept a speech requiring close analytical attention? If one is bound to advance an argument of some intellectual gravity, twenty minutes is not likely to do the job. This is a situation where the entertainment value of an address defers to the complexity of the content: one cannot dust off South Africa, for example, in zip time, nor breeze through the pros and cons of removing intermediate range ballistic missiles from the European theater. A public speaker has to learn to choose an appropriate forum. When I was booked at a community college, or some satellite campus of Podunk State U., I never failed to inquire what percentage of the student body majored in psychology, sociology, and education. When 30 percent or more of the students were engaged in these ersatz disciplines, I edited my talk accordingly.

After-luncheon speeches should be kept under twenty-five minutes, and addresses following supper banquets, depending on the length of the cocktail hour, the caloric scale of the fare, the wines (if any), the lateness of the hour, and the occasion, under thirty minutes. Almost all introductions should be less than two minutes, and if there are three speakers on the program, and you are among them, but not the featured speaker, it pays to find out approximately how long the star intends to hold forth, keeping your spiel to a minute for every five of his, and reducing that by fifteen seconds for every speaker on the program above four. Should you be the feature on the night's card, you have a right to half an hour. But if it is a heavy program; if the warm-up speakers hog the ring too long; show mercy. Slash your own address. (You are entitled to remark on the robust wind of those who preceded you.) Audiences will be grateful. Any after-supper program that exceeds an hour and a half total is twenty minutes too long.

The Length of the Text in Relation to Delivery

How long is long? In his book Mr. Valenti cites as a rule of thumb that "one 8 and ½ by 11 typed page, double-spaced, will hold about two minutes' worth of spoken material. Therefore you can usually judge that eight pages of script will run about sixteen minutes. But practice and practice again." He adds, "If you find your speech rhythms run more than two minutes per page, edit, cut, reduce." And he concludes, "Remember this maxim: *It is very difficult to make a bad speech out of a short speech.*"

Mr. Valenti's field, of course, is entertainment. But brevity is almost always desirable. Keep in mind that no matter how slowly one reads the text of one's speech, spoken—if it is properly delivered—it will consume as much as a third more time. This is even more the rule when one attempts to make a serious intellectual point, not merely pass people's time. Then twenty minutes for eight pages of text is scarcely sufficient.

Mr. Valenti has good things to say also on

Memorizing Talks

He does. Short ones. His method is excellent. He begins by committing to memory the first and last paragraphs, and then by memorizing the first sentences of succeeding paragraphs, proceeding in this manner until he has the whole speech meshed into his mind. Even for Mr. Valenti, however, this consumes many hours of concentration.

He can justify it because speaking is his business. To most people speaking is an after-hours chore, and they do not have an actor's mnemonic training. Winston Churchill improvised from notes, but Charles de Gaulle and Douglas MacArthur committed their orations to memory, which was the practice in their generation. Today, mental laziness prevails.

Speaking from a Text

In college, I memorized. Don't any longer. I quickly gave up trying to wing my talks extemporaneously, either, resorting to those three-by-five-inch index cards that are admissible in college debate and that Ronald Reagan made famous. I still use five-by-seven-inch cards (much easier to type on, they stack more discreetly, and more information can be packed into them) for important quotations, statistics, or lines of reasoning that may be pertinent to several topics, and therefore interchangeable, but these are accessories to the body of my talks.

Underscoring the Text for Extemporaneous Effect

Any executive putting in twelve- and fourteen-hour working days will sympathize with what I say next, and will be able to extrapolate from my experience what is useful to him. On tour, one is unable to rely on performing at all times at one's best. After a week or so traveling the circuit, cumulative exhaustion sets in. Booking A gets its money's worth; Booking B gets a subpar performance by a speaker whose jet from Los Angeles landed three hours late, having fought air turbulence the whole flight.

I therefore compromise. I write out all my texts from first word to last. Using fiber pens, I underscore heavily. I am a demon about this. I divide long words that tend to defy instant discrimination, or that tend to knot the tongue, into syllables—into discrete parcels, such as "de/tran/scen/dentali/zation." (The subject of that talk being conservative political philosophy, use of this and other brain-crunching terms was unavoidable.) Further, I score the emphasis as one does in poetry, with blips and dashes, as for example: "dé/trăn/scĕn/déntalized." When I want to make absolutely certain that I wrest from an assembly maximum attention to a line of reasoning, or to a single word, I speckle my text with little round polka dots that call for a caesura, thus: "Friends, ○ Romans, ○ Countrymen, ○ lend me your ears." "Magic markers" are a boon. Those gorgeous fluorescent hues swabbed over words or phrases cause them to leap into one's eye, so that a glance tells one where one is and where one must go next.

Color Coding

I established a color code. Chartreuse green is for proper names, sky blue for titles of books and articles, canary yellow for all quotations, and rose, orange, or magenta for content I want to emphasize. All this takes a lot of time. My palms end up splotched in most of the tints of the rainbow, and my shirts are often spotted at the breast and on the cuffs, but it pays. The very labor helps impress the talk into one's mind. In poor lighting conditions, one's place in the text is not lost—which can be a frantic feeling!

I then follow the Valenti prescription, committing to near memory first and last paragraphs. All anecdotes, asides, and most illustrations I leave as obbligatos—unwritten, providing an opportunity for free extemporization and for moving out from the pocket of the lectern (which, incidentally, one is prevented from doing when there are mikes, or if one is speaking at a banquet table—see below). The first sentences of paragraphs I repeat and repeat to myself until I have them almost pat. When preparing for a tour, I practiced the talks maybe a dozen times each before setting out—at first silently, reading the speech slowly while muttering the words, then reciting it out loud, to myself, into the mirror. (There are few exercises that make one feel so foolish, but humility accustoms us.) This is essential for establishing an easy flow.

II. Eleventh Hour Preparations

Rehearsing Before a Performance

When possible, I spend an hour before every lecture or debate in my motel room, running through the talk against a stopwatch. I observe this routine though I may have delivered the same lecture the night before. I faithfully do this though I may have delivered it twenty times in the two months past, or sixty times in two years. Rehearsing an entire talk immediately prior to the performance establishes rhythm and imparts to the speech ease and fluency. What one strives for is to give the impression of almost total independence of the text. One has to create the illusion of extemporaneousness even when plainly reading.

Apart from total familiarity with the text, one way of accomplishing this illusion is to glance down at one's papers with a kind of disdain. Flick the sheets with the backs of your fingers. Lift a page from the lectern and slap it down on the table as though stuffing it down into a wastebasket. "Who needs this?" is the attitude. (You do, desperately. But never own up.)

Privacy before a Performance

When possible, I beg for ten or fifteen minutes of total privacy—in a dressing room, or in the dark wings of the stage—before coming on. (It is at this time that relaxation exercises may be helpful: see under "Posture," below.) Some people are pleased to socialize before a performance. I detest it. It is to me unsettling one moment to be chatting about this and that, and the next to pop up and deliver what people have come (even paid) to hear. I feel a most pressing desire to withdraw, to be alone. It's, I guess, a matter of temperament. I need to psyche myself. I must tap the adrenalin. For this reason I dreaded, and dread still, luncheons and banquets. One can't escape. One can't muse to oneself, reflect on what one is going to say. One is obliged to prattle with host to the left and host to the right, and across the table, one's mind meanwhile grating as from a thumbnail being drawn across a blackboard in anticipation of the fell bell. "You say your aunt has phlebitic phlogosis in *both* legs and her toes too? How perfectly dreadful!"

It clangs. One is summoned as to one's doom, to rise from wherever one is seated and walk on stage, there to face three or four hundred people in the maw of a darkened theater. What first impression will those people conceive?

III. Getting a Good Start

Spring up those three steps to the stage; do not drag yourself to the speaker's stand. Once situated behind the lectern, facing the audience, remember:

Posture

The American slouch has no place on the platform. If one's body slumps, so will the audience. An attitude of fatigue will cause the folk out there to feel tired before one has opened one's mouth. Everybody sooner or later evolves his characteristic carriage, which conforms with his personality; but in the beginning one should try to stand classically at ease behind the lectern. That is: spine erect, but not military-stiff; feet comfortably apart, one foot a little in advance of the other, toes pointing slightly out; the weight of the body favoring the balls of the feet; knees limber, not locked; shoulders and arms loose and easy, the arms hanging naturally by the sides, elbows brushing the ribcage; neck and head a mite forward from the chest, with just a touch of belligerence; chest out, buttocks flat, belly tucked in, though not so severely as to constrict the diaphragm. Men: Practice standing with hands clamped to the hips, elbows wide, like cock-o'-the-walk offering to take on a local bully. Then, without altering anything else, let the hands fall from their perches. That's the air one wishes to convey, the very slightest suggestion of cockiness, or insouciance, that indicates adrenalin is flowing—a current of vitality that communicates *with* the audience, creating a Newtonian reaction *in* the audience. Nevertheless bear in mind: nothing that I say relating to posture should be taken as a recommendation to alter in anyone that manner of holding his body attractively peculiar to his or her type. There is a way of standing peculiarly suited to stoutness, which is further back on the heels. The long and lanky person should retain the long and lanky air, though guarding against what can degenerate into a lazy attitude. The short person, if she, a la Bette Midler and Goldie Hawn, or he, a la James Cagney and Edward G. Robinson, possess a corresponding pugnacity, should by all means come on like a bantam cock, standing squarely on the balls of both feet, chest out and mitts ready.

Relaxing before the Talk: Suggested Exercises

Acquiring an easy posture is where exercises to relax legs and arms and body may be vital, depending on one's temperament. If one has been granted the boon of half an hour to oneself in the dressing room, assume a stance (preferably before a mirror) with feet twelve inches apart, hands on hips, elbows sprung wide, rising up on the balls and toes of the feet, and then letting oneself slowly down. Repeat this several times. If one is already unspeakably bored, one may take advantage of the interim to say one's prayers, or count one's lucky stars, or compose a limerick. Roll the head on the neck, left to right, right to left, letting the head slump forward and hang over the chest, lolling there an instant every time it rotates to the front. This is delicious, truly. Then rise up in an alert attitude, spreading out hands and arms before you as though supporting a very large balloon chest high. Beginning from head and shoulders, permit your entire corporal frame to slump—chest sagging, knees bending, arms hanging from the sides, backs of fingers nearly brushing the floor—coming down like a collapsing scaffolding. The head should loll forward, mouth open, eyes closed. Remain in this utterly dilapidated attitude several moments, and then pull yourself together like one of those multi-jointed wooden toy dolls on tiny springs, activated by elastic threads, that children love to play with: the Plutos and Mickey Mouses that flop when the tendons are relaxed by depressing a button controlling them, and then pop back up when the pressure is lifted. You put yourself back together in the same manner, but slowly.

None of this requires that one break out in sweat. Repeat the flop at your pleasure. Now grab left wrist in right hand and stretch the arm, bending over from the waist to one side, until you feel the ligaments stretching under the armpit. Change wrist and hand, and repeat to the other side. Five or six times each. Place hands on waist and rotate the upper torso on the hips—loosely, comfortably, dreamily. Follow this with knee bends. Yawn exaggeratedly. Finally, if there is a wash basin handy, splash cold water on your face, grin stupidly at yourself, and you are set.

Everybody develops the therapeutic routine of his choice. Since what is expected of a speaker is a performance, anything that will relax the body but at the same time energize it will set up the mind. (I rarely do exercises before a speech, preferring either to lounge sleepily in an armchair while thinking furiously on the subject at hand, or to pace the dressing room, mouthing the major points as I mull through the text.) People who are short of stature especially need relaxation and stretching; they tend to get up on their toes too much, try too hard. Tall folk—especially tall women, who spent their early teens stooping to boys much shorter than they in order to spare them embarrassment—need to vitalize their bodies. Tall men and women must snap to it, consciously straightening their spines, extending their necks, lifting their heads high, and gazing out over the audience, chins up and eyes alive with kinetic energy. They should rehearse their speeches with books on their heads. That sounds so silly that I hesitate to mention it. But it works. A substitute is mentally to reach upward with the crown of one's head as though one could in this manner so lengthen the body that one touches the ceiling. This accomplishes the purpose also, and it is worlds more dignified.

Finally, it aids posture no end to have gone to the bathroom not later than half an hour before the dread tinkle of spoon against crystal goblet signaling that one's hour has come. Male speakers, zip up.

The Batters' Box

The *podium* is the elevated platform or stage on which a speaker performs; the *lectern* is the stand on the podium that one speaks at. This is the speaker's batters' box. Hope it fits.

Rare lecterns are adjustable, incorporating a good reading light, and shelved to accommodate water pitcher and glasses. Most are rudimentary rectangular frames, built to an arbitrary height, the surface set at an arbitrary tilt, accommodating some imaginary average male with perfect eyesight, who exists in mathematical mean form but in reality hardly ever—women being even in this day chauvinistically ignored by the manufacturers.

Take command of it. The lectern is the speaker's redoubt. It is his quarter deck, his bully pulpit. Approach it confidently and grasp it with both hands. Take possession of it with both hands. It's yours. Don't hang on to it as though for dear life, however. Don't plump one elbow down on its surface and lean on it so hard (tall people acquire this vice) that the audience may be tempted to swipe one's elbow off just to see if the whole scaffolding of the body will come down. Nor, as nervous short women tend to do, fold your hands on the near surface of the stand, palms down, fingers tightly closed, meanwhile pressing your chin close to the edge. The body from just beneath the chin is entirely cut off from view: the woman appears decapitated, her head floating on top of the hands as cherubs' heads are sometimes depicted floating on paired wings (see further below). But fuss a little with the lectern if you like. Do not pick imaginary lint off it (temperamentally tidy nervous women cannot seem to help themselves when the surface is upholstered in suede), nor with repeated sweeps of the back of one hand or the other wipe it clean of imaginary dust, or dry of imaginary water spills (tidy nervous people of both sexes fall prey to this tic). But go ahead and adjust the mike to about an inch below the level of your lips and three or four inches in front of them (do not make love to the mike after the manner of torch singers), switch the lamp on or off, check the water tumbler in the bin, contriving not to upset it when stuffing away briefcase or whatever else you may have brought to the podium (it is inelegant to present oneself before an audience thus encumbered—leave everything except maybe the manila folder containing your text in the dressing room or on your banquet table seat). Then flash a smile at your audience and begin. (I'll elaborate on this below.)

Tall people: pray that you are lucky enough to get a tall lectern, or one whose height can be adjusted. If it is too low, the tall person's tendency to stoop is irresistible; and if the tall person's eyesight is less than 20-20, he will be at pains to follow his text or read his notes. Raise it to the level of approximately the stomach, or to where, if one is nearsighted, one can easily prompt oneself. Short people pray for a lectern that does not cover them up to their throats. Women, as mentioned, typically experience this handicap, some being obliged to step up on stools, these being available. (Such perilous footing is never a good idea. The inconvenient alternative, which is not always an option, is to stand beside the lectern.) Women encounter another annoying impediment if they happen to be buxom. Unless their arms are proportionately long, when they grasp the lectern they tend to press their breasts against its ledge, which is awkward, or even o'erhang it, which can be risible. The alternative is to assume a position so far back from the lectern that one can't read one's notes or make use of it in other ways. The optimum height of the lectern, depending on a woman's eyesight, is a few inches below the level of her maidenform.

Attitude

Academics counsel that one should not fuss around at the speaker's stand—hitching up the knot of one's tie, patting one's hair, straightening one's skirt, or dressing one's trousers. "Above all," writes one of these gentlemen, "don't begin by looking [down] at your notes."

This advice is OK, contingent on happy circumstances. If the lectern has been set at just the optimum height for the speaker, and the mike at the convenient height and distance from his mouth, he has no problems. But it is better to fuss a little setting matters right at the beginning than to labor for a neck-wrenching half hour with one's head bent awkwardly to a low mike, or just the upper half of one's physiognomy visible to the audience.

Dignity

Professional entertainers make such adjustments with smooth assurance, while already addressing the audience, but they come on too glibly, and too eagerly, and with too naked a desire to ingratiate themselves, for what suits a speaker. Dignity isn't much valued these days, but the speaker who lacks it won't likely be accorded it. The president of a university, or of a major corporation, or a renowned scholar, or an eminent architect, or a person who amounts to anything at all should avoid trying to be "a regular guy." Leave that to nuns and priests in their sneakers and Lacoste tennis shirts, to office-seekers, and to other vain, pretentious folk of such little self-esteem that one is excused in wondering why anyone should conceive the most minimal esteem for them. Respect begins in self-respect. The speaker's attitude should be courteous, not obsequious. Though what one aims for is somehow arousing in an audience the presentiment from the moment one mounts the stage that a cargo of combustible energy is being kept in hold, the movements of the body at the beginning are best deliberate. Not lethargic: deliberate, calm, self-possessed. There is no hurry. This is when the audience sits bated with expectancy. Exploit these few seconds of suspense. It can pay to look down at one's notes, *appear* to study them a short while, keeping one's eyes lowered, before abruptly lifting one's head and straightening one's body, sweeping the auditorium with a long, penetrating gaze in which a smile may only reluctantly surface. And only then, in a good loud voice, beginning to talk.

(For heaven's sake do not smile at all unless you actually feel warmth and congeniality for your audience: the smile otherwise comes across as insincere, or even as insultingly condescending.)

Salutations

And go straight to the nap. Do not recognize every worthy at the banquet table, or half the dignitaries on a stage. That's both boring and pompous. Anyone of the slightest consequence whom one may inadvertently omit feels slighted. If there is an honored guest, make your obeisance to him or her right after addressing the chairman. (Get the name right.) Otherwise, "Mr. [or Madam] Chairman, ladies and gentlemen," suffices.

The Voice

If God gave thee a beautiful voice, fall on thy knees in thanksgiving. I can listen to a person with a fine speaking voice who has nothing in particular to say, oh, almost all of five minutes before my eyes begin glazing over.

Do not count on the natural gift alone. I remember a High Church minister from my childhood who drove his parishioners up the wall because of his infatuation with the orotund Anglicisms he affected. God was ever Almighty Gawd, pronounced invariably at a certain pitch and with the long vowel almost gargled. One struggled against onslaughts of instant atheism.

Exercises for the Voice—Professional Help

On the other hand, it is foolish to disdain cultivation of the voice. If one has problems breathing correctly, or in pronunciation, or because of a tendency to stammer, medical attention is indicated. One's bite may be incorrect, requiring orthodontistry; one may require surgery of the palate, or suffer from asthma, or labor under certain emotional traumas that can impair speech. Absent pathological obstacles, one may still be advised to hie to a professional voice teacher. Self-help isn't an exercise in futility. A true and tried way of cultivating one's speaking voice is to listen to recordings of fine actors, male and female, as suggested in the preceding chapter, and practice (into the mirror, with a tape recorder switched on at the same time) reciting poetry or passages of fine English prose. One must have an ear, and natural taste. God supplies both. But the bad mechanical habits can be treated. Closely watch the area of your mouth as you articulate. Is there something slovenly about the muscular movements there? Are *t*'s and *p*'s and *d*'s being slurred, present participles glottally gulped? If these faults in diction are evident (which you can check instantly by stopping and replaying the tape, listening attentively), and if in general the sound of your voice comes out muffled, its quality suppressed, beyond question tongue and jaw and lips are being activated stiffly, or slothfully, the throat is constricted, and the necessity of projecting one's voice from the abdomen ignored. Danny Kaye is wonderful for breath control and alleviation of faults in diction: try doing his song "Anatole of Paris." Auden's poetry is good for modern idiom, Ogden Nash superb. And the opening paragraph of *A Tale of Two Cities* is marvelous training against lapsing into singsong, as earlier mentioned.

Few American males are born with deep, resonant speaking voices. Women more than men have problems pitching their voices to reach the back rows without waxing shrill. And there are many women who aspirate in the breathless Jackie Onassis manner, which is inaudible without a mike, but whose sibilances produce wild distortions in public address systems. A voice therapist is indicated.

In fact, all speakers do well to check in with a professional every so often. We slip into poor habits. The Churchillian stammer becomes a mannerism, the wry rendition of an adversary's case coy, the humorous *moue* an affectation, the rhythmical rise and fall singsong, the dramatic intonation phony. A tape recording will alert us to some of these faults, but our sole ears are too often indulgent of our vices.

Personal Appearance

Women have the advantage of make-up. Men must contend with their natural skin tones. And with baldness. And with beards.

Men: Bushy-Faced and Dull-Eyed

Starting with the last, the heavily bearded speaker tends to look like a woolly caterpillar with lips. Most of the expressiveness in the face emanates from the thousands of tiny muscles surrounding the area of the mouth. When this is shrouded, what the audience discerns of the speaker's mug is precious little; what it gathers of expression is *nada*. Rubbery lips in their hairy casements open and shut, like vulva. Or writhe, like sea anemones. This gross effect is compounded if the speaker also happens to wear glasses. For some reason, heavily bearded men tend to prefer thick tortoiseshell or black plastic spectacle frames. With these the eyes—their sole remaining means of imparting intelligence—are occulted; the upper cheeks too, maybe even the brows. What the audience sees is a pair of weird refracting panes, the fleshy blob of a nose, a lot of bristly follicles, and the dark orifice of the mouth. Quite obscene.

If the nose of the bearded speaker is also long, and has a thin bridge, down which those heavy eyeglasses may keep sliding, the paw of one hand is continually lifting to shove the frames back up in place, so that what was sufficiently obscured is now blotted out. (All bespectacled speakers, bearded or smooth-shaven, male or female, who have this problem: use adhesive plaster.)

Shave the beard. At the least, trim it close. It is almost impossible for expression to transpire through a bush.

Bearded men, moreover, unless they are blond or redhead, tend to look dour, grouchy, even menacing; like Fredric March's Mr. Hyde. The ill-fated male with a heavy natural growth of black whiskers who shaves with meticulous care may still look saturnine. He is truly accursed. He must scrape a razor across his cheeks and chin shortly before every performance, and he is advised to use talcum powder.

Men: Skin Tones

Men with gray or sallow complexions must pay attention to the color of the clothes they wear. Browns are generally unbecoming, causing them to look unhealthy. Men who are sallow-complected and to boot balding must make every effort to keep their chins tilted high, because if they glance down at their notes too much, or as a matter of custom nest their chins on their breastbones, they will present a bulbous elongated doughy mass of tallow-toned flesh to the audience, with shiny accents on the knobby naked dome, giving them a megacephalic appearance. Elmer Fudd. These men, if they wear glasses, should favor the heavy frames that bearded male speakers ought to eschew; if they are able, further to break up the flesh tones, they should grow heavy eyebrows.

Men of gray or sallow complexion who do a lot of public speaking should wear pancake. I know. I refuse to. But I should also for my, by turns, pallid and choleric skin tones. But I don't.

Female speakers should contrive at all times to look perfectly cool, perfectly kempt, and perfectly lovely.

Clothes—Male and Female

This is a touchy subject, which we dread broaching at the school, but which we are obliged to do.

Outside of Savile Row, the three top haberdashers for men are Brooks Brothers, J. Press, and Chip. They have stores in Cambridge, New Haven, New York, and other cities. They also publish catalogs.

If the male speaker is not 100 percent sure of himself in the matter of clothes, he should guide by these tailors. They charge an arm and a leg, as well as for the inseam. The materials, however—especially the fine English worsteds and Harris or Shetland tweeds—are of superb quality. I bought a business suit at J. Press in 1951 for a very special occasion (a debate against a visiting British team) that I passed down to my eldest son, who was wont to go trout fishing in it, when he wasn't playing touch football in it, yet which is being worn by still another son to this day—his best suit, on the most formal occasions. That's over thirty-five years of use.

The style of these haberdashers is "Ivy League." Whatever one may privately think of Ivy League education, there is no doubt that the understated, round-shouldered, unpadded, loose-fitting two- or three-button cut in men's clothes associated with that clutch of Northeastern colleges, and hence with the tailors I've mentioned, is the *ne plus ultra*, otherwise known as the cat's pyjamas, for the business and professional worlds. People from Ohio and other Middlewestern states dress with taste and formality. The South and Southwest are notorious for having the gaudiest predilections in male clothing. California is in another dimension, reached by space warp. Men all over the States who subscribe to Ducks Unlimited will sport duckogrammed shirts and vests and hip pockets, by Duxbak, out of L. L. Bean, which is depressing, but probably does not reflect on their morals. Among public figures Johnny Carson dresses abominably— he is too natty, too Hollywood, too penguin-like—Bryant Gumbel on the whole well. Watch out for checks! The male speaker can hardly go wrong donning a well-cut soft wool midnight blue blazer and dark gray flannels, or a dark business suit with a discreet pinstripe.

As for what women should wear . . . Here goes.

Any woman confronting a mixed audience can be certain that among the men she is always the object of latent prurient attention. There is also latent, sexist, male antagonism. Nor will she be spared resentment by her own gender, who will decry her appearance because envying her brilliance. These realities have to be dealt with; they can interfere with getting one's message across. The formal clothes men wear are, in cut, sex-concealing. This is not always the case with women's formal clothes, which in cut and style are often sex-oriented. If the object of the woman speaker is to capture and hold the intellectual attention of the men in her audience, while giving minimum opportunity for the cats to meow, minimizing distractions must be her policy. If she has a "full," Jane Russell figure, she does well to avoid styles that emphasize the curves of the bust. Or, obviously, plunging necklines—unless, as the late British blonde bombshell Diana Dors cracked to newsmen who had crossed microphones in front of her when she swept down the gangplank of the Queen Elizabeth in New York harbor (endearing me forever), "Look out, boys, you're hiding what I'm selling." Women on an elevated podium should avoid dresses whose hems reach shorter than just below the knee. Generally speaking, women in tight short skirts or dresses should avoid leaving the protective pocket of the lectern. No slacks, please.

Using the Stage

The lectern is the fulcrum from which a speaker imparts dynamics to his presentation. It is the base of operations, the full stop, the *burladero*. It is the pad from which paragraphs are launched, important points emphasized. And it can become a trap.

When Rooted to the Lectern

The inexperienced speaker who languishes still in the panicky stage (not having been so fortunate as to come upon this book) grasps the lectern for dear life and will not relinquish it. That speaker would wish for a stand four feet wide and ten feet tall, behind which he can hide. That's not what it is for. But even the experienced speaker is nowadays often bound to the space immediately behind the lectern because of microphones, or because he talks from a banquet table and may not move around. This is inhibiting to anyone who likes to prowl the stage; but the speaker thus confined has to learn how to inject dynamics into his posture by use of body language.

He may lean slightly to one side or the other; he may tilt one or the other shoulder, advancing or withdrawing it; he may take a half step back (if so much is permitted), rearing the upper torso back and away from the audience, and then, in one motion, in a kind of swoop, bring head and torso forward while recovering that half step toward the stand. He may rise up on his toes, or even flex his knees slightly and crouch, depending on the tone and content of what he is saying. Here is a "speaking situation" in which the nervous temperament simply must be activated, because it must flow through the person behind the lectern, and outward to the audience, in body language that transcends his confinement.

Strong facial expressions are now vital, and may require some exaggeration, because mikes tend to impede the audience's view. And since mouth and zygomatic muscles can be blocked by the palisade of microphones, eyebrows assume greater importance, and such expressions as shock, or grim earnestness, or outrage, or mild disbelief, or sardonic disapproval require a heap of practice before the mirror. The dry or diffident temperaments are here at a disadvantage. People of this mold tend to indicate mood by the slightest inclination of head, or attitude of shoulders. Or the single raised eyebrow. Or the infinitesimally curled lip. Their expressions are naturally subtle. They have to work that much harder.

When Able to Move Freely: Quartering the Deck

When one is not confined to the space immediately behind the lectern, quarter that deck! Do not prowl it aimlessly, or nervously. Use the stage with deliberation, with restraint, and for the best dramatic effect. It is natural to paragraph one's talk from one to the other side of the lectern. Standing immediately behind it, in the cockpit: "There are two major arguments in favor of limiting the presidency to a single, six-year term. The first," leaving the word to dangle—moving now to the left or to the right, taking two or three steps without speaking, letting the audience hang pent with anticipation. When having walked perhaps to the lectern's side, continuing: ". . . is that no one the object of such relentless TV camera attention as a president, not even someone blessed with the rubber face of a Red Skelton, can survive more than six years of this exposure without boring the American people to tears, and . . ." Almost turning one's flank on the audience at this moment, perhaps lifting one hand in a professorial, attention-getting gesture, while strolling back to stage center, behind the lectern—there bringing the feet together in a stop: ". . . second, because," stepping off now to the other side, maybe not quite so far, nor so far stage front as before: ". . . no man or woman was born—certainly no seeker after public office—who has more than six years' worth of fresh ideas, or that many." At this point the speaker returns to the lectern, squaring himself before saying: "Let's examine the second point first." And so forth.

This is, of course, an exaggeratedly schematic illustration. But use that platform, and use the lectern as the paragrapher between major themes. Generally, do not talk while making a major move away from the lectern; but it can be effective to terminate a point in the act of moving back to home base—almost, though not quite, tossing the remark to the winds. It is good to cultivate a certain insouciance. For the life of me, I cannot answer why anyone should willingly suffer listening to a lecture; but since masochism is as American as cherry pie, and one has been invited presumably because people out there want to hear what one has to say, one is obliged—yes—out of courtesy to give one's best, but one's soul—no—never. Maintain a certain interior reserve, as suggested earlier, and permit this to peep through. Nobody appreciates what comes cheap.

Gestures

The writer, so far as he can make out, is one-eighth German, one-eighth Swiss German, and six-eighths Irish. From whence he gets his "Latin" propensity for speaking with his hands is a mystery. But he does. Too often with calamitous effect, having knocked eyeglasses off the noses of dinner partners, plates and drinking glasses from tables, and whole trays out of the hands of passing waiters. Once, many years ago, while twirling the light fantastic in the ballroom of West Palm Beach's The Breakers Hotel, he neatly hooked with outstretched pinkie of left hand the hair piece of an entertainer who was that very evening to perform, ripping it off the naked scalp, the writer stammering, "Oh, excuse me, is this yours?" thrusting the pelt at the poor guy, who vented a miserable, "Yes, thank-you," grabbing it, stuffing it in a pocket, clapping both hands to his skull, and fleeing the dance floor. (The writer also once lit Ava Gardner's lipstick with an absent-minded flick of his Bic, while quenching his own cigarette in the wine glass of her companion.) He cannot keep his hands still, nor out of mischief, not even by sitting on them, because they twitch convulsively under the pressure of his thighs and buttocks, plainly each endowed with a malignant genius of its own.

I have known maybe ten people who were able to talk with their hands and arms hanging so naturally by their sides that they neither called attention to themselves by spasms and aborted breaks for freedom, nor so inconvenienced the speaker by their slat-like weight that his upper torso stiffened, as though the appendages dangling from the shoulders had gone numb and become paralyzed. They must nevertheless be subjected to strict curbs.

The Five Principles

There are five constituents to the effective use of one's hands on which everybody agrees. First, gestures must arise from the emotions. They must therefore be generated, and come fully to flower, simultaneously with the emphasis or rise in pitch of the voice. The entire body must be put behind a gesture, following through—as for example, on the clenched fist and raised arm—just as it must follow through with a punch. When the voice rises, the tendency will be for the heels to lift slightly, and the torso to thrust forward; when voice (and the concomitant emotion or intensity) drops in tone, for the body to slump, the heels to descend to the floor, and a step backward to be taken. In your mind, sound out the word "eu-*ryth*-mics." That's the completed gesture, from initiation to end.

The second constituent of an effective use of the hands is individuality. Gestures will vary depending on personality type. The restrained temperament may employ few gestures (too few gestures), and these will be precise (too precise). It is incongruous for a person of this type to thrash around from the lectern like a deranged Rodney Dangerfield or excited John Madden. On the other hand, in a disciplined speaker, as in a disciplined actor, the extravagant gesture at a suitably climactic moment can have extraordinary effect. Recall Sir Lawrence Olivier in his film version of *Hamlet,* when he thrust one hand up at the heavens and fairly shrieked, "The *play's* the thing / Wherein I'll catch the conscience of the *king*"—spinning like a dervish on the stage. It startled. It shocked. But it worked.

This is a daring prescription. One may have to boast the histrionic talents of an Olivier so to do violence to the temperament to which one belongs. On the whole, people best execute gestures natural to them, developing a repertoire from which to draw.

Correct timing is the third constituent of the successful gesture. One doesn't shout at a friend across the street, "Hi, Fred!" and only then wave one's hand at him. It looks as foolish and awkward on the platform for the complementing gesture to lag behind or by too great an interval anticipate the sense of what one is saying.

Incongruity results also if the gesture is not consonant with the emotional pitch of what one is saying. That is, one does not pound the lectern when suggesting that maybe a compromise is the indicated course of action, nor shrug one's shoulders when one is petitioning Congress for a declaration of war.

Restraint is the fourth principle to observe. Suit use of the hands to the words; use them purposefully, and unless one is in the business of tripping the consciences of kings, without exaggeration. Speakers who windmill nonstop from the lectern tire audiences. Let the hands be when there is no need to emphasize a point; let them fall as naturally as possible to the sides, or grasp them behind you, or cock them on either side of the waist, or hook one thumb in the belt (never both, and *never* a thumb in the armpit of a waistcoat), or even place them on the lectern a little while. Do not, however, anent this last position, succumb to the habit of leaning into the lectern thus held, every so often flicking the spread fingers of left or right hand out to the sides, like a bird stretching its wings. This can drive an audience nuts.

The fifth and last principle is appropriateness. A gesture may fit one occasion but not another. Older people prefer parsimony in gestures: they don't like to be lectured to, and too much hand flinging about in their faces irritates them. (Children, on the other hand, respond to enthusiasm, the more exaggerated the better.) Fullblown gestures are out of proportion in a small room and before a small audience; the subtle gesture, on the other, er, hand, won't do in an auditorium. It passes unobserved as though lapped up by space. The energy of one's gestures, moreover, should be determined by the power of the voice. A weak voice accompanying a strong gesture is like a high voice piping out of a big man.

Let me sum it up. Gestures should be generated naturally out of the strength of emotion or intellectual heat. Do not force them. They should issue up out of the gut. Speakers must cultivate a certain kinetic energy in (1) choice of language, (2) inflection, (3) voice, (4) expression, (5) intensity of eye contact, (6) body language, and (7) gesticulation. These must all become one thing, working in unison.

Study drivers in Rome, Athens, Paris, or Madrid during rush hours. Their gestures are: appropriate to the provocation, expressive, energetically compatible with the tone of voice, complemented by the most eloquent body language, and obscene. The idiom is choice, trenchant, rich in imagery, sometimes imaginative, and obscene. Should you be the target of such an explosion when in Spain, France, Greece, or Italy, listen with bright ingratiating eyes, smile, and then, when the other driver has finally exhausted his insults, say to him, "And your mother." And run.

A subject that cannot be stressed too much is the make-or-break-a-speech importance of

Facial Expressions

Saith Professor Soper:

Practicing in front of a mirror is indispensable to your knowing what your face does as you speak. Study it. What do the eyebrows and forehead do? If frowning wrinkles appear, iron them out; if your brows are pulled down into a scowl, relax them. Perhaps most important, does your face *do nothing at all* as you speak? If you are a "deadpan" speaker, practice to relax and *lift* the muscles about the mouth and cheeks. Experiment in delivering sentences expressing various emotions: sorrow, joy, anger, curiosity, and so on.

Discover what is your natural, most relaxed expression. Should it be cloying, or coy, or offensive, or too gloomy, or too stupidly cheerful, or vacuous, modulate it. Do not try to assume an expression that is simply out of character for you. And use body language appropriate to each expression. For instance, if you have a happy thought to communicate, smile, rise up on your toes, lift your arms and shoulders.

Finally in the list of odds and ends before getting into the swim of things (sorry) there's the all-important one of

Audience Contact

Never permit the theater manager to douse the lights so that the audience is all in shadow, unseeable by you. Do not permit him, no matter what he says or pleads, no matter what the sponsoring committee chairman pleads, to throw blinding spots on you, and—or—intensify the footlights, which rim the edge of the stage, to the effect that once again you are unable to establish eye contact with your audience. Just as you should always, always, always demand to test the public address system and inspect the lectern for proper height and lighting before you go on, insist on being shown just how the auditorium will be illuminated. Worse than talking into the great dark cavern of an auditorium is the impression one can get that one is talking into a void. There is no better formula that I know for attacks of stage fright.

Find a Friend in the Audience

Rather than simply quartering the audience with a roving gaze, I try always to pick a person out. Some sweet-looking lady with her silvery hair freshly blued and permed, who seems to gaze back at one with an encouraging smile and maybe even a wink of empathy; or some young person whose expression of earnest attention helps one keep up a good feeling about oneself. We all need that, though we must try not to become upset by what may seem to be a hostile reaction to what we are saying, judging from the expression on the face of whomever our itinerant eye may light upon. I've known this to demoralize speakers, who become greatly disconcerted by the angry stare of someone in the first, or third, or seventh row, to whom, like a fatal attraction, their eye keeps being drawn back. It can induce a paralysis of fear and uncertainty.

Dealing with Hostility

It need not. First, one is often mistaken about people out there in the dim reaches of a lecture hall. Of all the States in the Union I used to dread touring Pennsylvania. I once asked my lecture agent to charge double for a booking in that state. Why? Because Pennsylvanians as a tribe can be, or can appear to be, about as unresponsive an audience as any speaker will conjure in his nightmares. The impression is that nuances of meaning utterly escape them, and that they are bereft of a sense of humor. One winter when I was booked at a college near Harrisburg, my path crossed with Russell Kirk's—that extraordinary man of letters—who, I discovered, also dreaded bookings in the Commonwealth. "I take what consolation I can," he said to me over lunch, "from the experience of Mark Twain. Were you aware that *he* feared and dreaded Pennsylvania as much as you and I do, and for similar reasons? Why, one night he was giving a talk to a rural York County audience, which never cracked a smile. There was a farmer in the front row who particularly unsettled him: a tall, gaunt, lantern-jawed, hard-knuckled, bony-kneed individual in his mid-fifties, who stared grimly at the speaker out of steel-gray eyes, arms crossed with the hands buried tightly under the armpits, hob-nailed boots solidly planted on the planks of the wooden floor. Mark Twain decided that he would concentrate his efforts on that man. He decided, by golly, I am going to crack that fellow's shell if it is the last thing I do. With this fervent purpose he aimed the final twenty minutes of his talk at that farmer and that farmer only, volleying his wittiest remarks at him, only to see them bounce off that impervious front and fall shattering to the floor. He had failed. He had done his darnedest, but he had failed.

"Afterwards, at the apple cider and doughnuts reception, Mark Twain's nemesis stomped up to him, declaring, 'Mr. Clemens, sir, I just want to tell you: that speech you gave was so funny I could hardly keep myself from bustin' out laughing.'"

One never knows, you see. But never permit hostility to unnerve you. Without sacrificing dynamism and sincerity, learn the trick of abstracting yourself from what you are doing. You must be like the actor: at one and the same time the passionate Hamlet, son of the foully murdered king, and the cold, skilled professional who is play-ing Hamlet. In the Cambridge Union, the British University debating society, the members hurl elaborate and sometimes blistering insults at one another. Americans are shocked when they visit Parliament the first time, for the jeers and catcalls and rude noises that speakers are subjected to by the back benches, so unlike our stilted, boring, and oh-so-respectable federal Congress. Oh, it's so much more fun in England. It is part of the game, and people play it in good part.

Mark Twain's idea of concentrating his fire on the person in the audience who seemed to be the most implacable is a good tip. Prac-tice individualizing your audience. If you happen to catch that sweet old lady in her fresh perm beaming with grandmotherly approval at what you are saying, beam right back at her. You will have won a favorable opinion that by contagion spreads. If you spot somebody frowning in concentration, as though finding what you say difficult to comprehend, focus your attention on that person while you ex-plain once again, slowly and carefully—intimately for his or her spe-cial attention—what it is you mean; you will be explaining yourself to many others, and your extra effort will be appreciated. Should you spot somebody who unmistakably evidences hostility, lifting his lip in a sneer, or yawning ostentatiously, or even making a great show of laughing at you, don't let him get your goat, which is what he dearly desires. Goodness, no. This is the time for a self-deprecatory comment, or a quip. Or simply shrug. "I sometimes find this as hard to believe as at least one of you in the audience, apparently," you might observe, with an easy, confidential smile. "Believe me, I've been there. It took an accumulation of evidence I simply could not ignore to convince me that thus-and-so is the case." Having served up this graceful concession to skepticism, harden your tone (you may be polite; you are no wimp), proceed to concentrate your energies, the fire in your belly, on that hostile person. Lay out the facts. Oblige him to acknowledge your sincerity and conviction; and if he is so ideologically congealed that your arguments do not win him over, or at minimum gain his respect, you will have wiped the sneer off his face. If failing even that, you will have so charged your remarks with intellectual passion that the majority of the audience is almost sure to be swept along.

IV. The Delivery

Speak clearly, confidently, expressively, and in good cheer. It is all right to be momentous when content calls for it, and grave, but do not be so deadly serious that you do to the death the audience's attention.

Humor

If you don't have a sense of humor, my counsel to you is run out and get one.

Don't waste a moment. Nothing is so essential.

What is humor? It's perspective. It is the first cousin of genius. It is keeping a catawampus eye out for the aberrant (can you guess on which syllable you are supposed to inflect that word?), for what does not quite fit. It is the ability to see things topsy-turvy, and therefore take their correct measure. It's a sense of personal and ultimate ridiculousness. From which should follow the ability to put things in their place. *No somos nada.*

That's humor. There are a lot of people who tell jokes all the time whose sense of humor is nil. They do not comprehend sophisticated puns. Shaggy dog stories confuse them and leave them feeling faintly unhappy, as though they dreamt their spouses were unfaithful to them but in the morning couldn't remember with whom.

It May Not Pan in Peoria

Be cautious of its use, however. Outside the metropolitan areas in the Northeast, spreading out in a fan across the North and Midwest, humor is viewed with dark suspicion. These are the audiences that like to have all speakers certified by some academic degree. These are the pedagogues who take profound offense if one neglects to address them as Doctor This or Professor That. (They keep high school basketball trophies in their offices, hanging the walls of their "den" with plaques from the Jaycees and Chamber of Commerce.) Levity in connection with serious matters tends to furrow foreheads and pitchfork brows. Grant Wood lives. Sinclair Lewis lives. There is such a thing as good taste, and bounds to that: we've mentioned that humor in connection with the tragedy unfolding in South Africa is out of place, as it would be about Buchenwald. But anyone who essays a pinch of irreverence in upper New York State, Vermont, Maine, New Hampshire, Indiana, Michigan, Minnesota, either Dakota, Missouri, and Kansas is foolhardy. Count your blessings if you are addressing a convocation of Jews, Southerners, Southwesterners, non-Slavic Balkans, and blessed-be-the-God-who-created-them Latins. In Texas and Louisiana the taller and more outrageous your story, the more tickled the audience. The people of Arkansas and Tennessee love a good yarn, and if you enjoy spinning them you will find kindred folk in the Carolinas, Georgia, and Alabama. But do you have trouble delivering or recollecting punch lines?

Not All Jokes Cut It

I got myself into a jam once. In the course of a debate before the Pennsylvania Library Association—a dignified affair, held in the great auditorium of the Heinz Hall in Pittsburgh, which looks something like the Paris Opera house done up with more money—as I was listening to my opponent's summation, a marvelously apposite story flashed into my mind, guaranteed prettily to spit and polish off his entire case, or so I hoped. Springing to the lectern when my turn came, I launched into it: to realize, to my horror, just as I got to the climax of the story, that the very last word, on which everything depended, was sexually obscene. The whole point hung on that vivid obscene expression, which stuck unuttered and unutterable in my throat.

Thank God this happened in Pennsylvania, because minimal damage was done.

Only before special audiences risk an off-color tale. To pass, it should be free of prurience. There's a nifty one about an old lady in Fort Worth who surprises her nonagenarian husband in bed with a doxy, in a hotel room. She grabs him by his wizened neck and tosses him out the window. The prostitute sits up horrified, crying, "But we're twenty stories up!" "So what!" snaps the old lady. "If he can *blank* he can fly!"

There is nothing prurient here—the point isn't to titillate the concupiscence—but I would still be wary about using it unless the audience were small and I knew it well, and even then I would flinch at the moment of truth, as I have here.

Jokes about any religion teeter almost always on the abyss of poor taste and invariably offend someone in the audience. Leave them off your repertoire. Ethnic jokes are dangerous, as are jokes about race. There is a lot of hypocrisy about this, especially within that strange territory circumvallated by the Beltway. (Oh my heavens—how one has to watch one's tongue in Washington!) These stories depend on stereotypes, true. But some carry no malicious freight. Nevertheless, in public one is advised to wait until the minorities in question have acquired sufficient self-confidence to tell these stories on themselves.

Alipori: 1. That State of Agonized Emotions One Suffers When One Watches Others Making Fools of Themselves 2. The Effect Produced by a Wretched Jokester

Are you a graceful raconteur? There's them that are not. Nothing can be more agonizing than an ill-told comic tale, or a botched punch line. Nothing can be more embarrassing than the smirk of a speaker who is enjoying his own story when maybe the audience is not, nor so excruciating as to hear a speaker guffaw at his story when the audience draws a blank. One has to ask oneself, "Am I naturally comical when I speak? Do I tell a story well, or do I usually have to repeat and explain the punch line, and do people generally titter thinly, if at all, when I'm through?" If so, quit trying to be funny. If you can't tell it so that people put on that half-explosive expression of appreciative expectation, don't. Play it straight. You can be an interesting speaker to whom people will pay the closest attention without cracking jokes. (People who are not good at humor can cultivate light sarcasm as a substitute.) I don't think anybody ever accused John L. Lewis, founder of the United Mine Workers Union, of being a funny man, yet he was galvanizing in an oration. If a comical thought ever occurred to General *(le Grand)* Charles de Gaulle, he probably brushed it off his cuff as though it were some insolent speck of lint, yet he was one of the great orators of all time, by a single television address probably saving France from going Communist.

When the Goodie Doesn't Come Off

Everybody misfires on occasion. There are two ways to handle this: one is to sail on unperturbed, as though the anecdote hadn't been meant to be funny (in which case one may leave the audience utterly puzzled as to the relevance of the digression); the second is to take the dud by its dead weight, so to speak, hold it up to the audience, and shout, "Hey, that's funny." And maybe shrug, with a despairing expression on your face. This will fetch a laugh when mayhap the story had no right to.

The "Happy Hour" Ramada Inn Comedy Routine

One-liners become wearisome. They can be like too repetitive couplets, causing one to flinch in expectation of the thud of the rhyme. We've mentioned in this connection Bob Hope, beloved that he is of us all, whose monologues have become decrepit, and Robert Dole, about whom many people hypothesized that he lost the 1976 presidential election for the Republicans during his debate with Mondale because of the way he kept dragging in his tired cracks.

Irrelevant Funnies

The very worst thing a person can do is tell a joke whose point is irrelevant to the theme of his talk. The next worse thing is to indulge in so many wisecracks that one antagonizes the audience into thinking one is being flippant, and that one is hence shallow.

The second best humor is that which rises naturally out of one's theme; the very best humor is that which stems from personal experience and at the same time illuminates one's theme. When speaking of the venalities and corruption that are inevitably engendered in the corporate state, at a time when Washington was rocked with scandals about peculation in high places, I recalled similar lamentations by the press in Mexico City many years back, in 1941, when my family was living there and I was a boy. The principal newspaper published a cartoon. One frame showed Diogenes, in Greece, with his lantern, looking for an honest man. The second frame showed Diogenes, in Mexico, looking for his lantern.

That kind of story not only gets a good laugh; it resonates in an audience's imagination, making the point, as in this illustration, about the corruption that inevitably attends Big Government better even than recounting the political history of New York, since the Indians grossly overcharged the Dutch for it.

When to Use Humor

Some people like to begin their talks with a touch of humor. That can be graceful, especially if it follows on a sally by the previous speaker, or by the program chairman. But don't tell a string of jokes right off, unless you mean to continue cracking jokes to the end: wrong expectations will be set up.

My preference is for a light touch—maybe no more than a wry observation—someplace within the first few sentences; and then to use humor exclusively for illustration in the course of the talk. Never digress into a story solely for "comic relief." It should always be suggested by the content, and it should neither absorb an undue amount of time nor upstage the text. What is peachy is when a speaker discovers some good humorous anecdote that fits perfectly into the conclusion of his speech, encapsulating its major ideas.

Oh, if there is to be a question and answer period, I try to reserve just such a story for the last question of the evening. It can clinch the case one wishes to make.

Related, but critically differing in its ingredients, is

Wit

Without wit a public speaker is mortally handicapped. In a scale of value, wit wins over humor. Decisions may more often be gained by the fortuitous turn of phrase than by the logic recommending them. Ronald Reagan quite clearly lost his debate against Jimmy Carter on domestic issues, judged by the soundness and coherence of the individual points raised; but he won the night, and the presidency, by his since famous summation, beginning, "There you go again!"

Something to remark about the witticism right away, because apropos, is how quickly it becomes tired. President Reagan fell into the habit of resurrecting that phrase in his second presidential campaign, and it palled, it was but tepidly responded to by crowd titterings. Fritz Mondale similarly overused his "Where's the beef?" crack, which, when he first let it fly, was inspired.

In what consist the differences between wit and humor? Webster treats the word exhaustively. The archaic, second meaning is given as: "The power of conceiving, judging, or reasoning; intellectual power; mental capacity; understanding." The fifth sense, also archaic, is given as: "Mental ability, esp. of high quality; lively intelligence; perspicacity; understanding." Wit is further defined as: "Mental sharpness and alertness; intellectual quickness and penetration; . . . now esp., such capacity along with lively fancy and aptness of talent for clever expression; readiness in seizing upon and expressing brilliantly and amusingly ideas which are startlingly incongruous in association." The ninth sense is closely related: "Felicitous perception or expression of associations between ideas or words not usually connected, such as to produce an amusing surprise. *Wit* consists typically in a neat turn of speech by which disconnected ideas are unexpectedly associated."

Note from these definitions the role that intelligence plays in wit. In the importance of this ingredient is where it differs from humor. Webster goes on to say under synonyms: "WIT is more purely intellectual than *humor* and implies swift perception of the incongruous; it is primarily verbal in its expression, and depends for its effect chiefly on ingenuity or unexpectedness of turn. . . . HUMOR commonly implies broader human sympathies than *wit.*"

Many warm people, filled with the milk of humankindness, are humorous, though they lack wit; many exceptionally witty people are dryly intellectual and are lacking in those instant human sympathies. Dickens was especially gifted with human sympathy, and his works are in part wonderfully funny; but had he had more wit, he might have been saved from his excessive sentimentality. Anthony Burgess today is a consummate comic writer, but his intellectuality typically subverts his novels because his characters are subjected to an excess of cruel wit. There is a quality of bloodlust in wit; one goes with one's witticism for the jugular. Sentimentalists may be slobs, but they are nice slobs; the person notorious for his or her sharp wit may not be a person one would care closely to associate with.

There are thousands upon thousands of examples of marvelous wit attesting to the ingenuity of the human mind. The English, to whom word play is so important, are superb at it. There was a minor poet by the name of Sylvester who kept pestering the great Ben Jonson to a contest of rhymed couplets, a challenge that Jonson was averse to accepting because he rightly suspected that Sylvester was after trading off his (Jonson's) name; but one afternoon at, I suppose, I don't recall, a coffee house, an exasperated Jonson said all right, you go ahead. Sylvester promptly extemporized, "I, Sylvester, slept with your sister." Jonson is said to have thought about that a moment, and to have retorted, "I, Ben Jonson, slept with your wife." "But Mr. Jonson, that doesn't rhyme!" objected Sylvester, to which Jonson replied, "Yes, but it's true."

Samuel Johnson was a notoriously sloppy dresser, and absent-minded besides. He often forgot to button up his fly. One afternoon when out walking in London a dowager acquaintance stopped him in shock and surprise, exclaiming, "Why, Dr. Johnson, your thing is sticking out!" To which he replied, "You flatter yourself, madam. It is hanging out."

Politics has always been rich soil for wit. On one famous occasion the conservative Prime Minister Benjamin Disraeli said of William Gladstone that he was a "sophistical rhetorician, inebriated . . ." and he paused right there, lengthily—permitting the chamber to fill with gathering shock. This was bending the rules of partisan badinage too far, even for the British, and cries rose up on all sides of "Shame, Shame!" Whereupon the imperturbable Disraeli completed his sentence, ". . . with the exuberance of his own verbosity."

Oh yes, the British are marvelous at this kind of thing. Churchill was, of course, famous for crushing turns of phrase. When Clement Attlee campaigned against him right after World War II, adopting the role of the humble man of the people, who, unlike the vainglorious aristocrat, was modest in all things, Churchill snapped that few people had more to be modest about. We Americans are not bad at that kind of put-down either. Was it Wayne Morse who cracked at Goldwater, "Barry, you're so handsome you should star for 18th Century Fox"?

The comforting thing to know is that one is not born with the gift for clever repartee. It is a developable talent for the speaker's arsenal. It does require keen intelligence—not profundity, a certain shallowness being more characteristic of the famous wit—and quickness. The natural intelligence cannot be augmented, but anybody's wit can be sharpened by use: by engaging in debate, by imagining before an event circumstances in which one might confront difficult questions, and what one might answer to them. (One can assume that Cyrano de Bergerac thought long and morbidly about the insults to his preposterous nose before ostensibly being inspired into his magnificent rebuke.) The mind must be subtle, and the acuity of its perceptions also cultivated. The habit of standing back and looking at matters from a different, what I have called in these pages "skewed," perspective is essential. And one must enjoy word plays, inventing them, testing them, exploring possibilities. (Read Anthony Burgess's masterful analysis of James Joyce's method, in his book with the word play for a title, *ReJoyce*.) One cannot produce a witticism on call; but when all these ingredients are present, and when the mind is heated in the course of a public challenge or debate, the witticism will occur in a flash of inspiration.

Now, witticisms can be even more dangerous than humor when they misfire. A heavy remark that just misses the point is gravely embarrassing. If one flubs a joke, the audience may shrug sympathetically, even laugh at one, perhaps—one may hope—with a modicum of sympathy. But the witticism that bombs is painful, intellectually uncouth, making listeners deeply uncomfortable, at once putting in question the smarts of the perpetrator. When what may sound like a witticism ignites in the mind, hesitate just an instant before delivering it.

We've barely mentioned

Statistics

I detest them so. They are dull enough reading; spoken, they are murder. Nothing quite shuts the eyes like reams and reams of statistics. I remember vividly that night in my junior year at Yale when my partner and I debated the All-England Team from Oxford and Cambridge, which toured the United States challenging all comers on the subject of socialized medicine. After I had got up (in my brand new suit) to fire a few salvos at the first Brit, the second rose to say, "Mr. Buckley, like the drunkard, leans on the lamppost of statistics not for illumination but for support." He was right. I have never forgotten that rich put-down, though we clobbered them anyhow.

Select one telling statistic that stands synecdochically (get that!) for the point you are trying to establish. This is difficult; sometimes two or three supporting statistics may be required. In rebuttal, the single telling statistic to each of one's opponent's assertions is best, though it may be just the thing to crush his argument under a load of hard quantitative testimony if he has been so temeritous as to challenge the statistics one called into evidence earlier, or if he has insolently riposted that they were merely exceptions proving his rule. The audience will absorb almost none of this heavy artillery, yet the impression will nevertheless be that one has the facts, the other fellow mere opinion. (Unscrupulous opponents in debate or in board rooms sometimes empty whole bagsful of irrelevant and even inaccurate statistics on the floor, hoping thus to impress peers or audience: which is dirtiest pool.) Just keep in mind that tables of statistics, unillustrated by visual aids, far from shedding light, will utterly baffle an audience.

One has to be careful, also, about

Appeals to Authority

There are rules for the use of authority as evidence. The most important are: (1) make no assertions on your own authority that the audience is unlikely to accept, and (2) when you cite an authority, be certain that he is a household name and not tarnished by association with some egregious lobby or ideological pressure group.

That is, one may cite Gloria Steinem regarding the latest direction in the feminist movement; one does not cite her regarding the goodness or rightness of that direction.

And just as one should avoid ambiguities of grammar and logic, avoid the ambiguous citation of sources. One may have it from highest authority, but name the guy. One's source may be of unimpeachable character and veracity, but who is he? All folk of exquisite taste may agree that peanut butter and banana sandwiches on rye toast are delicious, but who are they, and by what criterion may they be deemed gourmets, also by whom? When one is on the receiving end of this kind of garbage from a speaker, do not hesitate to challenge him.

A kind of appeal to authority is the use of

Visual Aids

The first thing to be said about these is that they are inelegant, never to be resorted to in a formal address before a large auditorium filled with a heterogeneous audience, unless inescapably necessary, and sparingly when conducting a military briefing, or a class, or a sales conference. Too many charts dull attention.

They do help give visual dimension to statistics. But do not turn your back on the audience and talk to the visual aid. That's not only bad manners: the audience begins to assume that the flip chart is more interesting and important than the speaker (one does not voluntarily risk such comparisons), and the speaker sometimes becomes so involved with the fascination of his beautiful graphics that he is totally oblivious of the audience. Stand to one side of the rack supporting the flip charts, not in front of it, obscuring the audience's view. (This can be aggravating in the extreme; some speakers manage utterly to block out the graphics that are supposed to illustrate their argument.) A pointer is handy. Refrain from brandishing it like a rapier, and do not let it slip out of your hands, as once a pointer did mine, nearly skewering a very frightened lady in the third row left center. When referring to the visual aid, do then turn from the audience, in order precisely to locate the significant datum, because it defeats the purpose of such dangerously distracting impedimenta to have a speaker slap hand or pointer in the general direction of the chart while he talks on, leaving his listeners to screw eyes in sometimes frantic concentration as they strive to single out the pertinent curve or fact.

If one is going to use the damn things, have an assistant bring them on stage at an appropriate time—at that interval in one's talk when one is actually going to refer to them, not before, because the attention of the hall will keep straying to the charts, even though they are covered, wondering what delights are contained therein. Close them up, or have them lugged off, immediately one is through.

I do not like these artificial supports. Who is to bring in the charts? A pretty damsel, on the order of those sleek sexual fantasies who display the prizes in game shows; a handsome young man? In either case components of the audience will fail faithfully to attend on one's urgent call for a new septic wastes disposal plant. A buffoon of either sex—someone who will trip coming on stage, or miss a step coming down from the stage, crashing with the easel? My more serious objection is that visual aids relieve a speaker of a burden properly his obligation to bear: which is to explain without assistance from the floor, by use of clear, clean prose, and by the power of his voice and personality, even the most refractory subject. Visual aids conduce to making the lazy speaker more lazy yet. I call to my witness those paralyzing hours spent in ROTC and basic training with nearly illiterate sergeants, or bored and sometimes not less illiterate commissioned officers, too long frozen in their rank, droning interminably on as they flipped over chart after chart, putting us all to sleep.

Against which fate the speaker must exert himself by all means at his disposal.

The Art of Public Speaking

Never forget—this is my last exhortation—that public speaking is a minor art form. It is a performance. As after any performance, when a speech is done a body should feel thoroughly wrung out— elated, moody, bonetired—if one has done a good job. It's like coming to the end of a long piece of work, an architectural plan, a market survey, a book. One has performed. One has pitched intellect and temperament to their highest levels, to the limit of one's capacity.

Above all, the public speaker must be entertaining. He has been invited to give the audience a good time. There was a schoolteacher back in the 1860s in my adopted town of Camden—a dour Scot schoolteacher called Leslie McCandless. Almost every evening of the week he would walk to the house of another Scot, McRae by name, a fellow with a reputation for being every bit as dour, and irascible besides, drink two whiskies with him, and leave. They never exchanged ten words.

This went on for years. One evening McRae complained irritably to his guest. "McCandless, I do believe the only reason you come to visit me is to drink my whisky!" To which McCandless replied, "Why the hell else would anyone come visit you?"

And why should anyone come listen to a speaker if he is not entertained?

11

Dealings with the Press
and How to Tell Mike Wallace
to Go to Hell and Make It Stick

There is the view that all businessmen are s.o.b.'s, and all members of the press and television are their illegitimate half siblings. News folk are lice to some, the Enemy to others.

They are failed novelists, or playwrights; they dream rotgutted pipe dreams of Pulitzer Prizes they will never achieve; they are the dregs of the tribe of scriveners, dealers in and panderers of gossip, scandal, and all the dreary venalities to which human flesh is heir. They are the fourth estate for no historical reason other than that they are fourth-rate failures as human beings and professionals.

There is the happier view: print and screen journalists are shining knights and sometimes avenging angels, who almost alone check corruption, corporate or private, defending the public good against abusive arrogations of power in government and elsewhere. They are Jimmy Stewart.

Then there is the moderate view—mine of course—that they are neither stereotype, just working stiffs like you and me, writing in prose as stylish as the toolbox of a garage mechanic between slugs of whisky, divorces, alimony payments, more whisky, sordid one-night stands, child support delinquency notices, whisky, and endless hangovers.

The truth is not probably less condemnatory than less flattering. They are paid miserably, resenting it—and hold the world accountable. Gore Vidal's wicked line, that every time he hears of the success of a fellow writer, he dies just a little bit, bites true applied to the men and women in almost any newsroom. They begrudge success in others, of whatever profession, assuming that it was ill got and ill deserved. As a tribe, few professions are filled with more vainglorious, complected, and cynical individuals.

I never said that. I deny that I wrote those words. Some goblin commandeered my fingers as they trickled over the keyboard. I am not responsible. The *public*'s estimation of the Press, nevertheless, ranges somewhere close to its estimation of used car salesmen and congressmen. That is not high. Anderson Bakewell, the famed Jesuit missionary, explorer, and hunter of man-killing beasts, writes me recently about his grandfather, Edward Everett Hale, of "Man without a Country" fame. A Unitarian minister, he was appointed at the ripe age of eighty-one chaplain to the United States Senate. Someone asked him, "In your capacity as chaplain, do you pray for the Senate?" Mr. Hale replied, "My friend, I look at the Senate and I pray for the country."

Encountering Ideological Bias: Can One Do Anything about It?

Which could be said of the Press. Studies over the past ten years have demonstrated that any relation between the social and political opinions of the vast majority of Americans and those of journalists in print and television is purely coincidental. If we can take the 1984 presidential elections as a fair plebiscite, 62 percent of American electors identified with Reagan's conservative policies, in broad terms if not in detail, whereas from their voting record since the McGovern-Nixon contest some 80 percent of the Press identify with the left-liberal wing of the Democratic Party—the Kennedy-McGovern-*senile-dementia* wing. There is in fact an adversarial relationship between Press and public. (I loathe the word "media," and won't use it. *Press* with a capital *P* covers television journalism in my lexicon.) Anyone who has ever been hostilely interviewed is aware of this. There is a well-documented animus against businessmen, the more successful (the bigger) the worse. There is scarcely less an animus against the other institutions of our society: lawyers, doctors, even churchmen. We are all to be distrusted; we are all liars, and probably crooks. It is their sacred duty to smoke us out, should they be obliged to fan a false blaze or two. *They* are righteous. Regarding these pretensions, a lot of us ask: who elected them to be our ombudsmen? The question is rhetorical. They are self-appointed.

Sound, Prudent Assumptions

I have private rules governing my conduct toward the Press that apply to newspaper reporters and television journalists equally:

1. Since as a tribe they count a disproportionate number of individuals who are ridden with envy and the malice that envy spawns, never trust them. The friendliest-seeming reporter—unless he or she is ideologically sympathetic with one's cause, or what one stands for (where the truth may lie has little to do with it)—will stab you in the back: will use confidences, or any unwary remark, or some foolish statement you may make when half overcome with fatigue, against you. Without compunction. Without remorse. And without mercy.

2. Saving those who make it in big city newspapers or in the first rank broadcast studios—and sometimes even there—they are ignorant, provincial, uncultured, and ridden with bias. You can count on that. They know no history.[1] Their intellects are undisciplined. Their standard of ethics is low. They don't listen and can barely read, so never for a moment be sanguine that your clear written or spoken statement will be paid the most minimal attention if it conflicts with their prejudices.

Malice: The Goldwater Example

I did not truly believe in the degree of malice and apparent inability of the Press to hear or see truth until I was asked to be a point man for the Goldwater effort in Europe during the 1964 presidential elections. The campaign for us began in Madrid, with its large American colony and the nearby air force base of Torrejon; and there we at once ran into the deliberate misrepresentation of just about everything Barry Goldwater said and stood for.

It is embarrassing today, twenty-four years after the events of the spring, summer, and fall of 1964, to recall the viciousness of the assault on this utterly honest man's reputation, but it is instructive, and serves as a warning: if the Press have it in for one, there are almost no bounds.

1. Sometimes not even recent history. When in 1978 I spearheaded a drive to feed starving Cambodian children in Thai refugee camps, I was asked by a young reporter why I obviously felt Americans bore some sort of special responsibility in the tragedy. Dumbfounded, I replied, "Why, because of Vietnam." She gazed at me puzzle-faced, asking me please to explain what the Vietnam War had to do with it.

The Curious Affliction of Blindness to Fact in a Profession
That Prides Itself on Its Devotion to Truth

In Goldwater's case, there was the ideological bias; but there was also—Goldwater's partisans were obliged to admit—honest concern about his apparently cavalier statements regarding the role of nuclear weapons in Vietnam. When asked by a reporter what he would recommend doing to interdict Communist supply lines that were occulted by the dense tropical canopy, he answered, in part, "defoliation of the forest by low-yield atomic weapons could well be done."

A storm of (jubilant) protest by his enemies greeted this declaration, which was at once interpreted as signifying that Goldwater would introduce nuclear weapons into the conflict. "Goldwater's Nuclear Plan to Win Viet," *New York Herald Tribune;* "Goldwater Urges New Vietnam Aid; Would Use Atomic Weapons to Clear Red Supply Lines," *New York Times;* "A-Attack on Viet Jungle Proposed by Goldwater," *Washington Post;* "Goldwater Proposes Atomic Fight in Asia," *Chicago Tribune.* In short, the GOP standard-bearer was a nut who would nuke us all to perdition.

Clarifications of his stand at once issued from Goldwater's camp, but they were useless. There was no way of dislodging the impression in the public mind of a trigger-happy cowboy, which was daily reenforced by loose allegations in editorials and looser, reprehensible charges in the public utterances of members of the Johnson Administration. Goldwater wanted to use atom bombs in Vietnam. Goldwater was a reckless character, a gunslinger, a warmonger.

The relentlessness of this smear played havoc with our efforts in Europe. Desperate, I had painted in large block letters on a placard four feet high by six feet wide the words that Goldwater actually uttered, carting it everywhere the campaign took me. Thus:

This is what Goldwater said when asked what one could do about the enemy supply lines in Vietnam:

"THERE HAVE BEEN SEVERAL SUGGESTIONS MADE. I DON'T THINK WE WOULD USE ANY OF THEM. BUT DEFOLIATION OF THE FOREST BY LOW-YIELD ATOMIC WEAPONS COULD WELL BE DONE. WHEN YOU REMOVE THE FOLIAGE YOU REMOVE THE COVER."

So: Goldwater never recommended using tactical A-bombs in Vietnam. He mentioned their use as a theoretical possibility, but he never—never— said we would or should resort to them.

We translated this statement into the language of whatever country we were in. We distributed copies of it to the press, native and foreign, and to everyone in the audience. From the podium, I pointed to the placard, and called attention to the fliers as they were passed up and down the aisle, repeating Goldwater's exact words in English, and then in Spanish or French or Italian. We might as well have saved our breath. The foreign press paid no attention, continuing to parrot the slanders as they came over the wire services or from their correspondents in the United States, guided by the *Washington Post* and the *New York Times*. Those reporters ostensibly covering our rallies for English-language newspapers invariably ignored the placard, the fliers, and my statements, repeating in one form or another the canard that Goldwater had—as was well known (you will recognize the fallacy)—recommended that we plaster Vietnam with nuclear bombs. It was as though we were dumb, and they blind and deaf.

Even a Written Statement May Be Unavailing

The helplessness one experiences is well-nigh indescribable. What can a body do? In Goldwater's case, the Press wanted to believe what they wanted to believe. It is not, however, extraordinary for journalists to get things incorrigibly wrong even when bias plays no part. I wince at newspaper accounts that have been sent to me of my lectures. Facts are got wrong, quotations garbled, connections between premises and conclusions elided, to the effect that the positions I am reported to have upheld are sometimes the diametric opposite of what I believe. But what cut maybe deepest are the clichés couched between quotation marks, including turns of phrase that never in my life dead drunk have I used because stylistically I detest them so. This is another advantage of writing out one's text: there is at least historical vindication in one's private papers—if anybody cares, which is unlikely.

How does one account for the disinformation that is our daily reading fare? The reporter was inexperienced, or confused, or tired, or in a rush. Or something. It defies explanation, except insofar as the modish subjective "truth of mood" school of history has infected courses in journalism, unseating the notion that objective accuracy is of any value. Once a young female reporter came to my motel room before a debate to plead that she simply had to get her copy in before a nine o'clock deadline. (By the way, it is not advisable to invite any member of the opposite sex to one's digs, unless one has a suite with a proper living room, for even the most legitimate reason.) She would not have the time to tarry long enough to hear anything except my opponent's opening statement, so wouldn't I please give her something written to guide by? Fearful for the salvation of her political soul, I therewith batted out on the Smith-Corona, a summation of my case, handing it to her. She thanked me profusely, departed: and next morning I read a version so scrambled that I could make nor head nor tail of it.

Innocence errs. What malice can do to one is as beyond repair as it is beyond one's darkest forebodings.

If one suspects that journalists of the printed word are dangerous, ideologically and politically hostile to one's middle-class values, or to one's radical spirit of reform, or to whatever: watch out for television folk!

They are not worse. The medium itself protects against the slipshod variety of inaccuracies, but when malice is a factor, the techniques for intentional distortion are manifold, and the power of TV journalists to influence opinion in the short term is greater. One can be vilified in newspapers; one is crucified on television. When those folk want you to appear on their program, they are sugar and spice. Once they have you on it, you are virtually at their mercy if the show is taped. If it pleases them, they will cut you up.

The Dread Ogres of Celluloid Journalism

I have met many thoroughly decent TV talk show hosts and "anchors." I have also met alligators that did not choose to drag me down into the muddy depths of a swamp, and serpents that skedaddled instead of burying their fangs in my flesh. We have, thank God, in this country no one except Phil Donahue to compare with the savageness of Spain's Mercedes Mila, renegade Catholic daughter of the counts of Montseny. (She also—like Donahue—abominates the Church and most of its teachings.) But every now and then one runs into a true reptile of the airwaves; and I do *not* agree with the policy we teach in my school that one should attempt to ingratiate oneself with them. I don't, and won't.

What Posture to Assume under Television's Magnesium Lights

There is a lot of advice about dealing with television interlocutors that amounts to blue funk. My instinct is to meet them head-on and intimidate *them,* which is surprisingly easy to accomplish when they catch on that one is not stupid, not easily disconcerted, and not a bit loath to give as good as one gets, and in language that they may not expect and would not choose to broadcast. I have heard of a wary industrialist who, when he is being taped, punctuates every phrase with the foulest four-letter word for copulation in the language, thus ensuring that what is used will look edited, making it less easy to frame him after the fashion made infamous by CBS—by the smooth splicing onto one question the answer given to another. I do not recommend this style of defense, please understand. The point is that in my opinion, contrary to conventional advice, one may unleash one's temper on the air, and go for the jugular of the host or interviewer, when the situation justifies it; but do so coldly, and with as deadly effect as you are able to muster. One should rehearse in one's mind all the likely, unlikely, and barely conceivable nasty jabs that a hostile (or merely news-hungry) TV interlocutor may throw at one. There is always the question one did not expect, notwithstanding. If one is able to give back as good as one gets in such a situation, give it by all means. If not, swallow hard, attempt to maintain dignity, and pray the "host" will go too far, antagonizing the TV audience.

Live, that is one's last defense: the audience out there. Play to the audience, not the TV newsperson. When an interlocutor badgers you in an increasingly rude manner—cutting your replies off short, or assuming the attitude that you are being devious, or lying—there is no reason to lose your composure. Go silent for ten seconds. Ten seconds is an interminable length of time on the airwaves. Count them: one-mississippi, two-mississippi. (A moderately paced Lord's Prayer almost exactly fills ten seconds, and it's good for the soul, too.) Television interviewers can't stand that. Smile thinly. Stare straight and hard at the man, until your eyes glitter. When he repeats his question—he may begin to stammer—widen your lips slightly, but allow another three or four seconds to elapse before deigning to speak. He will be frantic. He is no longer in control. His show is going to pieces. The audience out there may be laughing at him, thinking, "At last you've met your match, you son of a bitch." (You are the underdog. Most viewers itch to see show folk upended. Remember that. It is comforting.) Then say, for example: "Are you going to let me finish my replies to your questions, or do you care? I mean, because if you don't, why do you bother to ask?" Or, "If you choose not to believe what I tell you in answer to your questions, why should *I* bother?" Oh, he will be so grateful that you have broken silence! He is almost bound to apologize, and to gush, go right ahead, Mr. Smith, take all the time you want! Then turn deliberately and face the center stage camera. Ordinarily one should not do this: one should talk directly to the interlocutor, permitting the camera above the left shoulder to pick one up. But in this situation, swiveling in one's chair to address oneself to the other lens is a very evident act of disdain. One is ignoring the host. One is reducing him in size. One pitches one's appeal to the audience out there, the audience at large, beginning with something like, "For those of you who may be interested in answers . . ." Chances are the cameraman will zoom in on you. It is the cameraman's natural reaction. Your image then fills the screen. You continue with deliberately spoken but trenchant rebuttals, oblivious to frantic signaling about commercials, or whatever else may be pending, obliging the interlocutor to interrupt you once again, which he will now do miserably and abjectly. He will look bad, not you.

One is unlikely to fluster a pro of the caliber of Mike Wallace by this tactic. (There are by last count forty-one field producers for "60 Minutes": the chances of being interviewed by Mike Wallace, or Ed Bradley, are about on a par with drawing knaves to an inside straight twice running in a single night.) The big-time pro will know what you are up to. He will handle it. But you will have gained his respect. Watch former Secretary of Defense Caspar Weinberger; recall former White House Chief of Staff Donald Regan. They are expert at reducing interlocutors on television to pint-sized pests. They may make few friends, but TV newsfolk are wary of them. Their attitude, however, is—respecting the first—too arrogant, and—respecting the second, whose arrogance got him fired—truculent as well. When they appeal over the heads of anchors to the public, they do not win the sympathy for their positions that they would wish.

Responding to Insolences and Impertinences

When TV creatures wax not merely rude but become inexcusably personal in their questions, do not take it. Not for one moment. In a famous recent example Vice President George Bush was asked whether he had been popular in prep school. There is nothing but naked malice in such a question, which serves no legitimate journalistic purpose. The audience is at once disgusted. The only way to deal with prurience of this order is again to lapse into stony silence; and then, if thus goaded a second time, give this reply: "If you are capable of framing an intelligent question, I'll answer it."

Dignity

Maintain a healthy regard for your personal dignity, from which the correct, and comforting, attitude should follow.

You are the show. Remember that. You are doing them a favor by appearing on the program. And you are generally unpaid for it, too. Oh, sure: if one has just released an album one hopes will get on the charts, or if one has just written a book one prays publicity will help sell, there is a tradeoff. Those six minutes on "Today" or "Good Morning, America" should be a plus. Most people who appear on television, however, have nothing to sell. They are asked: because of their position, or authority, or personal experience in some tragedy— say a terrorist hijacking—or even assumed complicity in a scandal. In such circumstances (even the last) do not permit it to slip your mind that you are doing them a favor. They—the TV interviewers, the talk show hosts—are essentially nobodies, living off the fame, transient or lasting (it makes no difference to you), of others. Treat them therefore not like lackeys, but like servants very recently employed in your household. Be courteous. But be firm. Be neither unctuous nor obsequious: it is not fitting for the employer (this is your position in fact) to seek the favor of the employees. They are beholden to you, not you to them. If *you* were bid by *them* to appear on *their* show, *their show*, not *you*, would be the poorer without you, had you declined.

That is the fact of the matter ever to keep present in your mind, from which a dignified attitude on your part must be implicit. For the love of Heaven do not first-name them, and do not encourage them to first-name you. (Unless, of course, you do truly socialize with

They are *Mr.* Jennings, *Mr.* Brokaw, *Mr.* Rather. And you pointedly remind them that you are Miss/Mrs./Ms./Mr. .r, by addressing them formally and icily as Mr.-Miss-Mrs.-Ms. in return even though they may have addressed you as Sally or Peter. In fact, most anchor folk and TV talk show hosts will not err on the part of familiarity; it is their nervous, and sometimes distressingly fameglorious, guests who do this, incurring their contempt. Because next day, recall—your six minutes of celluloid fame having terminated—should you bump into them in the street, they will nod distantly at your overfamiliar greeting, and hurry on.

Fear of the Camera

People are terrified of the television camera as of an evil eye. The person who conducts himself with ease in a press conference suffers paralysis under the hot lights and claustrophobic environment of the studio. There is something forbidding and inhuman about all those cables and the moony, malevolent eye of the television camera lenses, which are like some obscene sea creature surfacing from the deep. Valenti recommends taking a small audience with one: one's wife, friends, associates. There is human contact then. But this cannot always be arranged. At our school, we are able to dissipate these fears by keeping a videotape camera trained on our conferees almost from the moment they register, and by simulating TV studio interviews. The camera finally becomes another piece of furniture, or a familiar surrogate human person with which at times to converse.

It can help to do this at home. Prop a camera on your desk or on the sink cabinet, preferably using a telephoto lens, and practice talking to it. (Draw down all shades first, else a neighbor may summon the police.) Court it. Cajole it. Convince it. Principally, get used to it. And as your confidence grows, cultivate that intimate communication with the camera at which de Gaulle in his time, and President Reagan today, are so expert. In the imperishable words of Franklin Roosevelt, we have nothing to fear but our phobophobia.

Rules Governing Relations with Print and Celluloid Journalism

Our professional consultants on these matters at the Buckley School provide conferees with rules of thumb that, as I've indicated, do not always jibe with my personal feelings about how to handle the despots of print and screen. They tell me I am grievously wrong, that it is suicidal to do combat against the Press, despite the rare exception, such as a Lieutenant Colonel Oliver North, who made hash of his tormentors in the summer of 1987 show on Capitol Hill. They make the sound point that if a gunfighter like Herb Schmertz of Mobil Oil thinks he gets away with taking on Fleet Street, his is the special case of an executive in a very large company with millions of dollars at his disposal for counter publicity. They insist also that I have formed an exaggerated opinion about the low ethics of the Press, who are no worse, they strive to convince me, than, say, the average klutz on the KGB. I growl, but I submit.

When Dealing with Merchants of the Printed Word

These are the Ten Commandments we hand out under the title "Dealing with a Potentially Hostile Press" (print journalists):

I. Be available. Return press calls promptly and never imply that your time is more valuable than the reporter's.

II. Be courteous and friendly. Don't act suspicious, or refuse to comment unnecessarily. Avoid pomposity.

III. Be brief and colorful in your language if you want to be quoted. Use plain words and avoid long-winded technical explanations.

IV. Be discreet. Never speculate or attempt answers when you are unsure of your ground. Never be afraid to say, "I don't know."

V. Be direct and straight. Journalists are generally skilled at detecting doubletalk. And if you have bad news to report, be the first to step forward with it so as to avoid the appearance of a cover-up.

VI. Be careful when you go "off the record." The reporter must agree in advance to receive information "off the record" or "not for attribution." If the reporter does agree, generally you can trust his or her ethics, but don't abuse off-the-record privileges. [They have come for news, not private elucidation.]

VII. Be witty, if you handle humor well, but never use sarcasm or wisecracks. Unless you are that rare person who is able to adopt an irreverent and pugnacious attitude inoffensively.

VIII. Be informed of your subject matter *before* you answer, collect your thoughts *before* you speak. Speak a little slower than you normally do, both as a courtesy to help the reporter who is taking notes and as a device to help you speak more carefully. [And because they are idiots: see above.]

IX. Be prepared to complain if an article appears that you feel is unfair. Complain first to the reporter, and, if that doesn't help, complain to his or her editor. Journalists are generally sensitive to complaints of unfairness. [I choke, but this is the advice we give.]

X. Be aware that you *cannot* dodge or stop a story. You can only try to influence how it is written with friendly persuasion.

Our experts—professional journalists—elaborate on these pointers, as follows:

The Press Isn't after You—The Press Is after News

[Unless you become the news, or blunder into making yourself the news.] What is newsworthy? The things people like to read and hear about. The flubs and foibles of our fallen condition. Readers are drawn to scandal, tragedy, disaster, and mayhem. They are more interested in an executive who filches floppy disks from the storeroom or bludgeons his wife to death with a tennis racquet after her tenth double fault in the country club doubles tournament than in one whose integrity is unimpeachable and never forgets his wedding anniversary. Supply and demand is operating in the news business just as everywhere else in the economy. But the press also rises to higher purposes and informs people of what they ought to know and need to know to improve their lives. A mix.

News Happens with or without You

Ducking the press, refusing to make a statement, "No comment," not returning press calls: these are all bad strategy because stories will be written anyway and your unwillingness to cooperate is likely to cause everyone (including the reader) to assume the worst possible interpretation. Your choice is not whether the story will be written. Your choice is whether you will have some impact on how it is written. "Mr. Jones's refusal to comment on charges that he beats his wife" is generally interpreted to mean that Mr. Jones beats his wife.

How to Handle Press Calls

Be available. Be friendly. Don't act as though you expect to be abused. Be as forthcoming as you are able. Don't withhold information unnecessarily. [Remember your own irritation when airlines simply refuse to tell you whether your connection is grounded on take-off, has been canceled, or has been rerouted to Nova Scotia—the answer to which they know, or can easily find out, but gratuitously keep to themselves.] Be straight (if you don't intend to answer a question, just say, "I can't say anything about that now, because I don't know, but I will get the answer to you as soon as possible.") Don't try to run around the question. Reporters have very sensitive bull— detectors, and evasions make them suspicious.

Journalists Have Ethics

Learn the differences between the two different modes of "off-the-record," the first being "not-for-attribution," which means that the newspaperman will protect your identity, though he may quote your words, and for "background only," which means to the newspaperman that you are filling him in on something he must know fully to understand the story, but that he is not in any way to write about. You cannot dictate these conditions. You cannot simply declare a remark "off-the-record." There must be an actual agreement in advance between yourself and the reporter before you make the statement—a verbal contract between you. Seldom will this be violated.

How to Make an Effective Statement

Be brief. Explain your position simply, using everyday words. Keep in mind that journalists look for short, punchy quotes that make readable copy. Excessive detail and technical explanations will be lost.

What Makes the Press Hostile?

Arrogance. Doubletalk. Refusal to return calls. A condescending attitude. The implication that your time is more important than theirs. Self-importance. Offishness. Journalists have egos too, about the size of city blocks. Give their professionalism its due. Treat them with respect. [But don't for pity's sake fawn on them.] Try never to intimate that you are easily intimidated or unsure of your position. Try not to appear nervous, which can be taken to signify that you are hiding something.

When Do You Do Battle with the Press?

Never. Because they are the ones who get to declare the winner. It's always a mistake to get into a fight with people who buy ink by the barrel, as the saying goes. But this doesn't mean you can't complain. If you get treated unfairly, talk to the writer. Tell him why you believe you were abused. If it happens again, go to the editor. Complaints work. Journalists do attempt to be fair. Fairness is a point of pride.

What Personal Style Is Most Likely to Result in a Good Press?

Journalists try to go beyond style to substance. But that's rarely possible. A winning personality always helps. Friendliness. A ready smile. A pleasant appearance and attitude. Wit and humor. These traits tend to come through, even when the press is hostile. Reagan is a good example. [Goldwater was too blunt and prickly.]

Adversarial Relationship Unavoidable

Your objective (to create a favorable image) and the reporter's objective (to produce news) are necessary, different, and at times opposed. So you should remain cautious. Don't become cocky or overconfident.

Get to Know Reporters Personally

Try to meet them socially, or at least cultivate friendly ties. Just as you are likely to do better with a bank where you have established good credit, you are apt to do better with the Press when reporters know you as a decent, credible person.

I have on occasion choked over some of these counsels, but I accept them in general.

When Dealing with the Deities of Celluloid Journalism

The Ten Commandments for avoiding crucifixion by television interviewers are:

I. Be comfortable with the camera. Think of it as a single person whom you hope to impress and make to like you.

II. Be sure to look at the interviewer when giving your answers. Just let the camera watch you and don't keep glancing at it.

III. Be steady. Keep good eye contact when the interviewer is talking. Don't drop your eyes or shift them nervously. [If you are bored by the interviewer, or by the show, conceal it. If you feel you are not going to be able to suppress a yawn, think an impure thought.]

IV. Be coherent. Speak slowly, taking care to enunciate your words properly. [Without condescending, treat the interviewer as you would a bright child: with patient affection. Often they know next to nothing about your subject, so take nothing for granted.]

V. Be friendly. Smile as frequently as possible when appropriate to the subject. [Don't smile if a leak in one of your chemical plants has just asphyxiated a few thousand people.]

VI. Be conservative in your dress. Avoid bright clothes and busy patterns. Also, avoid white clothing, which can create special problems for some cameras.

VII. Be BRIEF in your answers. Never give long, technical answers or make statements that require detailed explanations, because the statement will be used on the air without explanation. [If you are asked by the interviewer to describe the safety precautions in a nuclear energy installation, or what is meant by immanentizing the eschaton, or exactly the strategic balance of terror between the Soviet Union and the United States, politely decline unless your host or interviewer agrees to allot you five uninterrupted minutes. This he will never do.]

VIII. Be aware that you will be allowed to make only one or two short points. So: decide in advance what points you want reported and emphasize them singlemindedly.

IX. Be wary of interviewers who use silence to make you talk too much. When you have finished your answer, wait for the interviewer to speak, even if the wait is awkward. Do not rattle on to fill the silence.

X. Be unafraid to start your answer over again [if you are not on live television]. Just say, "Whoa. I got that wrong! Is it OK if I start over?"

The pros who teach our conferees how to handle themselves under klieg lights elaborate on these points as follows:

Think Visually at All Times When Dealing with Television

Think of the camera as a person watching, as an observer whose eyes are on you—and as someone you hope will like you and agree with you. You want to persuade that observer that you are trust-worthy and likable as well as knowledgeable.

At Whom Do You Look When Being Interviewed?

Always at the reporter or interviewer. Do not speak to the camera when giving answers. [You will note my exception above.] Speak to the interlocutor. And keep your gaze as steady as possible. Shifting of eyes comes across as nervousness (or worse).

[I have a bad habit of swaying from the fulcrum of my hips forward and back in my seat. This makes life difficult for the cameraman, who has to be agile with the zoom. Be vibrant, but sit still.]

How Should You Dress for TV?

In solid colors. Bright and busy patterns can vibrate. Pure white can create flashing problems for some cameras. Light blue, cream, beige or other pastel dress shirts are best. Ties should be solid or at least of a subdued stripe or pattern. Conservative, understated styling is desirable, so that the viewer is not distracted from your face or message. [No loud checks.] Brown, gray, and dark blue are good for jackets. Black is severe.

*What Techniques Can Interviewers Use to Fluster You,
and How Can You Deal with Them?*

The interviewer is generally more comfortable with the camera
than you are—and this is used to his advantage. The interviewer
assumes that you will be nervous, on edge. The best way to serve him
notice that you are not to be trifled with, therefore, and to gain the
confidence of the audience, is for you to appear perfectly at ease:
amiable, relaxed, comfortable, and calm. These traits enhance your
believability. You should smile frequently and salt your words with
humor when you can. Avoid sarcasm and wisecracks. [See comment
above.] Self-effacing humor wins over the audience. Be courteous at
all times, even under provocation, because the audience out there is
forming judgments regarding your character and person. [This
doesn't mean you have to be gnathonic.] Silence is a favorite technique of interviewers to work on your nerves and provoke you into
saying more than you intended to say. Remember that the burden
of filling in that silence is on him, not on you. [His rating is on the
line every bit as much as yours.]

The burden is on the interviewer. If you have answered a question,
yet the interviewer keeps looking expectantly at you, as though your
answer was not complete, or did not satisfy him, don't succumb to
the temptation of babbling on. Maintain your composure. Smile, and
wait him out. Or else say, "That's my answer. Do you have any other
questions?" Avoid repeating yourself, except deliberately, for emphasis.

Fast pacing of questions and interruptions of your answers with
still other questions can also be used as a technique to fluster you or
to trap you into contradicting yourself. Keep the pace of your answers slow and measured. Consider what you are about to say before
you say it. And if you are interrupted with an unrelated question,
continue your answer to the first, saying in a friendly manner, "Well,
that's a good point too, and I'll be happy to answer it. But would you
like me to finish my answer to your first question?" [Watch out for
the interviewer who reconstructs your answer in his own words,
putting a different, usually pejorative, slant on what you said. You are
a city parks manager, and there have been rapes. "Have you taken
any measures to provide for the safety of women and young girls?"
"We hire watchmen from midnight until five in the morning . . ."
"Most of these rapes took place between ten o'clock and two a.m.,

didn't they?" "Yes, but our budget . . ." "So what you're saying is that public safety takes second place to budget considerations." That sort of thing. Stop him in his tracks. Say, "Hold it. You're putting the interpretation you please on what I'm telling you. If the public is willing to pay for more nightwatchmen, providing me with the money to pay *them*, no one could be happier than I to double the force."]

Another technique is to lure you into speculating about things outside your competence. Resist the temptation. Do not opine where you have little knowledge—on matters beyond your expertise, or, if within it, on which you have insufficient information. Never be afraid to admit, "I just don't know the answer to that. The back-up alarm system failed. Just why I can't tell you. But I'll find out and let you know the moment I do." Or: "You're asking me to hypothesize about something I just don't have direct knowledge of. I don't think I should do that, do you?"

What Kind of Answers Should You Give?

Succinct. Anything you say will be edited later. Try to avoid statements that require elaborate explanations for sense to be made of them. The reporter is likely to use the broad generalization without its qualifications. [Remember Goldwater.] Use simple words in short sentences. Colorful phrases help, but always keep it snappy, especially for television news. Remember that the portion of the tape run on that evening's news program will probably be less than fifteen seconds, and usually around five seconds. [Even the Gettysburg Address wouldn't have survived the TV editors whole.] With practice, you can predict what short statement the reporter is most likely to use. He or she will be looking for a short, complete thought related to the story in which you express yourself colorfully. Decide in advance, therefore, on what you most want to be heard by the television audience: hit those one or two points hard, and couch them in imaginative language. A contradiction in terms is television and "in-depth" coverage.

Try to Be Comfortable with the Medium

It helps to perceive the camera as a single person rather than a window to millions and millions of unseen viewers. By thinking of it as a single person, you can relax and have fun with it. [This is an intimate medium.] And unless the broadcast is live (which it rarely is), you can also start over if you feel you have garbled an answer. Just stop and ask the reporter if you may do so. [He'll agree.] By yourself having interrupted the unsatisfactory answer, you will help assure that he won't be able to use that snippet of tape later on the air.

A Good Show

Recently, I happened to catch a TV interview that illustrates many of the attitudes and responses I personally prefer to anything that can be interpreted as courting favor.

The subject interested me. On the Monday evening NBC news program of 16 February 1987, Tom Brokaw ran an in-house clip about the Strategic Air Command's new B-1 bomber. Dear God, it was dreadful to watch! Here we evidently had one more military foul-up. The B-1, according to the report by NBC's Jim Miklaszewski, is unable to perform the mission it was designed for, and a rushed schedule of production has compounded the design faults, costing the taxpayer billions and billions of irrecoverably wasted dollars, and leaving U.S. defenses on this second most crucial leg of the strategic triad in perilous shape.

I groaned. When will the brass learn! Mr. Miklaszewski's documentation of these charges was impeccable—or so I assumed, retaining as I do a vestigial infantile respect for the good folk who serve the public weal in Congress. No less a legislator than Les Aspin, chairman of the House Armed Services Committee, predicted it would cost more than $3 billion to correct what was wrong with the B-1—four times the Air Force's estimate—and "that's just the tip of the iceberg." An expert witness was called to comment on the bomber's design. And oh what a dismal account he gave: "Its electronics do not work. There is not one B-1 today that has a complete, tested, full-up system on the airplane that works." Mr. Miklaszewski elaborated: "The B-1's offensive and defensive electronics jam each other, meaning the pilot can either defend himself or attack his target, but not both. The B-1 is designed to hug the ground—duck under Soviet radar. But the plane's terrain-following guidance system forces it to climb rapidly to avoid mountains that don't exist. And when fully loaded with the fuel and weapons needed to carry out its mission, the B-1 stalls under normal flying conditions."

For once I sympathized with Mr. Brokaw's expression of pained incredulousness, with which he so often silently editorializes at the conclusion of such NBC "special reports."

Next morning the Miklaszewski clip was repeated on NBC's "Today." I winced through it a second time as I watched in the bathroom mirror, while lathering my whiskers, asking myself, can the U.S. military do nothing right, ever? Bryant Gumbel then greeted General Lawrence Skantze, commander of the Air Force Systems Command. One glance at that frozen tundra of a military countenance was sufficient to prepare for the gelid responses it would issue, and for the blunders and contradictions that inevitably were going to ensue.

Mr. Gumbel went right to the grain: "By now, the question isn't if we should fix the B-1 but how much it's going to cost. The Air Force has asked for an initial 600 to 800 million to fix it, and yet Congressman Aspin, in a memo, says it could cost in excess of three billion. How do you explain this disparity?"

The camera swung to General Skantze, who wasted as little time smiling as had Bryant Gumbel getting to his attack. "Well, the information in Congressman Aspin's memo is wrong," he declared, that stiff mien imperturbable.

I had half turned away to scrape a fairway through the foam on one cheek, but these blunt words spun me right around. The good general was not a PR type, evidently. He did not attenuate his remarks by saying, as for example, "I'm afraid the information that was supplied to the distinguished Congressman is incomplete." Oh, no: he stated flatly that it was wrong—by his unwaffled assertion dealing the NBC case against the B-1 a blow that was reflected in the surprise on Nice Guy Bryant Gumbel's face.

Four more telling short sentences were tersely delivered by the general, anchoring his effect: "We signed the contract essentially with the Congress to do the program for 20.5 billion. We can still do that program for 20.5 billion. We're confident we can do it. The three billion relates to something outside that base line."

Bryant Gumbel scrambled. "Let's talk about some of the problems that exist," he said inelegantly, coming off to this listener as: now that you've smashed that point—the cost factor—let's hurry to something else. "The offensive and defensive systems that jam each other—how seriously do you regard that?"

SKANTZE: "The jamming problem is behind us now." [Implication: this is old stuff. Inference suggested to the listener: the special report by NBC's Mr. Miklaszewski is purest muckraking, its interest sensational rather than what might in fact be a military snafu endangering our defenses at outrageous cost to the public pocketbook; alternatively, Mr. Miklaszewski was misled by Congressman Aspin, who has felt obliged to run hard in a certain ideological direction since so nearly losing his job as chairman of the House Committee to a defense wimp. Continuing:] It's a matter of . . . you can have radio frequencies which interfere, but you [indistinct] radio frequencies. We know how to fix that problem."

GUMBEL [sensing an equivocation]: "You say you know how to fix it. How long before it's fixed."

SKANTZE: "It's a matter of changing software, and that's not a difficult problem."

Mr. Gumbel does not indulge in sneering at his guests; but he was clearly flushed by this man's nearly disdainful coolness. He asked sharply, "Why are you so confident it can be fixed, when it hasn't been fixed to date?"

SKANTZE: "We have started out on this program very rapidly, to put both development and production on line as quick as we could. With that sense of urgency, we went into a program where we were doing some flight testing at the same time we were doing production. Both of them are manageable, both of them are coming along, and they're moving very well."

This wasn't the most felicitous of General Skantze's statements, but it blocked that gambit for Mr. Gumbel, whose sails were now clearly luffing.

He assayed a more favorable tack: "Let's talk about the other problem that Jim Miklaszewski alluded to in this report. The terrain-following radar that sees obstacles where there are none. How major a problem do you see it?"

"That's already been fixed," came the devastating rejoinder, which General Skantze followed up on smartly: "The Chief of Staff of the Air Force flew the plane last week at two hundred feet on automatic terrain following, on range and off range. It worked fine."

Gee, thinks the listener, a three- or four-star chief of staff doesn't go risking his skin scraping ground level at supersonic speeds in a piece of equipment that's likely to imagine mountains where there are none and maybe—worse—Grand Canyons where there are none either! Mr. Gumbel was getting a little frantic, now. "What about charges [no longer incontrovertible facts] that, as flying machines, the planes lack maneuverability, they stall under normal flying conditions?"

SKANTZE: "Well, they have great maneuverability and they don't stall, and I think if you talk to . . ."

GUMBEL: "You're saying they don't stall and yet you are in the process of developing a stall inhibitor."

SKANTZE [utterly unfazed, terminating what he was interrupted in saying]: "I think if you talk to the professionals who fly them, you'd find the planes fly very well and have lots of maneuverability. [Having planted this compelling point in the minds of the audience, addressing himself to Mr. Gumbel's insinuation:] To get the last few bits of capability out of the airplane, to take some of the workload off the pilot, we're going to put a stall inhibiting system in. But that airplane is not in a situation where it's going to be stalling around the air, and I don't know where the data comes from."

Bryant Gumbel flashed, here. The general had made him plenty hot under the collar. The brassballed s.o.b. had reversed roles. Now it was as though *his*—Bryant Gumbel's, the network's—integrity and veracity were being challenged, whereas the proper format, as everybody in the business knows, is for the guest to play the supine victim in an auto-da-fe. "It's [the data] coming from experts in the field," he said, "like Mr. Evans, there."

He referred to a third party featured by NBC as an authority on the B-1, one other detractor of the bomber. General Skantze stared, as it seemed, straight through the camera into the gentleman Bryant Gumbel called to witness, declaring: "Mr. Evans is not an expert. He's a retired Marine Lieutenant Colonel. He wrote an article in the *Washington Post.*"

Was there ever a more deflating put-down?—he wrote an article. A mere scribble. A guy—probably a malcontent—who never even made full bird.

GUMBEL: "I saw the article."

SKANTZE [brilliantly briefed; he too had read the piece, and knew just how to characterize it]: "Totally a diatribe on the program. I think he's more concerned about manned bombers than the B-1, per se. The [indistinct] B-1 B [first currently operational production model?] is on alert at [indistinct] Air Force Base. It is capable of doing its mission. It is capable of penetrating the Soviet Union, and we could put twenty-five airplanes on alert tomorrow if a crisis develops."

GUMBEL: "You keep talking about its capability. Was it not designed as a low-level bomber designed to penetrate Soviet air space and successfully complete the mission?"

SKANTZE: "That's exactly . . ."

GUMBEL: "Can it do that?"

SKANTZE: "It can do that today."

GUMBEL: "It can do that today despite the fact that the system's offensive and defensive counteract each other?"

SKANTZE [speaking as to a slightly wayward amateur, yet avoiding condescension through his scrupulously controlled tone]: "What you have to understand, Mr. Gumbel, is that when you lay down a mission for a B-1 B, and you lay out that penetration route, and you do that analysis, you take into account the B-1 B as it is today. It has an excellent offensive capability, and based on that analysis, there isn't any question in our minds the B-1 B today can penetrate against the threat it faces."

Mr. Gumbel had also done his homework, countering to this not altogether intelligible statement: "But those ECMs, those electronic countermeasure systems, those EMCs, I'm sorry, countermeasure systems—are they not outdated, as they exist right now?"

SKANTZE: "We have a capability on board today which isn't matched by anything else in the world."

GUMBEL [sharply, almost rudely]: "I didn't ask you that. Are they not outdated as they exist right now?"

SKANTZE: "No, they're not outdated. There're pieces of 'em that've gotta be refined. The point you've got to remember is we run a flight test program. A test program is designed to take the very good design and find out where the bugs are and fix them. That's what we're doing in the test program. That's not unusual. It's been done in every test program on every airplane we've ever had."

Bryant Gumbel was getting a bit desperate at this point: "But in retrospect [no longer was this a scandal that should have been foreseen and avoided], you've made the job much more difficult by doing production and development concurrently."

General Skantze had his interlocutor. The tempo of his speech pattern accelerated just perceptibly, the slightest tinge of passion audible in his deliberate voice: "Yes. But let me remind you that when President Carter was in office, the Congress in 1980, under

President Carter, wrote an authorization bill that directed the secretary of defense to develop a new bomber for multi-role, conventional and nuclear, and do it as rapidly as we could and have it on line before 1987. So before President Reagan ever came into office, the Congress of the United States [of which Les Aspin was a voting member] set the sense of urgency to do this program as rapidly as we could. And [addressing himself to the audience] a lot of people don't understand that, and that's a fact."

Bryant Gumbel was not quitting quite yet. "But then, having foreseen these problems, they [the Congress] tried to back off and reoutfit the B-52s for less of a cost, because it could've been a stationary weapons firing system, which is what some would say your bomber has become today."

This statement, apart from being syntactically confused, signaling Mr. Gumbel's loss of control of the interview, insinuates a disingenuous point. General Skantze—whose composed professionalism had by now fairly won over the audience, I assume—declined to be put off stride. "No," he said firmly, "that's incorrect," he stated flatly: "The B-52 has gone through a series of updates, even before the B-1 was brought on line. We have continuously updated the B-52 bomber force. We would do that independent of whatever we did for B-1 or any other bomber."

So much for the tongue-tied Neanderthal military stereotype. And so much for the special NBC report by Jim Miklaszewski. General Skantze had turned the tables: he was no longer defensively vindicating the Air Force; he was exposing the shallow and inaccurate investigative habits by a major network. Bryant Gumbel was reduced to truculence: "One [final?] note, General. You have complained loud and long about the media's fairness in reporting on the B-1. And yet, the Air Force has put endless obstacles in the media's effort to get the true story of the B-1. Why?"

SKANTZE [gimlet-eyed]: "What are the endless obstacles?"

GUMBEL: "Refusal of requests to shoot it in operation. Refusal of requests to talk to those operational people who've flown them. Refusal of requests for anybody to speak on it with the exception of one general at Wright-Patterson Air Force Base. Those obstacles."

Alas, the general did not recognize them as such: "Well, I think, there is no refusal on the part of the Air Force to expose the media to the people who operate this airplane. General [indistinct], who is the Commander in Chief of SAC, has spoken out on it. He's available to people who want to talk to him about the system. The reason we had General Thurman at ASD and the Chief do it in the Pentagon is ya don't need more than several spokesmen. But, there is no refusal on the part of the Air Force to talk about this bomber, and [in those final seconds neatly coming back to, and reminding the audience of, his strongest point—a veiled challenge hurling Mr. Gumbel's accusation back in his teeth, and calling into question the sincerity of the whole NBC report] you talk to the crews who are the professionals who fly it, and it's one hell of an airplane."

That ended the interview. Bryant Gumbel cracked with feeble jocularity, "The Air Force has had its say. General Skantze, thank you." To which the general replied with laconic courtesy, "Appreciate it very much," to the last courting no favor, asking no quarter.

This is not to signify that I am now swung over to the Air Force's side of the B-1 controversy by General Skantze's able handling of Bryant Gumbel. The general's several flat assertions are subject to investigation and verification; but he did do a remarkable job in taking the wind out of the sails of critics of the program, at least temporarily, and under heavy professional pressure. In jeopardy were both the reputation of a major U.S. defensive weapon, and thus popular support and funding for it, and the general's personal standing among his peers. By his unshakable composure he demolished the millions-strong TV audience's uncritical trust in NBC reporter Miklaszewski's investigation of the matter, casting such critics of the program as Congressman Aspin in a questionable light. He accomplished this though eschewing any attempt to fawn on his tormentor (Bryant Gumbel is simply too genial a human being to discharge this role, which would suit a Ted Koppel of ABC better), with nary the ghost of a smile, and with no dissonant attempt at levity. He played his appointed role as a soldier. He was straightforward, blunt, tenacious, cool, master of the facts, disdainful where he had a right to be, and very, very adroit.

Of course, all these sterling personal qualities and clever tactics are worth not two cents when a show is to be taped, not run live. One is then truly at the mercy of the networks. The safest way to deal with the Press is never to deal with it. The best way of foiling Mike Wallace is never to appear on his show. Assign a subordinate. (Coward.)

Appendix I

Recommended Source and Reference Books

Public Speaking

Principles of Public Speaking

Raymond G. Smith's *Principles of Public Speaking,* (The Ronald Company, 1958).
Paul L. Soper's *Basic Public Speaking,* 3rd ed. (Oxford University Press, 1968).
Jack Valenti's *Speak up with Confidence* (William Morrow & Co., 1982).

The Art of Argumentation

Max Black's *Critical Thinking* (Prentice-Hall, 1946).
Michael A. Gilbert's *How to Win an Argument* (McGraw-Hill, 1979).
William O. Rusher's *How to Win Arguments—More Often Than Not* (University Press of America, 1985).

Dealings with the Press

Herb Schmertz's *Good-bye to the Low Profile—The Art of Creative Confrontation* (Little, Brown and Co., 1986).

Grammar and English Usage

Dictionaries

Words Most Often Misspelled and Mispronounced by Ruth Gleeson Gallagher and James Colvin (Pocketbooks, 1972: a concise paperback that is absolutely essential).
The New York Times' Everyday Reader's Dictionary of Misunderstood, Misused, Mispronounced Words (Weathervane, 1972: also essential).
Webster's Ninth New Collegiate Dictionary (1983).
Webster's New International Dictionary (get the 2nd ed., 1957, if you can).

American Heritage Dictionary, Safire's *Political Dictionary* (Random House, 1978), *Oxford Dictionary of Quotations* (1974).
Everyman's Dictionary of Shakespeare Quotations (Dent & Dutton, 1953).
A Dictionary of Euphemisms and Other Doubletalk (Crown, 1981).
The Quintessential Dictionary (Hart, 1978: rare, out of print, wonderful).
O Thou Improper, Thou Uncommon Noun (Potter, 1978: great fun).
The Glass Harmonica (Macmillan, 1967: ditto). *A Dictionary of Symbols* (Philosophical Library, 1983).
Dictionary of Word Origins (Philosophical Library, 1985). Adrian Room's *Dictionary of Confusibles* (Routledge & Kegan Paul, 1979).

Literary References

Bartlett's Familiar Quotations.
Oxford Dictionary of Quotations.
Granger's *Index to Poetry and Recitations.*
Home Book of Quotations.
Brewer's *Dictionary of Phrase and Fable* (Harper & Row, 1970).
Hoyt's New Cyclopedia of Practical Quotations (for a wider range of popular passages and phrases).
The Oxford Dictionary of Quotations.
Dictionary of Foreign Terms (Crowell, 1975).

Authorities on English Usage

Wilson Follett's *Modern American Usage* (Hill & Wang, 1966).
Fowler's *Modern English Usage,* as revised by Sir Ernest Gowers (Oxford University Press, 1963: paperback ed. 1983).
Gowers' *Plain Words, Their ABC* (Knopf, 1954).
William Strunk's *Elements of Style,* as edited by E. B. White (Macmillan, 1959).
James J. Kilpatrick's *Writer's Art* (Andrews, McMeek & Parker, 1984).

Appendix II

Terms and Word Usage

Rhetorical Terms

Allusion: An indirect reference, a hint, reference to something by passing mention.

You are operating under an illusion if you believe that one out of five of your classical allusions will be understood by today's ill-educated audiences.

Enthymeme: An argument in which one of the propositions, usually a premise, is understood but not stated.

We are dependent; therefore we should be humble.

Epiphonema: An exclamatory sentence, or striking reflection, which concludes a passage. Webster, 2nd ed. (Good epiphonemae are hard to come by.)

Eristic: The noun refers to a philosopher of the Eristic school. It means disputatious or controversial argument, arguing for the hell, or sake, of it. The adjective derives from this, as in "The court of eristic logic." Plato was against teaching young men under thirty the "dear delight" of dialectics for fear they would use it to argue for eristic pleasure.

Eurythmics: The art of harmonious and expressive bodily movements; as in dance; as in acting; as in public speaking.

Exordium: The introductory part of a discourse or composition. It is said that the length of an alligator can be estimated from multiplying by fourteen the length of its head.

Heuristic: Arguments and methods of demonstration that are persuasive rather than logically compelling, or which lead a person to find out for himself.

Hyperbole*: An overstatement or exaggeration. The horse can run like lightning.
He was more powerful than a bulldozer.
Jane was dead drunk.

Litotes*: (ly'-toh-teez) An understatement made to increase the effect.

GM still has a small part of the car market.
Honesty isn't impossible, even for you.
She is a student of no mean ability.

Metaphor*: A compressed simile; the *like* or *as* are omitted.

The waterlilies were ivory stars.
The red squirrel was a ribbon of fire.
Henry was the fashion plate of his town.

Metonymy*: When a cause is used for an effect, or an effect for a cause, or a sign for the thing signified, or the container for the thing contained.

He traveled by water to Hawaii.
The cowboy reached for his shooting iron.
Have you ever read Shakespeare?

Oxymoron: A combination for epigrammatic effect of contradictory or incongruous words.

cruel kindness
industrious idleness
Riunite wine

Paralipsis: A passing over with brief mention so as to emphasize the suggestiveness of what is omitted.

I come to bury Caesar, not to praise him.
I confine to this page the volume of his treacheries and debaucheries.

Parrhesia: *boldness or freedom of speech.* As in guts for intestines, sweat for perspiration, asshole for dunce. Be careful!

Peroration: The concluding part of a discourse. That portion of a discourse for which audiences are most grateful.

Simile*: A comparison of two unlike things, introduced by *like* or *as*.

He wriggled like a worm when accused.
The pussywillows are like silver mice.
Eating is to weight as reading is to judgment.

Sorites: An abridged form of stating a series of syllogisms in a series of propositions so arranged that the predicate of each one that

Principles of Public Speaking, by Raymond G. Smith.

precedes forms the subject of each one that follows, and the conclusion unites the subject of the first proposition with the predicate of the last proposition.

The soul is a thinking agent;
A thinking agent cannot be severed into parts;
That which cannot be severed cannot be destroyed;
Therefore, the soul cannot be destroyed.

—Webster, 2nd ed.

From a tile by Mensaque Rodríguez y Casa, of Seville:

El que bebe se emborracha
El que se emborracha duerme
El que duerme no peca
El que no peca va al cielo
Bebamos para que al cielo vayamos!

The pedestrian translation:

He who drinks gets drunk
He who gets drunk sleeps
He who sleeps sins not
He who sins not goes to Heaven
Let us therefore drink that to Paradise we may go!

Synecdoche*: (sin-ek'-duh-kee) When a part is used to represent the whole, or the whole a part, or a species a genus, or vice versa.

That freshman is a real brain.
What a beast he is.
The red nose staggered out of the tavern.

Words Commonly Confused

Acidulous/Sedulous: The first means slightly sour; the second means diligent, or persevering. Sedulous is not to be confused with solicitous. One is solicitous about the health of one's spouse, sedulous in one's attention to one's business. In the interest of one's own health. See *assiduous,* below.

Addled/Muddled: Addle once had the sense of putrid, as in a rotten egg, in that the addled egg has lost the power of development. It has therefore become fruitless, empty: which brings us to the contemporary meaning of the word, which is unsound, or confused, or even, yes, muddled, as in addlebrained. Muddle is to make turbid, or muddy; to confuse, or stupefy; to cloud, or fog, as in the brain; to render stupid with liquor; to make a mess of. Addle empties a thing of goodness or meaning, muddle invades good sense or sound action with its turbidity.

Admission/Admittance: Admission carries first the sense of admission in, say, guilt, then of permission or right of entrance into a place or society, which edges over into admittance. Admittance can denote admission, but one properly gains admittance to a place or royal presence, not admission to same, and one gives admittance—entry—to a state of mind, such as fear or happiness, not admission. Webster: "In present usage *admittance* is mostly confined to the literal sense of allowing one to enter a locality or buildings. . . . *Admission* has acquired the figurative sense of admitting to rights [and] privileges. . . . When entrance into a building or a locality carries with it certain privileges, admission rather than admittance is used. . . .

Adverse to/Averse to: Think of adversity when adverse pops into contention: serious business. A man who is struck by adversity has at least lost his spouse, his job, and his fitness club *admission* (see above) card (without which he cannot gain *admittance*). That same man may be averse to Mel Brooks films, yogurt, and regimental ties.

Alternately/Alternatively: People take turns when they do things alternately; when they do things alternatively, they are making a choice, usually one of two courses of action, propositions, etc. One visits one's favorite singles bar on alternate days of the week; one weighs the alternative whether to continue being such an ass (as to frequent a singles bar) or not.

Asseverate/Assert: To assert is to affirm or declare with confidence; to asseverate is also to affirm or aver positively or earnestly, but when one uses this ugly word to describe the position maintained by another, of which one does not approve, a connotation of falseness is implied. When a body is said to assert something, he may be proved mistaken, but there is no implication that he was being false, devious, or insincere. When a body is held to asseverate, he is tinged with pomposity, and the implication is that his confidence is braggadocio.

Assiduous/Sedulous: One of the synonyms given for assiduous is sedulous, but there is an obsequiousness about the first word that is happily absent in the second. When one is assiduous, one is brown-nosing, or groveling. It is beneath dignity. Solicitous is also given as a synonym, but one would like to be solicitous of one's spouse, not assiduously so.

Beautiful/Beauteous: The latter is technically defined as fraught with beauty, especially sensous beauty, and this is its true meaning; but the word has come to carry a sarcastic connotation, because it has come to be considered an overly fancy, Romantic poet's term. Beauteous in today's usage may be far from a compliment.

Donkey/Ass: The donkey is an ass. He/she is a stupid or obstinate fellow/gal. An ass can be the female of the species *Equus asinus;* and an ass is also a stupid person, a dolt. In current usage, however, an ass is dumber than a donkey, more perversely a jerk and stubbornly stupid.

Dominating/Domineering: The first is to rule, to predominate over, to control; the second is to rule tyrannically, imperiously, insolently, overbearingly.

Factual/Factitious: Factual is after the fact of the matter; factitious is "engineered" evidence, with a sense of being trumped up. It is not naturally or spontaneously created, but it is not for those reasons necessarily not genuine. Factitious is often confused with:

Fictitious: which as far as evidence or reality go means totally phony: sham, counterfeit, unreal. Remember, factitious evidence may be genuine, fictitious evidence never.

Infer/Imply: They are in the wrong order here; one infers *from* an implication.

Liable/Likely: In connection with liable, think of liability; in connection with likely, think of likelihood. One is likely to enjoy the circus; one is liable to break one's neck if one tries to emulate the high wire act off one's backyard clothes line.

Meritorious/Meretricious: There is *merit* in meritorious; there's *mere* only in meretricious—close, but no cigar. Meretricious is a sham—it even sounds like one, a made up word posing as the real thing. Would you be surprised to learn that it derives from the Latin *meretricius,* through the French *meretrix, -icis,* a prostitute, literally, one who earns money? Of course not. Hence its first meaning: of, pertaining to, characteristic of, or being, a prostitute; having to do with harlots; as, *meretricious* traffic. From which the second meaning: alluring by false show; gaudily and deceitfully ornamental; tawdry; as, *meretricious* dress, style, composition.

Militate/Mitigate: When there are circumstances mitigating an offense, they serve to extenuate it, they lessen it. The word derives from *mitigatus,* the past participle of *mitigare,* which is to soften. Think of military in connection with militate (the word derives from *militare, militatum,* to be a soldier: its first listed meaning in Webster is in fact that: to serve as a soldier, to engage in warfare—though this has fallen into disuse). One is on the march. One militates *against* something (rarely *for* something).

Official/Officious: An official is a generally detestable creature who is more than likely officious—a busybody. He may send out official orders that are interpreted by citizens as being officious intrusions into their private lives. We have given officious a bum rap in current usage, intending it almost exclusively as meddlesome. Its first dictionary sense, however, remains the obsolete "disposed or eager to serve or do kind offices; kind; obliging . . ." It is in the second sense that word gets tarred: "Volunteering, or disposed to volunteer, one's services where they are neither asked for nor needed." One feels sorry for officious.

Referee/Umpire: From Webster: c. A person appointed to decide any issue or question; an umpire, as in certain games or sports; sometimes, specif., a judge of certain points of play, as, in American football, an official whose decision is final in all matters under dispute, *but who is esp. the judge of matters connected with the progress of the ball, as distinguished from the* umpire, *who is, in general, judge of the acts of the players.* (Emphasis added.)

Transpire: The real meaning of this word is self-evident from the text, but Sir Ernest Gowers in his *Plain Words, Their ABC* has the most concise definition: "It is a common error to use transpire as [though] [tsk tsk, Sir Ernest: he used *if!*] it meant *happen or occur*. It does not. It means *to become known*."

Turgid/Turbid: I go to Kilpatrick for this one. "*Turbid* means muddy, opaque, unclear. Gobbledegook is turbid stuff. *Turgid* means swollen, pompous, overly resplendent. [Former] Sportscaster Howard Cosell in full flight is often *turgid*. He's often amusing too."

For other confusing words and usages, of which there are plenty, refer especially to the recommended books by Sir Ernest Gowers, William Strunk, Jr. (E. B. White), and James J. Kilpatrick.

Appendix III

The Buckley/Lerner Debate Format

The Stage

A. Two lecterns are required, one stage left, the other stage right.

    1. Opening and closing statements are delivered from these lecterns.
    2. The lecterns should be provided with good light.

B. A long table should be placed between the two lecterns (or two shorter tables), with a mike on either end.

    1. The periods of "Cross-Examination" and "Questions and Answers from the Floor" are conducted from this table.
    2. The moderator sits at a chair in the center of this table. (In the case of two small tables, the moderator sits in a large heavy armchair center stage, to the rear.)

Essential Personae

A forceful moderator must be chosen. He should explain at the beginning of the program what form it will take. He should subsequently announce each segment of the program: viz., "We will now begin the cross-examination between Mr. X and Mr. Y, and Mr. Y will ask the first question." The moderator must make every effort to discipline the debaters and help them with their time limits. This is especially important during cross-examination and question and answer periods.

A timekeeper with large time cards is absolutely necessary. He should be seated prominently in front of the debaters, facing them, front row center of the auditorium. His time cards should show 10' (to go), 5', 3', 2', 1', 30", STOP!!!!! When he raises the STOP card he should stand up, holding it aloft and high. The moderator should point out to the audience beforehand that when this happens the speaker is permitted to wind down his sentence, without excessive use of the relative clause. (At a signal from the moderator, the timekeeper should turn his back to the speaker and face the audience with the raised STOP card, indicating that the speaker is abusing the latitude to finish off a thought.)

The Sixty-Minute Debate

A. Opening Statements: 30'

    Affirmative: 15'
    Negative: 15'

B. Cross-Examination: 10'

    The cross-examination begins with the Affirmative and ends with the Negative. It consumes 8' to 10', at the moderator's discretion, during which the contestants toss curve balls at each other. Each has a total of 90", in the course of which, ideally, the first 30" are used to rebut some point made by the opponent, 30" are used to advance the argument, and the final 30" are used to pin the opponent to the wall with another question. A fast pace is of first importance. This calls for the moderator to exert his authority.

C. Questions and Answers from the Floor: 10'

    The moderator fields all questions from the floor. He may run this segment of the debate, which is generally quite spirited when following the cross-examination, from 8' to 10'.

    1. The moderator must insist that these questions be limited to 20" or less.
    2. Each debater may take 90" to answer a question.
    3. Questions may be addressed to either debater, or to both. (If a question is directed to both debaters, each may take 60" to answer.)

D. Summations: 10'

    Negative: 5'
    Affirmative: 5'

The Ninety-Minute Debate

It has been our experience that the 90' debate is much the better program.

A. Opening Statements: 40'

    Affirmative: 20'
    Negative: 20'

B. Cross-Examination: 20'

C. Questions and Answers from the Floor: 20'

D. Summations: 10'

      Negative: 5'
      Affirmative: 5'

Appendix IV

Three Myers-Briggs Personality Types

Hail Fella, Well Met!

This fellow is forty-five years old and a successful executive, who may have founded his own real estate development company. He is worth two million dollars. He is a big, booming, macho-type (he hunts ducks and uses irons only playing golf), he is a joiner of all sorts of clubs, and he enthusiastically chairs the annual Boy Scouts "Elder Pathfinders Last Campsite" Retirement Home appeal.

He is married to a florid, blonde, bosomy mate of two score years (the duration of their marriage, not her age) (she is a closet drinker, but that's beside the point), and they have three children, two strapping sons who are the image of their daddy, and a brainy, beautiful daughter who is the image of her mother (when her mother could be said to possess any image of her own, having over the years become a kind of female extension of her spouse). The whole family attends church every Sunday, sitting at a pew he fully paid for ten years before he was able to tear up the mortgage on his first house. They play tennis. They jog. They vote whatever can be identified as the moderate ballot. They chew granola. They subscribe to the *New Yorker* and, daringly, the *Village Voice,* and they are in innumerable other ways obnoxiously *comme il faut.*

If one identifies with this character type; or if one's physique, looks, and platform attitude correspond to this type; or if the audience perceives of one as hewing to this type; herewith (1) the strengths, (2) the weaknesses, and (3) what one should work on.

Strengths

This man (or his female equivalent) steps up smartly to the platform and takes command of the lectern with confidence and some polish. Assumes good stance, good posture, shoulders thrown back slightly, head thrown back from the fulcrum of the neck, and chin raised slightly above the plane of the audience's heads. He is the personification of an American Success story, which consciousness radiates from him to the audience. Opens with a pleasant, often cheery, smile, and exudes the impression of being supremely assured that the audience will be interested in what he has to say. The voice is strong and clear; square molars crack his jokes right to the kernel. If he wears glasses, especially bifocals, he tends to peer out at the audience through the lower halves of the lenses. His eye contact is generally as warm and personal as his virile handclasp. It does not occur to him that an audience will find serious difficulty with whatever opinions he expresses, which lends to his pitches a plausibility greater than is perhaps merited, but he steps down from the platform almost invariably satisfied that he has instilled into the audience a packet of good sense for which they are properly grateful.

Weaknesses

This character type tends to assume too much on his (or her) public standing. Audiences are not necessarily hostile, but almost all sit there waiting to be shown. There will be people who are not impressed and not charmed, who react antagonistically to anyone so sure of himself. A certain arrogance—maybe not real, maybe imaginary on the part of the audience—is conveyed, which is reenforced by that strong confident voice, by the (slightly condescending? slightly insincere?) smile, by the hearty jokes and manner. The speaker tends to self-satisfaction, and to be enamored of his platform self, talking too long or belaboring obvious points. He speaks in a single (loud) key that becomes a kind of high-decibel monotone. His C.-of-C. optimism wears, and finally the pith of what he is saying gets lost. Upon reflection, audiences conclude: the speaker is not altogether to be trusted, the speaker is platitudinous, the speaker is a bore, the speaker condescends, the speaker is superficial, the speaker is running for some office.

Deficiencies and Opportunities

This character or personality type should watch out for the big hype impression. His success as an executive or professional in a given career field, he must ever keep in mind, does not necessarily translate to other matters. He must climb right down from the high horse. He comes across too big. He may be used to getting his way, and having other people harken respectfully to the least indication of his will, but on the platform he must tone down the absolute trust in his own judgment that serves him so well in his business, must temper his forcefulness, must compel himself to do some hard thinking not only in the preparation of his speech but on the floor itself, in order to eliminate the glabrous impression. He must be careful to arrange the content of his speech so that he builds evidently (to the audience) from lesser points to points of greater importance and significance, seeking (either from the resources of his own mind, or from reading and carefully pondering the words of eminent thinkers on the subject of his address) the unusual perception or original insight with which to climax his address. (This will surprise the audience, even unto murmuring among themselves: hey, this guy is a lot deeper than we woulda believed!)

This speaker need not fear that he lacks stage presence, nor that his voice may suffer for conviction. He should turn his attention to moderating tone and attitude, keeping careful watch against any trace of condescension or arrogance. He must never make the mistake of attempting to play Hamlet on the stage: this interiorly inquiring attitude will not suit him. On the other hand, he should check himself from assuming that whatever he says is self-evidently correct. If he is good at humor, that which is self-deprecating becomes him.

The Sensitive Neurotic

This woman is thirty-five years old and looks as though she just lost her job, her lover, her husband, her car keys, her Tums, and her Bi-Lo Charjit-Card all at one fell swoop. A body might imagine of her that were she one-handed she would shut the door of her car on the good hand in the parking lot of a Los Angeles shopping center the morning of New Year's Day. Her presence reeks of the impression of desperately desiring some hole into which to crawl and hide. She is plain. (Her male counterpart continues to erupt in adolescent spots.) She is too young to show the symptoms of osteoporosis, but she stoops terribly just the same, hunching her narrow shoulders toward each other, not because she is big-breasted (she is the reverse), but because she feels she deserves to be deprecated, insulted, or actually struck by any total stranger, and is almost certain that she will be. (Her male counterpart is pigeon-breasted, also narrow-shouldered, prematurely balding, prone to dandruff, and habitually wears a worried frown, regarding the other males in the office with trepidation when not fear.)

She possesses a laser-sharp mind, but one would never know it, anxiety having seated on her features and possessed her psyche with such force of habit that she can actually seem retarded, her replies to simple questions come so hesitantly, so apologetically, and are so slow in issuing forth. She is miserably conscious that she provokes the greatest impatience in her contacts with fellow human beings, a kind of pitying contempt from men who can boast one quarter her perceptions, merciless contempt from good-looking women with a quarter her brains. By dint of midnight labor she has risen in her company to Board status—not as a manager, needless to say, but in a consultant capacity; her written reports are as though drafted by another person, but she is mortified by her ineptitude in phrasing what she wants to say, or articulating and defending her point of view, and when she opens her mouth no one can find the experience more painful than she.

Strengths

From a forensic point of view, this person (along with her male equivalent) is a hard case. This speaker must concentrate on content, relying upon the intelligence of what she has to say to carry her. Mind is her principal strength. From it she must develop a platform personality that with practice grows in confidence.

There is something else for her to exploit, if she can bring herself to do it:

the sensitivity to suffering that her intimate personal experience potentially has taught her. Not every shy, sensitive, introverted person learns to extrapolate from his or her experience with suffering: major effort must be bent on eliminating morbidity, and thus the cocoon-prison of total engrossment with self, which can prevent anyone from profiting from one's experience. This person must cultivate both qualities, keen intelligence and tender feeling: speaking humbly to the audience out of her own awareness of inadequacy, but very directly to each individual in that audience, conveying in the most intimate fashion her personal distress, or commitment, which will mitigate that perception of inadequacy (in herself as well as respecting others) and enlist the audience's sympathy; complementing that fine sensibility with the superior intellectual faculties of her mind, subjecting her arguments to its critique, so that the content of her speech is flensed of any trace of sentimentality.

Weaknesses

Oh, they are legion! Her posture on the platform will be dreadful. She will stoop. She will clutch the lectern as the capsized sailor clutches an orange crate. Her voice will be tremulous, falling sometimes to a whisper, with many glottal stops. Her eyeballs will jump about like Mexican beans in a heated pan, never fastening on anyone, her gaze fleeing to the rafters. Her expression of purest misery will incite in the mercifully-minded the desire actually to put her out of it—to commit on her some kind of forensic euthanasia, maybe by pulling the plug out of the public address system, or shorting the lights—and in the sadistically inclined the desire to crush her like a bug. Any statement she makes will invite contradiction; not even hard facts, tumbling from her lips, will command the conviction of their indubitable existence. (Her attitude invites these responses, understand.) She will flounder desperately through her talk, not so much terminating as, at the end, or what passes for an end, collapsing. Yet would she be a public speaker!

Deficiencies and Opportunities

To put it mildly, this lady (or gent) needs help, and some of it may have to be sought from a psychologist, depending on how profoundly rooted the trauma has become. Saving that recourse, some elementary steps can be taken. This person must make the conscious effort to cultivate her (or his) confidence by first cultivating both the attitudes of, and a real basis for, confidence. She must (shades of Dale Carnegie!) train herself to wake up in the morning and think, God-damnit to Hell, I *am* Somebody, and that Somebody I am ain't half bad! She isn't deceiving herself, remember. She has a basis: that good mind. She has to earn for it the respect it deserves by herself according it respect. Her market analyses are pretty good, after all—if she says so herself. Didn't she first spot the weakness in the sales potential of that new skin lotion, though she got no credit for it? Even though somehow she was unable to argue successfully for a scentless soap at the last meeting of the market research staff, did not her written analysis of trends clearly call attention to this unexploited niche?—that ass Joe Ferguson putting her down, ridiculing her arguments as though they were without foundation, which somehow they came out sounding when she articulated them, becoming (as usual!) flustered, though in their written form they were closely reasoned. Damnit, her analyses stood on their own. Upper management did recognize that, as her private file of letters of appreciation attested, though somehow the writers of those warm testimonies never offered to take her out to lunch, not even once. (She kept the letters in a manila folder at her Ninety-seventh Street apartment, tucked under the Yellow Pages tome of the Manhattan telephone directory; when she was feeling a little weepy, she embarrassed herself by pulling it out, poring over the contents.)

Her written professional work stood on its merits. And if this was so, why, the content of her speeches should be—easily ought to be—just as impeccably researched and cogently constructed, so what was there for her to fear about them? She need not be embarrassed by the content of her speech, by what she had to say and how, on paper, she said it. She simply had to keep in mind when rehearsing a talk that she should ruthlessly strike out the niggling little qualifications of fearful humility that creep in, instead trusting in the cogency of her thesis and expounding her arguments in a sequence of unflinching declarative sentences. Her written texts could stand on their own, could they not? Of course. Well, so can she stand on her own two feet! The same intelligence for which she need apologize to no one was the architect, and the same intuitions, deriving from her extreme sensitivity, acted on the arguments to illuminate them.

Come to think of it, that sensitivity of hers is an asset. It need not embarrass her, and she need not apologize for it. She brings perception to the evidence she derives from statistical tables. What did that old rascal Montaigne have to say about this? "In truth, knowledge is not so absolutely necessary as judgment; the last may make shift without the other, but the other never without this." Sure: she possesses a gift that in itself is of rare value.

This is the way for a person of such a character type to go, building on active and latent strengths. She must never try to emulate Mr. Hail Fella, Well Met. She will never be naturally so smooth, nor naturally so self-assured. The traces of tentativeness and hesitancy may never desert her; she may never contain her blushes, nor master her shyness, nor fully conquer her suspicions of personal inadequacy, but she can profitably raise her self-esteem by recognizing what is truly estimable about herself, and her humility can be tremendously attractive to audiences, at once bringing them over on her side. Few such personalities—admittedly, not without a lot of help—are going to make it this far; but if this woman is able to convince her psyche (remember: she is not deceiving herself) of the objective reality of her strengths, then it is less difficult for her to extrapolate from her confidence in the written text to the "speaking situation." She will find it easier always, true, to bang out a confident text (thanks to that good mind) than to acquire the ability of self-confidently delivering that text, but the first itself will nonetheless aid her cultivate the second. As her proficiency in the written argument increases, so will her self-esteem, helping her take courage in the delivery.

Mental attitude necessarily comes first, but it can be reenforced by such physical matters as posture. To enhance her new frame of mind this character type must also practice before the mirror throwing her shoulders back, standing as tall as God gave her the inches, lifting her chin, and—thick and smeared though her trifocals be—forcefully gazing out on the (imagined) audience. A woman especially is advised to consult specialists in such matters as the most becoming hair style, make-up, and clothes; but let not the male of this personality type neglect consultations in this order. The right clothes, a new hair style (for the male maybe a toupee) can do wonders for the appearance and for inner serenity.

Attention must also be paid to the ring and clarity of the voice, using a tape recorder. She is now fully conscious that what she has to say is worthy of being heard; she must concentrate on doing her text justice by articulating the sentences in a fashion as lucidly clear as their sense. The lectern must no longer be something to clutch for survival, or to hide behind: it is her— this is the attitude she has to cultivate—bully pulpit. She deserves to occupy the lectern, possessing it as her own for twenty, thirty, forty minutes, because she by God has something worthwhile to say, and is standing there by right of merit. She therefore steps up to it familiarly, takes possession of it by tranquilly (she is never going to be *that* tranquil) placing her text on its surface and maybe adjusting its tilt or height, takes a half step back from it, drops her hands to her sides, comes to an easy, erect stance, and . . . we trust she will begin, not collapse in an epileptic seizure. (Nothing, Dale, in this valley of pain, is dead sure.)

Eeyore

Audiences dread this sad creature. He is the doleful, mournful soul, who climbs on the stage with weary step and shambles to the lectern with hands hanging lassitudinously from the wrists, shoulders slumped, eyes downcast. He is forty years old. He is dressed in black. If he were a she (as plenty are), never would some Spanish gallant say of her, "Who has died in Paradise, that the Virgin goes dressed in mourning?" Maybe he is an accountant on the staff of the Long Island Railroad. He is not an undertaker, because they are a cheerier breed. (Actually, he is a physicist.) Is that a text he is extracting from his jacket's inside breast pocket? Oh, how it seems to weigh in his hand; oh, what a weight he lays on the lectern, and what distaste he seems to have for it himself. He has difficulty peering through his glasses, which he rubs between thumb and index finger. The lenses reflect greasy smears. He has difficulty seating his spectacles on the insufficient bridge of his long droopy nose, they keep sliding down perilously to the upper tip of the nostrils, his left hand lifting only just in time to nudge them back up that thin ridge, whence they at once recommence their downward slide. He hawks. He gargles. He goes "Huh," and "Ahem," and finally he croaks, "Good morning." The morning has by now quite gone dull and gray. The audience prophetically suspects that the Law of Entropy will make the next thirty or forty-five minutes well-nigh unendurable. This is Ichabod. This is Enderby. (In female form, she is Hepzibah.) This person is that weight on the spirits that never lifts.

I almost neglected further to relate that this speaker has a set of heavy black eyebrows and (in the male version) wears a full (and very black) beard that almost entirely masks his features except for the red lips, the nose, and the luctual dark eyes.

Strengths

Are you kidding? Actually, there do exist exploitable virtues. Audiences tend to believe gloomy folk and gloomy prognoses. (One guesses from our experience in the human condition, though eco-freaks should make note that audiences soon lose patience with professional doomsayers.) The melancholy temperament is attractive to us; it can be romantic; we tend to assume that anyone who has evidently suffered, or who appears to bear the scars of suffering, has gained in wisdom, has cast off foolish illusions. (Actually, damn fools persist in being damn fools all their lives long, but this is beside the point.)

Weaknesses

The audience is depressed by the speaker, whose doleful looks and voice put it to sleep. Further, the audience can scarcely make out the features of the speaker behind bushy black eyebrows and the black barricade of beard, not to speak of any welcome variation in his expression.

Deficiencies and Opportunities

A person of this character type must make a conscious effort to gladden his appearance, put bounce into his step, pep up his voice, and in general imbue his entire being with energy. This speaker really must dig for that first species of temperament—the nervous temperament—we have been talking about. He must develop a sense of urgency about what he is saying, which not only communicates itself to the audience but which instills his own person with a sorely needed kind of nervous apprehension. The subject for such a speaker can never be bland: it has to matter. If he is blessed with a sense of humor (such personality types often are, possibly because they play the Mercutio in their own gardens), he should capitalize on it for wry, mordant commentaries. But he must be vigilant against his temperamental laziness, which will undo him. He must look himself in the mirror with an attitude more constructive than the dissatisfaction most of us experience when we first get up to greet the grisly morning, made more grisly by the sight of our unkempt, unwashed, untoothbrushed visages as we film the very surface of the bathroom mirror with our matinal halitosis. We wipe conscious sight of ourselves out of our minds as we plunge into our ablutions, but the speaker of this character type must practice making faces at himself, by turns (though the exercises will pain him) gay, comic, eager, hopeful, optimistic—compelling his facial muscles into these, for him, unnatural contortions (he will look to himself as though he is grimacing absurdly) until the muscles are actually sore. He must nevertheless persist: every morning, until his cheeks feel stretched to the point of cracking. (One might prescribe that he Lear at himself, might one?) (Moan. Groan.)

Using a tape recorder, he must also consciously—self-consciously—force expression into his tone of voice, practicing a passage from any text over and over again until the appropriate modulations in tone of voice resound in his own ears as less and less forced. This person will never come off like a Willard Scott, whose effervescent exuberance was made in Heaven. But it is within the possibilities for him to teach himself to sound a little like William Cosby. That wry, semi-cynicism (graced always by transparent goodness of heart), is the platform personality to strive for.

None of this will avail if he remains in the chronically hirsute state. This speaker must either rid himself of his beard or trim it away from the lips and down the cheeks as far as he can bring himself to do so. It is commonplace to remark that a heavily-bearded man resembles a bear. That's because he, like the bear, is immutable in expression. The bear is feared by animal trainers more than the big felines because the beast lacks those thousands of tiny subcutaneous nerves and muscles that alter expression: the lion will *look* bad tempered; when the bear attacks, it is without warning. Much of the expressiveness of the human face resides in the zygomatic cheek muscles and below—in the lips, near the lips, at and around the chin. A bearded speaker, especially if the beard be dark brown or black, has an almost insuperable task in attempting to convey to the audience whatever expressiveness he is able to endow his face with, other than the stern or gloomy expressions that come naturally to the bushy state. He can lift his eyebrows in surprise, or in quizzical alarm, but there is not much else he can do there either if he permits his brows to grow so thick that they obscure the audience's vision of the eyes and brow. (When spectacled, such men typically compound matters by wearing thick black or tortoise-shell frames.) (The woman whose face tends to disappear into her hairdo—heavy bangs, the cape buffalo look—has similar problems.) A speaker, unless he is Vincent Price, or Mephistopheles, is at an advantage clean-shaven. (See Chapter 10.)

Index